THE SCHOOL EXHIBITION — PLAN OF STAGE.

THE

EXHIBITION SPEAKER:

CONTAINING

FARCES, DIALOGUES, AND TABLEAUX,

WITH

EXERCISES FOR DECLAMATION

IN

PROSE AND VERSE.

ALSO, A TREATISE ON ORATORY AND ELOCUTION, HINTS ON DRAMATIC CHARACTERS, COSTUMES, POSITION ON THE STAGE, MAKING UP, ETC., ETC.,

WITH ILLUSTRATIONS.

CAREFULLY COMPILED AND ARRANGED FOR SCHOOL EXHIBITIONS,

BY P. A. FITZGERALD, ESQ.

TO WHICH IS ADDED A COMPLETE SYSTEM OF CALISTHENICS AND GYMNASTICS, WITH INSTRUCTIONS FOR TEACHERS AND PUPILS, ILLUSTRATED WITH FIFTY ENGRAVINGS.

NEW YORK:
SHELDON, LAMPORT & BLAKEMAN.
ROCHESTER, D. M. DEWEY. PHILADELPHIA, LIPPINCOTT, GRAMBO & CO. BOSTON, JOHN P. JEWETT & CO. BUFFALO PHINNEY & CO. DETROIT, KERR, MORLEY & CO. CLEVELAND, S. KING & CO. CINCINNATI, APLEGATE & CO. CIRCLEVILLE, A. BEACH & CO. CHICAGO, KERN & BRO. ST. LOUIS, E. K. WOODWARD, AND KEITH & WOODS.

1856.

STEREOTYPED BY
J. & C. E. FELTON,
BUFFALO.

PREFACE.

THERE have been, during the last quarter of a century, many books printed for the use of schools, academies, and literary associations, containing addresses, dialogues, etc., proper to be spoken on, as they are commonly called, exhibition days, by tyros in oratory, and embryo statesmen, to the edification of strangers, and the delight of relatives and friends, which have been justly popular with those for whose use they were intended, and productive of good equal to the highest expectations of all interested in their adoption and success. Believing, however, that there yet remains room for the introduction of other volumes, devoted to similar purposes, yet differing somewhat from those that have preceded them, in that they contain several entire farces, dramas, etc., easily represented, and capable of furnishing much amusement when produced, the compiler of the present volume offers the result of his labors to the consideration of the public, in the sanguine expectation that a candid judgment will allow him the benefit of that approval, without which all efforts tending to advance the cause of general education must be rendered entirely futile.

To make the rough way smooth, to scatter flowers along and upon the track which, well followed, guides the weary yet hopeful student to the portals of that great temple from whence the light of knowledge shineth ever, is the first duty of all who feel a proper interest in the high and holy cause of popular education — that education, without which, Progress must stay her advance, and fall nerveless beneath the blight of Error, the poison of that deadly moral sirocco, Ignorance. The materials of which the compiler has availed himself in furtherance of his design, have long been in the possession of the public; but this fact can not injure their worth, if the selections prove to have been made with judgment. The plan of the volume will, he thinks, commend itself to approbation; of this, however, success must be the sole criterion.

The remarks on Elocution, if well studied, can hardly fail to assist. Accompanying each farce, and some of the other selections, including the tableaux, will be found explanatory remarks. These, as they may tend to assist the student to a proper understanding of the sentiments uttered, the characters represented, will, it is believed, be found worthy of, and receive their due share of attention. The fair hope and honorable ambition to be thought worthy to rank with those whose time and labor have been devoted to the encouragement and development of our native eloquence have urged the compiler to proceed in his undertaking, hopeful that it may be blessed to the benefit of some, who study that they may become worthy citizens; men in intellect, as well as form; men who, while living, will do honor to their country, their kind, and themselves; dying, leave to their children the inheritance of a legacy worth treasuring for aye, in the fame that grows in radiance as the light of time beams brightly over their oft visited, their quiet resting place, beneath the green turf, that on

> "The heroes breast lies soft, as though
> In reverence for the dust, sepulchred where
> Was from all time decreed its final home."

CONTENTS.

CHAPTER IV.

CHAPTER V.

CHAPTER VI.

PART I.

PART II.

PART III.

PART IV:

PART V.

PART VI.

INTRODUCTION.

As the work here submitted to the judgment of the public is somewhat novel in its design, a few remarks in reference to the plan adopted may not be inappropriate. It has long been held by the enlightened friends of education, that, while the mind is being prepared by a gradual development of its powers to exert, when matured, all the faculties wherewith it was endowed, it should not be forced in its growth, or subjected to influences which must impair its strength, and render that weak and languid which should be strong and active. Each recurring day brings with it, to the young, as they emerge from infancy, the experience of something new, something calculated to excite the reflective faculties, to force the exercise of the reasoning powers. To be curious as to causes and effects, is a characteristic of the human mind, as well in infancy as in maturity. As reason dawns, as the morn of life with its unclouded sky, giving goodly promise of a glorious future, opens to youth, the process whereby its meridian may be rendered glorious, its closing blessed, begins to unfold itself. The imagination, free from the curb of practical knowledge, bounds away into the distant future, regardless of naught save the brilliancy of the panoramic illusion that unrolls before its advance. The stern realities of life present themselves not to the unpracticed eye; it needs that years should roll away, ere the dreams indulged can be forgotten; or if remembered, thought of but as the whisperings of the infantile soul in communion with itself. Each man's destiny crouches abjectly to his command; he may make or mar his fortune as he pleases. If, recreant to his high calling, he devotes his time to pursuits foreign to virtue, opposed to his well-being, the result must be a melancholy one. Instead of standing before the world a model in his career, for all to emulate, all to admire, he grovels in deserved ignominy, companionless, despised. Education, to be entirely beneficial, should be as far as possible practical, such as will enable its possessor to go out among his fellows, and dispute with them for supremacy. In this age, no man, if his acquirements warrant him worthy of such high vassalage, is safe from being made the public's servant; and, acting in that capacity, he may often be called upon to explain to his masters the plans by which he intends to advance their interests. If he would do this well, he must be taught how, and for such tuition he must look to the school-room. Practice in reciting the written thoughts of others will give him confidence to speak his own when needful. Subject to the criticism of rival school-fellows and the strictures of his teachers, he can not fail to acquire that ease of action so indispensable to a public speaker, a command of voice not otherwise to be obtained, and a fluency of speech which will set stammering at defiance. Every man is liable to be called upon, perhaps at a few moments' notice, to explain his opinions on certain matters, important or otherwise, and to do so with ease is most requisite. Ease implies knowledge, and "knowledge is power."

To offer the young student facilities by which to acquire confidence in expressing his thoughts in public, is the object of this work. Should this be gained, much will have been accomplished worthy of commendation.

Elocution, as a branch of education, deserves great consideration, from the fact that it can be applied advantageously nearly every moment. Speech being a faculty common to all mankind, the most expeditious method by which to convey ideas, it follows that it should be cultivated, its scope enlarged, its system perfected. Civilized nations have always been aware of the great importance of a study pertaining to this design, though they have in many respects failed in giving it its due share of attention. The ancients, particularly the Greeks and Romans, seem to have been fully conscious of the great benefits resulting from a close attention to, and practice of such rules as are fitted to advance the orator in his profession. Their schools for the study of eloquence were frequented by students from all parts of the known world. They established prizes to be awarded to those who, contesting for the palm of excellence, were the victors. Nor were their greatest orators ashamed to acknowledge, that, apart from the mere influence of genius, to the external part of oratory —the management of the voice, expression of the countenance, and the gestures of the head, body, etc. —were they indebted for a large portion of their success. They found that to work systematically was to insure them expeditious progress; that the art of delivery must be studied with particular diligence. Pronunciation, or delivery, as we call it, Demosthenes considered to be the charm of oratory; without which it must fail in its effect upon those sought to be convinced or moved. A composition teeming with defects, false in its reasoning, vicious in its moral, if delivered by an accomplished orator will take precedence in most minds over one noble in sentiments, profound in object, spoken by one incapable of investing it with the charm of delivery. Can it be wondered at, in view of this fact, that to the art of delivery the ancients attached an importance almost equal to that of composition? The failure of Demosthenes before he cultivated this art with sufficient care, and his extraordinary success afterward, induced him to value delivery in preference to every other requisite which goes to form the perfect orator. We would not have our students emulate the ancients so far as to render themselves liable to the charge made by Cæsar against some of his cotemporaries, who, he averred, in their practice went so far as to take to themselves the drudgery of the theater; but we would impress upon the understanding of all, that, without giving to the external part of oratory the important consideration it demands, they will signally fail in their desire for eminence. We would say to the young man, study. You may be called upon to occupy a seat in those legislative halls whose walls yet echo with the speeches of a Clay or a Webster,—those mighty dead, the thunder of whose eloquence, reverberating through all time, shall monument their memory in the hearts of all. You may chance to stand, in the exercise of your vocation, before a jury on whose decision rests the life of a human being, the happiness of anxious friends; then, versed in your profession, if you call to your aid the magic charm of that oratory which convinces and subdues by its exercise, moving to mercy the stern law, rescuing from its grasp an innocent victim and restoring him to the bosom of his friends, you will find a sweet reward for all your toil. Perhaps you may, as a preacher of the gospel, become an expounder of its lessons. To you will then belong the task of winning from the pursuit of error your fellow-man; and to do this requires in you the exercise of every persuasive art; you must be competent to lead, whom you would persuade. No matter if your compositions do "smell of the lamp," they will be the better for it; for it is in the opinion of weak intellects alone, that sound logic, correct rhetorical ornament, lucid order, and laborious research, are fit only for the drudgery of dullness. Allow such prejudices to prevail, and though possessed of all the learning, all the genius that Heaven has lavished upon man, our public speakers will ever fall short of the orators of antiquity, whom they must be content to admire at an humble distance.

THE

EXHIBITION SPEAKER.

CHAPTER I.

THE ELEMENTARY SOUNDS OF THE ENGLISH LANGUAGE.

Elocution has been defined "the art of reading and speaking well;" therefore, to acquire this art the reader or speaker must have a perfect knowledge of the elementary sounds of the English language. Without this knowledge he will be unable to articulate correctly, and errors in articulation deprive a language of all its force and beauty. No matter how correct and worthy of attention a speaker's sentiments may be, if the words used in delivering them are hurried over precipitately, drawled, or allowed to slip out carelessly, their effect will be dissipated and entirely lost.

There has been too little attention bestowed upon the study of the elements, and to this cause may be attributed the fact that there are so few really good readers or speakers among those whose profession does not imperatively demand that they acquaint themselves perfectly with the elementary sounds of our language.

To cultivate the voice by exercise upon the elements, will give it a melodious fullness that can not perhaps be acquired by any other process; when thus cultivated, it will take such inflections and intonations as the speaker may desire to give it, without effort on his part.

The number of elements in our language is thirty-eight.

They are divided into *vowels*, *subvowels*, and *aspirates*; or, as classified by Dr. Rush in his "Philosophy of the Human Voice," into *tonics*, *subtonics*, and *atonics*.

There are fifteen *vowels*, fourteen *subvowels*, and nine *aspirates*.

Table of the Elements.

VOWELS.

A	as	heard	in	*a*le, f*a*te, m*a*y.
A	"	"	"	*a*rm, f*a*rm, h*a*rm.
A	"	"	"	*a*ll, f*a*ll, orb.
A	"	"	"	*a*n, ide*a*, p*a*n.
E	"	"	"	*e*asy, im*i*tate, m*e*.
E	"	"	"	*e*nd, l*e*t, m*e*nd.
I	"	"	"	*i*sle, *i*ce, fl*y*, m*i*ne.
I	"	"	"	*i*n, p*i*n, *E*ngland.
O	"	"	"	*o*ld, m*o*re, *o*ats.
O	"	"	"	*oo*ze, l*o*se, t*o*, f*oo*l.
O	"	"	"	*o*n, l*o*ck, n*o*t.
U	"	"	"	m*ew*, f*ew*, t*u*be, p*u*pil.
U	"	"	"	*u*p, t*u*b, h*e*r, h*u*rt.
U	"	"	"	f*u*ll, p*u*ll, w*o*lf.
OU	"	"	"	*ou*r, fl*ou*r, p*ow*er.

SUBVOWELS.

B	as	heard	in	*b*ow, *b*oat, *b*ar*b*.
D	"	"	"	*d*ay, bi*d*, *d*are.
G	"	"	"	*g*ay, fi*g*, *g*ilt.
L	"	"	"	*l*ight, *l*iberty, a*ll*.
M	"	"	"	*m*ind, stor*m*, *m*ate.
N	"	"	"	*n*o, o*n*, *n*i*n*e.
NG	"	"	"	si*ng*, fi*ng*er, lo*ng*.
R	"	"	"	*r*oe, *r*a*r*e, o*r*b.
TH	"	"	"	*th*en, wi*th*, benea*th*.

V	as heard in *v*ice, *v*ile, sal*v*e.
W	" " " *w*oe, *w*ave, *w*orld.
Y	" " " *y*oke, *y*e, *y*onder.
Z	" " " *z*one, hi*s*, *Z*enophon.
ZH	" " " a*z*ure, enclo*s*ure.

ASPIRATES.

F	as heard in *f*ame, i*f*, li*f*t.
H	" " " *h*e, *h*ut.
K	" " " *k*ite, ca*k*e.
P	" " " *p*it, u*p*, a*p*t.
S	" " " *s*in, *c*ell, ye*s*.
SH	" " " *sh*ade, *sh*ine, flu*sh*ed.
T	" " " *t*ake, oa*t*s, i*t*.
TH	" " " *th*in, tru*th*, mon*th*s.
WH	" " " *wh*en, *wh*ich, *wh*at.

There are many words in which there are difficult combinations of the elements; they, as well as those in which the combinations are easy, should be practiced upon until the pupil is able to articulate each element correctly. The following is a table of the *analysis* of *words*, in which there are easy and difficult combinations of elements. Let the pupil spell the words, uttering separately each *element*, and not the *name* of the word, as is the practice which generally obtains in our schools.

Table of the Analysis of Words.

WORDS.	ELEMENTS.	WORDS.	ELEMENTS.
ale,	a-l.	sky,	s-k-i.
day,	d-a.	lamb	l-a-m.
fame,	f-a-m.	oak,	o-k.
crew,	k-r-u.	eve,	e-v.
call,	k-a-l.	once,	w-u-n-s.

WORDS.	ELEMENTS.
deeds,	d-e-d-z.
wool,	w-u-l.
isle,	i-l.
dare,	d-a-r.
ink,	i-ng-k.
pause,	p-a-z.
mow,	m-o.
nature,	n-a-t-sh-y̆-u-r.
lose,	l-o-z.
pray,	p-r-a.
spell,	s-p-e-l.
breadths,	b-r-e-d-th-s.
twists,	t-w-i-s-t-s.
waste,	w-a-s-t.
awful,	a-f-u-l.
up,	u-p.
flirt,	f-l-u-r-t.
awe,	a.
power,	p-ou-u-r.

WORDS.	ELEMENTS.
mulcts,	m-u-l-k-t-s.
John,	d-gh-a-n.
exchequer,	e-k-s-t-sh-e-k-e-r.
objects,	o-b-d-zh-e-k-t-s.
George,	d-gh-a-r-d-gh.
projects,	p-r-o-d-d-gh-e-k-t-s.
thousandth,	th-ou-z-a-n-d-th.
wives,	w-i-v-z.
noise,	n-a-e-z.
nostril,	n-o-s-t-r-i-l.
softness,	s-o-f-t-n-e-s.
shrugged,	sh-r-u-g-d.
themselves,	th-e-m-s-e-l-v-z.
dredged,	d-r-e-d-zh-d.
church,	t-sh-u-r-t-sh.
betrothed,	b-e-t-r-o-th-t.
vanquished,	v-a-ng-k-w-i-sh-t.
mouths,	m-ou-th-z.

CHAPTER II.

OF THE VOICE.

The voice is the organ of eloquence, and has the entire dominion over one sense. The necessity for its proper management must be obvious to even the least reflective mind; for no one can fail to perceive that the understanding is more vividly impressed and influenced by language and tones, than by the countenance or gesture, as the ear is more easily interested than the eye.

The qualities and management of the voice are therefore of the greatest advantage to the public speaker, as upon them depends his success in the practice of eloquence. The qualities of the voice being the gift of nature, are, as are all of nature's gifts, bestowed to be improved, subjected to the training of art. The majority of our public speakers pay too little attention to the cultivation of the voice. Often when we look to hear their sentiments delivered in a bold, sonorous tone, we are, instead, stunned by vociferation, or compelled to tax our hearing in order to comprehend their whispers. Vociferation often carries the day, for all men are not judges of fine composition, nor are all capable of estimating the just weight of argument; therefore it is that superficial speakers make up in loudness of voice for lack of matter in the compositions they utter. Like the Roman Novius, they bawl themselves into credit.

The sound of a powerful human voice carries with it an imperiousness that often terrifies as well as convinces. Homer in speaking of Achilles, attributes to the voice of his hero an irresistible effect:

> "He stood and shouted: Pallas also raised
> A dreadful shout, and tumult infinite
> Excited throughout all the host of Troy."

But the shout of Milton's rebel angels is still more magnificent than that of all Homer's heroes and gods:

"At which the universal host up sent
A shout, that tore hell's concave, and beyond
Frighted the reign of Chaos and old Night."

The voice is considered first, as to its nature; secondly, as to the management of it. The nature of the voice is again divided into quantity and quality.

In the quantity of the voice are considered

The Perfections.

The body or volume. The compass.
The soundness and durability.

The opposite — Imperfections.

Smallness, feebleness. The narrow scale.
Weakness, liable to fail by exertion.

In the Quality of the Voice.

Clearness,	Flexibility,	Monotony,
Sweetness,	Indistinctness,	Rigidity.
Evenness,	Harshness,	
Variety,	Broken,	

That a voice decidedly imperfect can, by any art, be improved so as to answer every effort of oratory, is altogether hopeless; but if the ear be not wholly depraved, the power and qualities of the voice, if they be moderately good, may be much improved. Though there are some methods by which the nature of the voice itself may be improved, yet it is to the management of the voice, such as it may be, which he possesses, that the orator should chiefly direct his attention. By due exertions in this way, though he may not absolutely improve the natural qualities of his voice, he will give them the highest effect of which they are capable. With certain management, few voices are so bad as not to be rendered capable of discharging tolerably well the functions of public speaking in our assemblies; and few, perhaps, are to be found so perfect as not to require some alteration; or which may not derive benefit from the observation of some of the general rules for the management of that organ. These rules, in the order of their importance, may be considered under the following heads:

1. Articulation.
2. Pronunciation and accent.
3. Emphasis.
4. Pauses.
5. Pitch.
6. Quantity.
7. Modulation and variety.
8. Tones.

Articulation.

The first point in the management of the voice, and that of the most indispensable necessity, is *articulation;* because imperfection in this respect, would obscure every other talent in a public speaker. According to Sheridan, "good articulation consists in giving every letter in a syllable its due proportion of sound, according to the most approved custom of pronouncing it, and in making such a distinction between the syllables of which words are composed, that the ear shall, without difficulty, acknowledge their number, and perceive at once to which syllable each letter belongs. Where these points are not observed, the articulation is proportionally defective."

The importance of a correct articulation will be recognized, when we consider that a public speaker, possessed of only a moderate voice, if he articulates correctly, will be better understood, and heard with greater pleasure, than one who vociferates without judgment. The voice of the latter may, indeed, extend to a considerable distance, but the sound is dissipated in confusion: of the former voice, not the smallest vibration is wasted, every stroke is perceived even at the utmost distance to which it reaches; and hence it often has the appearance of penetrating even further than one which is loud, but badly articulated.

Good articulation is not only conducive to the improvement of the voice in clearness and strength, but it is the criterion of a speaker's knowledge of his language; hence the almost unconquerable imperfections in the utterance of those who, in their infancy, have been given up to the care of vulgar speakers. As the difficulty of acquiring a correct articulation is unusually great in the English language, the foundation must be laid at that age when the organs are most tractable. Would parents and instructors direct their attention to this matter, a manifest improvement would quickly follow; yet to acquire a correct articulation, is not so difficult as to defy the assaults of labor, where nature has not placed a barrier in the form of an impediment, such as lisping or stammering.

Impediments, Stammering, etc., with infallible Rules for Cure.

As connected with the subject of articulation, it appears necessary to say a few words concerning impediment of speech. In cases where a small degree of hesitation breaks the fluent tenor of discourse, much may be done by due attention. In seeking for a remedy, it must be considered that as persons of delicate habits are more generally subject to it, it no doubt proceeds from a constitutional trepidation. Care of the health, then, is the foundation of every hope of cure. All excesses should be avoided; all irregularities guarded against. All the powers of the mind should be enlisted in the combat with the defect. A young person should, therefore, speak with deliberation, and when alone, practice frequently those words or letters which he finds it most difficult to enounce. He should also furnish his mind with a copious vocabulary of synonyms, so that if he finds himself unable to utter a particular word, he may substitute some other in its place, and above all, he should be encouraged to exert the energy of his own mind, and assume a courageous command over himself. Let him do this, and if the evil be not entirely eradicated, it will at least be palliated in a considerable degree. To avoid stammering or stuttering, a person should always speak with an expiring breath. To do this, he must speak deliberately, and with the mouth sufficiently open to prevent the suppression of those sounds which are made by the proper exercise of the organs of speech. By strictly following this rule, namely, to speak with an expiring breath, the most inveterate cases of stammering may be effectually cured.

Why is it that persons afflicted with stammering, always avoid it in singing? It is because they utter the words deliberately, with a full supply of breath, and with the mouth open.

Whenever one reads or speaks, he should commence with a sufficient supply of breath, which he should renew at the intervals of all the pauses. Persons are not so apt to stammer in reading poetry as prose, because they are under a kind of necessity of taking breath both at the cæsural pause and the pause at the end of the line.

One very disagreeable imperfection of articulation is the guttural sound of the letter *r*. This imperfection is best overcome by removing the articulation from the throat to the proper organs, the tongue and the palate; and by practicing to continue the sound in its proper place, or rather nearer the teeth. This may be effected by forcing the breath between the palate and the tip of the tongue, and by causing the tongue to vibrate rapidly.

The hissing of the letter *s*, that reproach to our language, is, as far as possible, to be moderated, both by attention to composition and enunciation, and should not be exaggerated as some are found to do.

The letters *m* and *n* are also subject to be imperfectly sounded. Instead of passing the sound of *m*, when produced by closing the lips, entirely through the nose, it is stopped or resisted, apparently between the bony and cartilaginous part of the nose, and does not issue freely. This defect is called by a contradictory appellation, speaking through the nose, and is seldom difficult to remove. The sound of the letter *n*, when formed by pressing the upper part of the tongue against the palate, should also pass entirely through the nose, but more gently than that of *m*.

In its general combinations, imperfect articulation is not so disagreeable as when combined with the letter *g*. The words *ringing*, *singing*, sound as if the *n* was omitted, and are uttered most disagreeably, as if they were *riggig*, *siggig*. The defective articulation of both these letters may be successfully got over by attention and practice, except in cases where nature or accident may have denied the sounds a passage through the proper organ.

Pronunciation and Accent.

Pronunciation is the mode of enouncing certain words and syllables. By accent is understood the stress laid on particular syllables, or in a more extended sense, the tone or expression of voice with which sentences are delivered. As pronunciation varies with the modes and fashions of the times, it is sometimes so fluctuating in particular words, and high authorities are often so much at variance, that the most correct mode is hard to be determined: hence to acquire a correct pronunciation, this irregularity, whatever be the cause, must be submitted to. Accent is also subject to the caprice of fashion. Its effect on our syllables is either to lengthen or shorten their quantity. When the accent is placed on the vowel, the syllable is uniformly long, as *glory*, *father:* when placed on the consonant, if it be a mute, the syllable will be short, as *battle, habit;* if it be a liquid, the syllable will be long.

Emphasis.

Emphasis discharges, in sentences, the same kind of office that accent does in words, ennobling the word to which it belongs, and presenting it in a stronger light to the understanding. The necessity of observing propriety of emphasis is so great, that the true meaning of words can not be conveyed without it. Great attention should therefore be paid by the student or speaker in the discrimination of those sentences which, referring to some predominant idea, require to be emphatically rendered.

Pauses and Breathing.

The common pauses necessary to be made according to the rules of punctuation are so obvious, that a reader or speaker must be very careless, who offends against them. The ordinary pauses which are marked in writing serve principally for grammatical discrimination; but in public speaking, pauses somewhat different are introduced. These are termed rhetorical pauses, and require to be adjusted by correct judgment and feeling. They are placed either before or after important matter, in order to introduce or leave it impressed upon the memory with stronger effect.

The reading of verse requires certain pauses, which differ, in some measure, from the pauses used in reading prose. The first has been named the *pause of suspension*, or final pause, which takes place at the end of each line; in this pause there is not to be any inflection of the voice. The second is the *cæsural pause*, which divides the verse into equal or unequal portions; upon the right management of which the melody and harmony of versification in a great measure depend. Mr. Sheridan's rules for reciting verse are the following:

1. All words should be pronounced exactly in the same way as in prose.

2. The movement of the voice should be from accent to accent, laying no stress on the intermediate syllables.

3. There should be the same observation of emphasis, and the same change of notes on the emphatic syllables as in prose.

4. The pauses relative to the sense only, are to be observed in the same manner as in prose.

The usual fault of introducing sing-song notes, or a species of chanting, is disagreeable to every ear, and should be studiously avoided.

Pitch.

The voice in speaking, as in singing, is observed to move within a limited compass, above or below which it can not move without disagreeable straining. But the mode of moving within this compass is different in each: the musical tones are placed at considerable intervals, which are passed by complete leaps; the speaking tones are at very small intervals, through which the voice slides by ascending or descending inflections. Certain favorable stations within the limits of the excursions of both are preferred for the pitch or key note; from whence the intervals are calculated, and to which the modulations are referred. The middle tones are most advantageous for this purpose, as well because the voice has the command of the tones both above and below, as that these tones are generally used in common discourse; and the organs must therefore be strengthened in them by habitual exercise.

Upon the proper pitching of the voice depends much of the ease of the speaker. He who shouts at the top of his voice is almost sure to break it, become a mere brawler, and stun his audience; he who mutters below, soon wearies himself, becomes inaudible, and altogether oppresses his hearers.

In order that a speaker may succeed in choosing the proper key or pitch of his voice, he should begin low, and ascend gradually till he reaches the pitch that suits the place and his own power best.

Quantity.

Loud and soft tones are altogether different from high and low. *Piano* and *forte* have no relation to *pitch* or *key*, but to *force* and *quantity*, and when applied to the voice, they relate to the body or volume which the speaker or singer can give out. This depends upon the power of the lungs, and not upon the adjustment of the organs of articulation. A voice is powerful according to the quantity it is able to issue, and is soft or loud according to the quantity which it actually does issue.

Modulation, Variety, and Rate of Utterance.

The modulation of the voice is the proper management of its tones, so as to produce grateful melodies to the ear. Upon the modulation of the voice depends that variety which is so pleasing, and so necessary to relieve and refresh the ear. The opposite fault is monotony. To the variety, so grateful to the ear, not only change of tones is requisite, but also change of delivery. According to the subject the rapidity of the utterance varies, as the time of the different movements in music. Narration proceeds equably; the pathetic, slowly; instruction, authoritatively; determination, with vigor; and passion, with rapidity.

Tones.

The vital principle of the voice consists in those tones which express the emotions of the mind. Without this language of the passions as an addition, the language of ideas, however correctly delivered, will prove cold and uninteresting. As there are other things which pass in the mind of man besides ideas, and he is not wholly made up of intellect, but, on the contrary, the passions, and the fancy compose a great part of his complicated frame—as the operations of these are attended with an infinite variety of emotions in the mind, both in kind and degree, it is clear, that unless some means be found of manifesting those emotions, all that passes in the mind of one man can not be communicated to another. To feel what another feels, the emotions which are in the mind of one man must be communicated to that of another by sensible marks. These can not be words, which are merely signs of things and ideas, perhaps exciting emotions, but not of emotions themselves. Anger, fear, love, hatred, pity, grief, are terms that will not excite in man the sensation of those passions, and make him angry, afraid, compassionate, or grieved. The true signs of the passions are tones, looks, and gestures. These are understood by all mankind, however differing in language. When the force of these passions is extreme, words give place to inarticulate sounds; sighs, murmurings, in love; sobs, groans, and cries, in grief; half-choked sounds, in rage· and shrieks, in terror.

CHAPTER III.

GENERAL PRECEPTS.

The general precepts which relate to the voice may be classed under the following heads:

1. The Preservation, 2. The Improvement,
3. The Management of the Voice.

The Preservation of the Voice.

1. The first rule for the preservation of the voice is, that the public speaker should be habitually "temperate in all things;" not given to any personal excess.

2. The voice should not be exerted after a full meal.

3. The voice should not be urged beyond its strength, nor strained to its utmost pitch without intermission. Frequent change of pitch is the best preservative.

4. At that period of youth when the voice begins to break, and to assume the manly tone, no violent exertion should be made; neither should the voice, when hoarse, be exerted at any time, if it can be avoided.

5. Certain things are found injurious to the voice, and therefore to be avoided. Butter and nuts are so accounted; also oranges and acid liquors. The use of cold drinks, and dry fruits, was considered injurious by the ancients.

6. In case of hoarseness, warm, mucilaginous, and diluting drinks, sugar candy, barley sugar, and the various sorts of lozenges, which modern ingenuity prepares so elegantly, may be used; a raw egg, beat up, is considered the best substance for clearing the voice. Onions and garlic are excellent, but their offensive odor is apt to injure their use.

Improvement of the Voice.

1. The great means of improving the voice is constant and daily practice.

2. The second rule has been anticipated, which is bodily exercise. Walking about a mile before breakfast is recommended.

3. In order to strengthen the voice, it is advised that a person that has weak utterance should daily practice to read or recite, in the presence of a friend. His friend should be placed at first, at such a distance as he may be able to reach in his usual manner; the distance is then gradually to be increased, till he shall be so far from him that he can not be heard beyond him without straining. Through this practice, he should proceed step by step daily; by which he may be enabled to unfold his organs, and regularly increase the quantity and strength of his voice.

Management of the Voice.

1. The first principles of the proper management of the voice depend on due attention to articulation, pronunciation, accent, emphasis, pauses, and tones. These have already been treated of in a former chapter.

2. The actual practice of the various inflections and pauses, of the pitch and tones to be adopted, should take place previous to the public delivery of a written oration. When time or opportunity does not permit this practice, the manner in which the voice should be managed in the different parts of the oration should be considered and determined. This practice has been called the silent preparation of the voice.

3. The speaker should begin rather *under* the ordinary pitch of his voice than *above* it.

4. Every speaker should endeavor to deliver the principal part of his discourse in the middle pitch of his voice; or,

using an appellation more intelligible to the inexperienced speaker, the ordinary pitch.

The tones of the speaking voice, ascending from the lowest to the highest, may be considered in the following series.

1. A whisper, audible only by the nearest person.
2. The low speaking tone or murmur, suited to close conversation.
3. The ordinary pitch or middle, suited to general conversation.
4. The elevated pitch, used only in earnest argument.
5. The extreme, used in violent passion.

The lungs are to be kept always, to a certain degree, inflated, so that the voice shall not, at any time, be run out of breath; and the air which is necessarily expended must be gradually and insensibly recovered, at the proper times and in the proper places.

Estimation of the Powers of the Voice.

1. The speaker discovers that his voice has filled the room by the return of its sound to his own ear.
2. He will judge of the ability of his voice by the degree of exertion necessary to enable him to fill a room of any particular size.
3. And he may form a judgment concerning the opinion of his audience by the degree of their attention.

CHAPTER IV.

OF THE COUNTENANCE.

It may be considered as an established point, that a public speaker should attend to the expression of his countenance, as well as to that of his voice. Every public address should bespeak the favor and attention of the audience by due respect; and as the looks of the speaker precede his words, so it should be an established maxim, that an orator should temper, with becoming modesty, that persuasion and confidence, which his countenance should express of the justice and truth of what he recommends.

Every circumstance that can indicate respect for an audience should be studied. The speaker should rise up in his place with modesty, and without bustle or affectation; he should not begin at once abruptly, but delay a short time before he utters a word, as if to collect himself in the presence of those he respects. He should not stare about, but cast down his eyes, and compose his countenance; nor should he at once discharge the whole volume of his voice, but begin at almost the lowest pitch, and issue the smallest quantity, if he desires to silence every murmur, and to arrest all attention. These are precepts long established, and held in respect by the greatest critics of ancient and modern times.

The art of *feeling* is the true art which leads to a just expression of the features.

> "To this one standard make your just appeal,
> Here lies the golden secret, learn to *feel*."

The true expression of the countenance is well described by the poet:

"A single look more marks th' internal woe,
Than all the windings of the lengthened oh!
Up to the face the quick sensation flies,
And darts its meaning from the speaking eyes;
Love, transport, madness, anger, scorn, despair,
And all the passions, all the soul is there."

To the expression of the countenance all the features contribute a share, but by far the greatest is derived from the eyes. The management of the eyes, therefore, is important. To them, among their other powerful expression, belongs the affecting effusion of tears; and though some have doubted whether an orator should at any time give way to this proof of his feelings, his so doing should not be considered as a mark of weakness, but rather of that sensibility which is the test of his sincerity in what he utters.

The mouth is, next to the eyes, the most important part of the countenance. "The mouth," says Cresallius, "is the vestibule of the soul, the door of eloquence, and the place in which the thoughts hold their high debates." It is the seat of grace and sweetness; smiles and good temper play around it; composure calms it; and discretion keeps the door of its lips. Every bad habit defaces the soft beauty of the mouth, and leaves indelible on it the traces of their injury.

The speaker should never thrust out the lips, stretch them and expose the teeth, draw them aside almost to the ears, fold them over each other with a sort of self-sufficiency, let them hang down, or make the voice issue from one side of the mouth. To bite or lick the lips is also disgusting; and even in articulation their motion should be moderate; for we should speak with the mouth more than with the lips.

CHAPTER V.

ON GESTURE.

The third division of the external part of oratory, or of delivery, is gesture. Under gesture is comprehended the action and positions of all parts of the body; of the head, the shoulders, the body or trunk; of the arms, hands, and fingers; of the lower limbs, and of the feet. The gracefulness of rhetorical action depends partly on the person, and partly on the mind. Most forms of the human figure are capable, in a considerable degree, of graceful motions; but, if not trained and educated in the most perfect manner, are apt to imitate the awkward and the vulgar. The grace of oratorical action consists chiefly in the facility, the freedom, the variety, and the simplicity of those gestures which illustrate the discourse. To the gracefulness of action, facility and freedom are necessary; for if a man were obliged to address an audience from a narrow window, through which he could not extend his arms and his head, it would be in vain for him to attempt graceful gesture. Confinement, in every lesser degree, must be proportionably injurious.

In standing, the speaker should place the foot which, at any instant, sustains the principal weight, so that a perpendicular line let fall from the hole of the neck, shall pass through the heel of that foot. By so doing, he has a change of position always at command.

To present to the mind correct ideas of the manner in which important matter has been delivered, ordinary language is almost inadequate. We say of a speaker, "He used the gestures of a graceful orator, of a dignified hero;" yet these expresssions no more convey to the mind an idea what particular gestures were used by him, than could the description of an oration, said to have been well and elegantly composed, be comprehended as to its arguments and ornaments.

The young man who would acquire the art of action, must note the manner of accomplished orators; being careful, as no one can be considered perfect in this art, to avoid the practice of what may, to him, seem faulty, while, to all that is excellent and proper, he gives his closest attention.

If the public speaker desires to give to the composition which he delivers more interest than it can derive from mere reading; or rather desires to give it the highest interest of which it is capable, he must commit it to memory, and adorn and enforce it with all the aids of the various modulations of the voice, expression of the countenance, and suitable gesture; so that, even though he should deliver the sentiments of another person, he must appear altogether to adopt, and feel, and recommend them as his own. When the composition thus delivered is poetical, this mode of public speaking is called recitation. When it is argumentative, and pronounced or composed on an imaginary occasion, for the purpose of exercising the speaker's rhetorical talents, it is called declamation. And when the speaker delivers, in this manner, a composition of his own on a real occasion, it is oratory; for the acquiring of the external art of which recitation and declamation are chiefly practiced. As a rhetorical exercise, recitation should receive the attention of the young; as by no other, excepting the practice of declamation, can they so expeditiously fit themselves in those appointments, which, in the lists of oratory, may earn them the approbation and respect of their opponents. Let our American youth, conscious of their high destiny, lose no opportunity that may advance them on their way; let them, while carving out their way to fame and fortune, remember that however great they may become in the estimation of their fellows, the approbation of their own hearts, speaking to them always in pleasant dreams by night, or during the busy turmoil of their daily duties, is the sweetest, noblest reward that man can claim, or his Great Protector grant.

Exercise in Simple Gestures,

FOR A CLASS OF FROM FIVE TO TWELVE BOYS, IN WHICH THE GESTURES SHOULD BE MADE AS REPRESENTED IN THE ACCOMPANYING CHART.

The numbers 1, 2, 3, etc., refer to the proper gestures; the letters [a], [b], [c], etc., to that word in the sentence upon which the hand or hands, in making them, should pause for an instant, to prepare for the one that is to follow.

(1) Know ye this, my friends, that He who reigneth in [a]Heaven, (2) whose footstool is the solid [b]globe, (3) who at a glance taketh in all [c]things, (4) whose essence filleth all [d]space, (5) the immensity of the [e]universe, (6) regardeth [f]us, (7) the creatures of his creation, his [g]bounty, (8) not as objects to be cast [h]away (9) or repelled from his [i]presence, (10) but as beings to whom his [k]heart is ever open, (11) his hand ever [l]extended. (12) He will take us to his [m]arms, as a mother taketh her child!

Exercise in Complex Gestures.

A PIECE TO BE SPOKEN IN CONCERT BY A CLASS OF FROM FIVE TO TWELVE BOYS.

The teacher should see that the gestures are made firmly, at the same time, and in the same manner; and that the tones of the voice are kept in concert. He must be careful not to allow his pupils to indulge in the sing-song tone so common not only with young and inexperienced speakers, but with many of mature age, who have not, as they ought, studied the rules pertaining to elocution and oratory.

Though this exercise is intended to be used as a key by

No. 1. No. 2. No. 3. No. 4.

No. 5. No. 6. No. 7. No. 8.

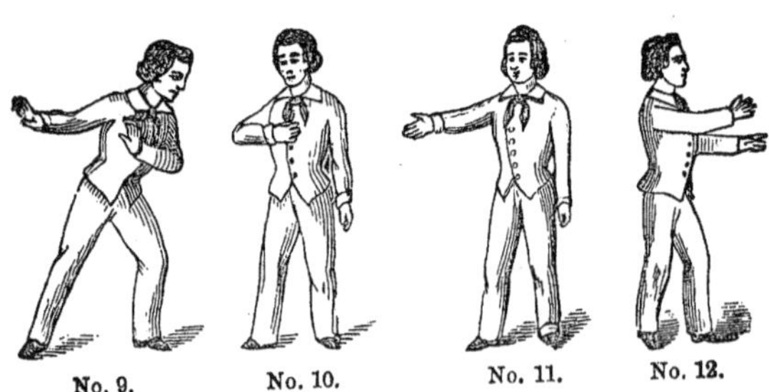

No. 9. No. 10. No. 11. No. 12.

which the pupil may be enabled to judge of the appropriateness to the sentiments he is delivering of any gesture he may wish to adopt, he must remember that there are no fixed laws governing the art of oratory, as far as gestures are concerned; and that it is only by strict attention to his subject, and an analysis of its sentiments, that he can hope to succeed in so calling to the aid of his language "the eloquence of motion" as to entitle him to the designation of a "perfect speaker."

Tell's Address to the Mountains.

(1) Ye crags and peaks! I'm with you once [a] again!
(2) I hold to you the hands you first [b] beheld,
(3) To show they still are [c] free! (4) Methinks I hear
A spirit in your echoes answering [d] me,
(5) And bid your tenant welcome to his home
[e]Again! (6) O sacred forms, how proud you look!
(7) How high ye lift your heads into the [f]sky!
(8) How huge you [g] are, (9) how [h] mighty, (10) and how free!

(1) Ye are the things that [a] tower, (2) that [b] shine; (3) whose smile
Makes [c] glad, (4) whose frown is [d] terrible—(5) whose forms,
Robed or [e] unrobed, do all the impress wear
(6) Of awe [f] divine. (7) Ye guards of [g] liberty,
(8) I'm with you once [h] again. (9) I call to you
With all my [i] voice! (10) I hold my hands to [k] you
(11) To show they still are [l] free! (12) I [m] rush to you
(13) As though I could [n] embrace you!

KEY TO FIRST VERSE OF TELL'S ADDRESS.

1. Raise both arms, extending them in front; as the sentence progresses, drop, and fold them across the breast upon

the word marked [a], at the same time throwing the body into a proud, perfectly erect position.

2. Unfold and extend the arms, keeping the hands about eighteen inches apart, and allow them to remain thus until the sentence is completed to the word marked [b].

3. Elevate the hands slightly, and, describing a half circle right and left, suffer them to rest a moment on the word marked [c]; then allow them to resume their natural position.

4. Draw both hands up toward the face, keeping the palms outward. The right arm should be a little more extended than the left. Finish the gesture on the word marked [d].

5. Extend the arms, and, dropping them, make a slight sweep to right and left; then finish the gesture on the word marked [e].

6. Raise both hands as high as the head, keeping the palms in front.

7. Extend the right arm and drop the left, at the same time, completing the gesture on the word marked [f], by a sweep of the hand upward.

8. Elevate the left hand, at the same time dropping the right a few inches; then, without any cessation in the motion, raise them both higher than the head, describe a half circle to the right and left, and stop on the word marked [g].

9. Bring the hands in toward each other, at the same time raising them till, on the word marked [h], they acquire their complete elevation.

10. From the last position let the arms be thrown out, describing a circle right and left. Finish the gesture with emphasis on the word marked [i], and suffer the arms to fall easily to their proper position.

NOTE. The teacher and pupil will observe that the gestures in the last three lines of the address, as marked above, are continuous, with the exception of some few pauses that should be made so as to be scarcely perceptible, running one into the other.

KEY TO SECOND VERSE.

1. Raise the right hand about as high as the face, pausing for an instant on the word marked [a].

2. Continue the gesture in the same direction, turning the hand, meanwhile, until the palm is up; finish the motion on the word marked [b].

3. Raise the left hand and drop the right, completing the gesture by placing the arms across the breast on the word marked [c].

4. Extend both arms a little, keeping the palms of the hands turned outward, at the same time avert the face from the right shoulder. Finish gesture on word marked [d].

5. Elevate the right arm and drop the left, until they are brought into a line, on word marked [e].

6. Raise the left arm and depress the right, at the same time drawing the hands in toward the face with the palms outward. In connection with this gesture, the body should be bent slightly forward, and the eyes raised. Complete the gesture on the word marked [f], and after a slight pause suffer the arms to resume their natural position.

7. Extend and spread both arms, pausing on word marked [g].

8. Draw the hands in, and, folding the arms across the breast, throw the body into a proud, erect position.

9. Continue in the same position to the end of the sentence marked [i].

10. Extend both arms, and, keeping them about eighteen inches apart, finish the motion on the word marked [k].

11. Bring the hands together, with the palms turned downward; then raise the arms, and, describing a half circle, finish the gesture on the word marked [l].

12. Raise, spread, and extend the arms, on the word marked [m].

13. Draw the hands in toward the shoulders, keeping the

palms toward each other; then extend the arms, and, at the same time dropping them, finish the gesture on the word marked [n].

NOTE. Every part of the human frame contributes to express the passions and emotions of the mind, and to show in general its present state. The head is sometimes erected, sometimes hung down, sometimes drawn suddenly back with an air of disdain, sometimes shows by a nod a particular person or object; gives assent or denial by different motions; threatens by one sort of movement, approves by another, and expresses suspicion by a third.

The legs advance or retreat, to express desire or aversion, love or hatred, courage or fear, and produce exultation or leaping in sudden joy; and the stamping of the foot expresses earnestness, anger, and threatening.—*Sheridan.*

CHAPTER VI.

DESCRIPTION OF STAGE.

The stage should be elevated some two or three feet above the level of the floor, so that the audience may have a full view of all that occurs upon it. Common pine boards, placed upon trestles of the height required, should be firmly held in their places by nails or otherwise. To conceal the front of the stage, some drapery may be tacked along, and allowed to fall as low as the floor. At each corner of the stage, should be placed an upright piece, of some six or eight feet in length, to support another, the length of the front of the stage, from which is to depend the curtain.

The curtain should be made in two pieces, closing in the center, and so arranged, by means of rings running on a thick wire, fastened to the horizontal bar from which it hangs, as to admit of its being drawn asunder, and closed again when required. The drawing of a stage accompanying this work will enable the reader to understand the description more perfectly.

Exit and Entrances.

R. means *right;* L., *left.*

Relative Positions.

R. means *right;* L., *left;* C., *center;* R. C., *right of center;* L. C., *left of center.*

Hints as to position and action upon the stage. Also, as to "Making up" for characters.

A constrained attitude must, on all occasions, be studiously avoided. Let the speaker endeavor to act as if there were none present to observe his gestures or appearance: his positions will then be natural ones, and such ever are the most graceful. In gesturing, all angular movements must be discarded: whatever the movement, it should be made in a curved line. Be careful not to make too many gestures, and, above all, learn to stand still. (The pupil, on reference to the piece entitled "Tell's Address to the Mountains," will find a description of the gestures in most common use.)

There are a few articles necessary for the toilet of one who is dressing and "*making up*" for a character, of which the following is a list, as complete as can be desired on ordinary occasions. A box of Chinese vermillion; a rabbit or hare's foot, dried—used to put the paint on with; prepared chalk; India ink, and a small camel's hair pencil; a piece of cork, with one end charred; a little gum Arabic, dissolved in a small bottle; and some crimped hair, white and black.

Having the above named articles, you are prepared to "*make up*" for the character you desire to represent, as far the face is concerned. By "*making up*" is meant painting and marking the face, so as to give it the appearance of age, or any other that may be wished.

To make the face appear wrinkled, mix some Indian ink with vermillion,—a dark brown is the color requisite,—dip your pencil in the mixture, and draw a line wherever you wish to have a wrinkle. By observing the face of an aged person, you will be able to see where the lines should be drawn to produce a proper effect. Hollow cheeks, red and sunken eyes, and pinched lips, give a person's face an emaciated appearance. To produce this effect, proceed thus: rub a little burnt cork on each cheek, being careful to blend it in well with the color of the skin, so as to present no abrupt edges. This causes the cheeks to appear hollow. To heighten the effect of the cork, the other portions of the face, those about the cheek-bones especially, may be thrown into relief by the application of the chalk. Painting the outer corners, and under lids of the eyes with red, gives them a swollen appearance, as if caused by weeping. To sink the eye, tinge the under lid with burnt cork. Now apply a few wrinkles, and the face is "made up." In representing *old men*, whiten the eyebrows and beard.

A cropped, light-colored wig, a red nose, and eyebrows heightened by a dash of red above them, give the face a comic appearance.

Much artistic skill may be shown in "making up" the face; therefore, practice is the only means by which the pupil can learn all that is necessary. Let him remember that, to look like the character he would represent, attention must be paid as much to the externals which would mark the character, if it really existed, as to the language it is supposed to utter; and that to identify himself with it in all respects is the only way by which he can produce a proper effect upon those before whom he is playing.

When a piece is ended, the persons remaining upon the stage should so dispose themselves as to produce a picturesque effect, if a tableau is needed; if no tableau is necessary, they should range themselves at equal distances apart,— those in the centre being a little further back than the ones at the side, so that a slight curve may be formed in the line upon which they are standing.

In studying dialogue pieces, such as farces, dramatic extracts, etc., it is not necessary, nor indeed expedient, for the scholar to whom any one part may be assigned to study all the others. He should study the sentence, or a portion of it, consisting of four or five words, immediately preceding each speech or exit and entrance of his own. The sentence to be so learned is called the *cue*, or hint to what follows it. To make our meaning perfectly plain, we will illustrate it by an example.

In the play of William Tell, in reply to a speech of Tell's, *Gesler* answers:

Gesler. Darest thou question me?
Tell. Darest thou answer?
Ges. Beware my vengeance!
Tell. Can it more than kill?
Ges. And is not that enough?
Tell. No, that is not enough!

Tells *cues*, or *hints* for his speeches would be as follows:

Ges. *(cue,)* —question me?
Tell. Darest thou answer?
Ges. *(cue,)* —my vengeance!
Tell. Can it more than kill?
Ges. *(cue,)* —that enough.
Tell. No, not enough!

The pupil will see that by following our directions in that matter, he will save himself a great amount of study.

PART I.

DRAMATIC.

A RACE FOR A DINNER.

A FARCE, IN ONE ACT.

DRAMATIS PERSONÆ.

DORIC, A lover of architecture.
MEASURETON, An architect.
SPONGE, A gentleman in want of a dinner.
DALTON, A merchant.
LOVELL, His friend.
FRANK, Servant to Dalton.
FEEDWELL, A landlord.
GAMMON, A fictitious character.
WAITERS, etc.

COSTUMES.

DORIC, Dress coat, black pants, and vest.
MEASURETON, Frock coat, light pants, and vest.
SPONGE, Shabby black suit.
DALTON, Frock coat, black pants, etc.
LOVELL, same as Dalton.
FRANK, Jacket, buttoned up, white pants, hat with gold lace band.
FEEDWELL, Vest, pants, etc., white apron.
GAMMON, White hat, overcoat, black belt.
WAITERS, Pants, vests, and white aprons.

SCENE 1. *Representation of an arbor in the center of the stage at the back; on the* R., *a post with a board, on which is written "Dinners Dressed on the Shortest Notice—Robert Feedwell." On the rising of the curtain,* FEEDWELL *and Waiters enter from* R. H.

Fee. Take care, there, take care! Mind you don't break the dishes or spill the gravy: this is the most particular dinner I ever had to provide in all my life.

Wai. We shall be careful, sir. *(Waiters exeunt* R. H.*)*

Fee. This is the long-looked for day, on which my former master, and now my near neighbor, Mr. Doric, gives his daughter in marriage to Mr. Measureton, the architect; and purely, as it would seem to me, because he has been seized himself with a mania for building. That house, which he seems almost to adore, is the first fruit of his sublime imagination; but here he comes.

Enter DORIC, L. H.

Doric. (L.) Well, Robert, how proceeds the dinner?

Fee. (R.) Charmingly, your honor.

Doric. That is right. Here comes my son-in-law.

Enter MEASURETON, L. H.

Meas. (L.) My dear father-in-law, the company are waiting: your presence is expected.

Doric. (C.) I'm coming; but do you know the news? Mr. Dalton has bought the manor-house, upon the hill.

Fee. (R.) What! Mr. Dalton, the rich merchant, who never dines with less than forty or fifty covers?

Mea. What! The rich merchant, who is always building? I wish I were his architect; but as I was saying, the guests will arrive, and —

Dor. And if they should arrive ten minutes too soon, you can show them over the house; let them see the grand saloon, and my new designs. But come, neighbor, I will just pop into the kitchen, take a glance at the eatables,— and then for the guests.

Fee. This way your honor.

(*Feedwell and Doric exeunt* R. H., *Measureton* L. H.)

Enter SPONGE, *cautiously from back of the stage*, L. H.

Sponge. No dinner yet! and nearly ten miles from London. Alas! tired of admiring, with an empty stomach, its parks, museums, streets, and cook-shop windows, I have come to try my fortune in the country; but the hour of dinner approaches, and not one invitation yet. Hallo! (*Looking off* L.) I believe there is to be a wedding in that house; a wedding, and I not in it? They always have good dinners at weddings! 'Tis there *(pointing off* L.*)* that Hymen lights his mighty torch, and there *(smelling and pointing* R.*)* the cook lights his mighty torch. I must have a dinner; but how am I to get it? *(Feeling his pockets.)* Nothing there! *(Feeling his stomach.)* Nothing there, and in fact nothing everywhere! and, unfortunately, this is a country in which nothing is to be had for nothing. But who comes here?

Enter DORIC, *from* R. H.

What a fine figure to work upon; yes, yes, we'll dine together.

Dor. There, there, not yet ready! I'm sure the guests must be quite impatient. *(Looking off* L.*)* It's astonishing what an effect my building produces at this distance; never was such a piece of architecture in this world. How beautiful the coach gates, and the two posts; then, the coach-house, the pump, the laundry, and the larder, all in the fore-court. It's really a little palace.

Sponge, (aside.) Oh, you're there, are you? This is the proprietor.

Dor. Provided that coaches don't lose their wheels in going in: that gate is delightfully narrow. I shall never leave off admiring it. Eh! what's that fellow about?

(Sponge looks off L, *and appears, every now and then, to write with a pencil in a small pocket-book.)*

Sponge. (L.) Suppose we say twenty-three feet?—twenty-three—that will bring us there; we put the dining-room into the kitchen,—

Dor. What!

Sponge. The laundry into the pantry, and the nursery into the cellar!

Dor. Why, he's turning my house out of the window.

Sponge. We put that back some ten feet, and we shall have a straight line.

Dor. (interrupting him.) Sir, sir, might I take the liberty of inquiring what you're about with that house?

Sponge. A thousand pardons, sir; I had not the pleasure of seeing you before, — I am the surveyor general of the county, employed at present in conducting the works of the new road.

Dor. (R.) And pray what has the new road to do with that house?

Sponge. (L.) Ah! I see you 're not acquainted with the new plan. It is now determined to continue the new road, in a line with the Thames, up to that point; we then cut horizontally, you see, in that direction. *(Pointing toward the house,* L.*)*

Dor. Hey! why, that will take away one side of my house.

Sponge. What, sir! does that house belong to you? I'm quite distressed. However, it's not the intention of Parliament to injure any private person, and there is certainly one comfort, we only want about twenty-three feet, for which you will be paid, and all the remainder of the house is your own, which you will then find in the middle of the great road; the dust may be rather inconvenient at first, perhaps; but I've no doubt you 'll consider it an improvement on the whole.

Dor. An improvement? nonsense! Why, you 'll leave my house without either doors or windows.

Sponge. By which you will save the taxes.

Dor. What! cut away that beautiful front, that triumph of the art! What an event! and in such a time — on my daughter's wedding-day.

Sponge, (aside.) How! the father of the bride! happy rencounter! *(Aloud.)* I 'm really grieved that my duty compels me to intrude upon you, and on a wedding-day, too! perhaps at the very moment you were going to sit down to dinner.

Dor. It 's distressing! but tell me, Mr. Surveyor General, are there no means by which it might be avoided?

Sponge, (musing.) Hem ! it's a very delicate affair. I don't say, however, but that with some exertion, and the uncommon appetite — I mean interest, with which you have inspired me —

Mea. (outside, L.*)* Mr. Doric! Mr. Doric!

Dor. I'm called; they wait for me; and really it's the most distressing thing in the world to keep people waiting for their dinner, when, perhaps, their appetites are as keen as the carving-knife.

Sponge, (aside.) I know mine is. *(Aloud.)* My dear sir, make no apology: I know the horror of having to wait for a dinner as well as any man who ever swallowed one.

Dor. I dare say you do. But, my dear sir, you have the appearance of a gentleman. *(Aside and looking at his dress.)* A little out at elbows, or so; but never mind that — and if you would be so condescending —

Sponge. Now he's coming to it. *(Aside.)*

Dor. As to take a bit of dinner with us, in a friendly way, and without ceremony.

Sponge. Really, you overpower me, — I — I — I can't refuse, but —

Dor. Now, no buts, I know what you're going to say; you wish to step home to change your coat; but there's only my own family present, and this will do very well, so let's in! My son-in-law is an architect, and he'll be delighted to have the surveyor general at table, whom, indeed, I have heard him say, he is perfectly acquainted with.

Sponge. Hey! *(Aside.)* I'm done for!

Dor. And fortunately here he comes.

Sponge. Yes, *(aside,)* fortunately for your dinner.

Enter MEASURETON, L.

Dor. (C.) Come, come, son-in-law, we shall have a host of friends. Here's the surveyor general, Mr. Wideacre, will do us the honor of sitting at our table.

Mea. Nonsense, father-in-law; he sent me an apology an hour ago, to say he could not come.

Dor. Well, well, judge for yourself; there he is.

Mea. How, Mr. Wideacre! No, no, that's not he — you're deceived, father-in-law. I know Mr. Granite, who has the superintendence of the new road, as well as I know you.

Sponge, (aside.) Hang the fellow! he knows every body.

Dor. You're really wrong, son-in-law; for I'm certain that Mr. Granite never said any thing to you of the last plan adopted for the new road, by which I shall lose half my mansion.

Mea. Depend on my information, father-in-law, the new road runs half a mile the other way.

Dor. (to Sponge.) What, then, have you been telling me?

Sponge. Wait for one moment, and I shall be able to explain —

Mea. Do n't listen to him, father-in-law; that fellow's some impostor.

Sponge. Seriously, you are deceived; but I'm no impostor. What, Mr. Measureton! have you not the least recollection of me?

Mea. Not the least in the world!

Sponge, (aside.) Considering we never saw each other before, that do n't astonish me. To say the truth, I have an affair of importance to communicate to you, *(crosses to Measureton,)* and wishing to find out some new, sharp, clever way of introducing myself to you, I thought the manner I adopted quite original. Ha, ha, ha! *(Aside.)* He won't laugh.

Mea. Well, sir, may I have the honor of knowing to whom I am speaking.

Sponge. I wish to be alone with you a moment; I have a most important affair to mention.

Mea. (crosses to Doric.) Father-in-law, will you excuse us for a moment?

Dor. Certainly. *(Crosses to* L.*)* This fellow, with his twenty-three feet, has put me quite in a flurry. However, with all his new roads, he shan't find his way to my dinner-table. *(Exit* L.*)*

Sponge, (aside.) Hang his dinner-table! However, there's no time to be lost. Sir, sir, you are Mr. Measureton, an architect of distinguished talent, to whom my worthy friend, Mr. Doric, has at last obtained me the honor of an introduction.

Mea. (L.) Sir, I really—

Sponge. (R.) How strange you do n't know me; but I know you, there's the difference: you're established; you're a husband; you've married a beautiful and charming woman;—

Mea. Not very beautiful—merely decent, to say the most of her.

Sponge. You're too modest! you have prepared every thing to celebrate the wedding. The invitations, the bride-cakes, the bridemaids, fiddles, flutes, horns,

Mea. Horns!

Sponge. Yes, yes, horns, you know, French horns—you understand me, *(imitates blowing a horn,)* and in fact you fancy you have thought of every thing, but there is one thing you have forgotten.

Mea. Not that I remember.

Sponge. I dare say not; no, you don't recollect that you have forgotten,—where is the occasional ode, the song of love, in which the soul is to pour forth its heaven-felt raptures in soft poetic strains? *(Looking at a rent in his dress.)*

Mea. Right, I have no occasional verses yet, though I've been poring over the Little Warbler full two hours, in hopes of finding some

Sponge. A wedding without a song! that will never do. No sir, you must have an amatory poem written on gilt-edged vellum paper, filled with grace, energy, and tenderness.

Mea. But where am I to find such a poem?

Sponge. There is the occasion of my visit—I have thought seriously of your embarrassment, and without letting you know a word about it, I have written the said verses, which I now bring to you.

Mea. Hem! you have taken the trouble, and without even knowing me!

Sponge. Oh, I'm much more your friend than you think me; but I reckoned on coming without ceremony, and announcing myself, perhaps, just at the moment dinner was on the table. Ah! it is in those moments that a man finds out his real friends.

Mea. I must confess to you, I never met with such attention in my life.

Sponge. Don't be astonished—it's a recreation—it's meat and drink to me. I'm delighted with the wedding of love, and the sight of a wedding—*(aside,)* dinner—is enough to set me on fire. Oh it's a day of love and pleasure! how delightful the bustle of the morning, the coming of the bridegroom, the arrival of friends, the welcoming of the parson, the hugging of relations whom you never saw before, the kissing of the bride, the call to dinner, the dinner itself, the dessert, the tea, the ball; but that's not all! then the delights of the bridegroom, the modesty of the bride; then comes the supper,—no one can eat excepting me. *(Aside.)* Then the nods and winks of the gentlemen, and the blushing of the ladies, and, and,—*(aside,)* but I musn't go any further, or he'll forget the dinner. *(Crosses to* L.*)* You see I understand my subject, and there are some few of the ideas I have attempted to throw into the verses I have written for the occasion, and here they are. *(Gives him a paper.)*

there it is — it's set to a beautiful air; but that need not embarrass you, for I shall be by your side to encourage and give you the key-note.

Mea. And you have written them expressly for me! I'm delighted! though I really believe it's the first time that verses were written expressly for the marriage of an architect.

Sponge. Listen,— it begins thus:

"On Richmond hill, there lives a lass
More bright than May-day morn,
Whose charms all other maids surpass,
A rose without a thorn.

"This lass so neat, with smiles so sweet,
Has won my right good will.
I'd crowns resign to call her mine,
Sweet lass of Richmond hill."

Mea. (R.) Do you know, I'm afraid I've heard something like that before.

Sponge. (L.) Oh no, never — you're mistaken — I wrote it expressly for the occasion. You see the locality struck me, and —

Mea. Well it's a singular coincidence. *(Opens his book and repeats the second verse.)*

"Ye zephyrs gay that fan the air,
And wanton through the grove,
Oh, whisper to my charming fair,
I die for her I love.

"This lass so neat, with smiles so sweet,
Has won my right good will;
I'd crowns resign to call her mine,
Sweet lass of Richmond hill."

(Measureton laughs.)

Sponge. Confound the Little Warbler! To think I should hit upon nothing but that!

Mea. Ha, ha, ha! I'm exceedingly obliged to you for the trouble you've taken on my account but you and your muse had better beat a retreat, unless you wish that the retreat should be beaten upon your back. When you have any new occasional verses, *(crosses to* L.,*)* I'll listen to them; but don't pop in just as the dinner's put upon the table. Ha, ha, ha! Well, one thing I will say for you —

Sponge. And what is that?

Mea. That you look like a poet, at all events.

(Exit L., *laughing.)*

Sponge. And I, unfortunately, feel like one. Five o'clock by my appetite! Now they are seating themselves at table, and I not among them. Oh, my genius! oh, my appetite! inspire me, both of ye. Eh, who comes this way? *(Looking off* L., *and going up stage.)*

Enter FRANK, L.

Frank. Landlord! landlord!

Fee. (entering from R.*)* What do you please to want?

Frank. I've come to order dinner for my master and two of his friends.

Fee. What will they please to have?

Frank. Soup, beefsteaks, a fine fowl, a salad, a few tarts, and every thing for three persons.

Fee. It shall be all right. May I be permitted to know whom I have the honor of speaking to?

Frank. (L. C.) I am Mr. Francis, valet de chambre to Mr. Dalton, the rich merchant.

Fee. (R. C.) Mr. Dalton! bless me, but pray when may I expect Mr. Dalton to come?

Frank. In about an hour, more or less.

Fee. Every thing shall be ready as you require; and depend upon it, Mr. Francis, I shall not forget your kindness.

Frank. And depend upon it if you do, I shall not fail to remind you of it. To insure against failure, here is the money for the dinner. *(Exit Frank* L., *Feedwell* R.*)*

Sponge, (coming forward.) All the world will dine

to-day—except me. What shall I do? My appetite is prodigious, and to satisfy it I must dine. The proprietor of the dinner will not arrive in less than an hour; yet, if I understand right, he may come sooner. Every thing warns me to hasten the execution. Hallo, waiter! landlord! *(Reckoning on his fingers.)* Mr. Dalton, a merchant, paid in advance,—soups, fowl, beefsteaks, tarts, dessert, etc. Ah! what a fine memory fasting does give me.

Enter FEEDWELL, R.

Fee. (R.) Who calls?

Sponge. (L.) What, sir, can't you guess? However, when we take the trouble to order in advance every thing is neglected. I see how it is: that careless fellow, Frank, has done nothing right; and so every thing's wrong.

Fee. (aside.) Oh, this is Mr. Dalton, no doubt! Mr. Dalton, a thousand pardons,—though your servant told me you would not arrive in less than an hour.

Sponge. He made a mistake. He has paid you in advance, has he not?

Fee. Yes, he has, sir.

Sponge. I hope he did not forget to tell you what I wished to have for dinner?

Fee. (thinking.) No, sir; no, sir;—soup, a fowl, beefsteaks—

Sponge. A few tarts and a salad.

Fee. Right; and, as the dinner's all ready, I'll serve it up the moment your two friends arrive. *(Going R.)*

Sponge, (aside.) My two friends! I had forgotten my two friends; I was making a pretty blunder; a dinner ordered for three. I don't doubt I could eat it all myself,—but that won't do. *(Aloud.)* They can't be long.

Fee. Then in the meantime I'll lay the cloth.

Sponge. Yes, lay it here in the arbor. I'm fond of dining in an arbor.

Fee. I'm afraid you'll find it very cold in the arbor.

Sponge. So that the dinner's hot, never mind; and, I say, landlord! though the dinner's ordered for three, let there be a sufficiency for six. *(Aside.)* I'll put some in my pocket for to-morrow. I shall reward you for your trouble.

Fee. I have no doubt of it, your honor. *(Exit* S. C.*)*

Sponge. I have. That fellow's like me,—he's ready to swallow any thing. But where am I to find my two friends! I must have two friends. Let me see—is there any one coming on the great road? *(Looking off* R.*)* No. Well, well, somebody must be found, and the two first decent people that I meet with, I'll take by the collar; and if they won't dine with me, I'll cram it down their throats by force. *(Calling.)* Holloa! halloa, there! *(Exit* R.*)*

Enter DALTON *and* LOVELL, L.

Lovell. (L. C.) In truth, Dalton, I admire your happy disposition, you are contented with every thing.

Dalton. That is what I call true philosophy.

Enter SPONGE, R.

Sponge. I can't find a single creature; it's becoming desperate. Eh, what do I see? These are my men; whether they've dined or not, they shan't escape me. *(Bows to them.)*

Lov. *(rather up stage,* L.*)* What can this fellow want?

Dal. *(rather up stage,* C.*)* A seedy coat, and making his bow at the door of an inn. Depend upon it, he wants to ask us for a dinner. What say you? We are only two, the dinner is provided for three, and we can, on such an occasion, take pity, and give a meal to a poor fellow who is not fortunate enough to be able to pay for one himself. *(They advance.)*

Sponge. Gentlemen, not having the pleasure of your acquaintance, my proposal may seem somewhat odd, and, to say the truth, I find myself in a very extraordinary situation.

Dal. *(aside to Lovell.)* It's just as I said.

Sponge. I have a peculiar habit of judging people at first sight; and, strange as it may appear, from the first moment I beheld you, the strongest symptoms of a growing appetite — I mean friendship.

Dal. I understand you — come to ask us to —

Sponge. Do me the honor of dining with me.

Lov. Eh?

Dal. This is an invitation I certainly was not prepared for.

Sponge. How strange! *(Aside.)* I'm always prepared for an invitation. No doubt, you look upon me as an original; but I love company, and, in fact, if I do not find two companions to sit at table with me, in all probability, I shall not dine at all.

Fee. (entering from R.*)* Mr. Dalton, your dinner 's ready, and shall be served the moment you wish it.

Sponge, (with importance.) It's all right, my dear fellow.

(Exit Feedwell, R.*)*

Dal. (with astonishment.) How, sir! are you Mr. Dalton?

Sponge. I'm sometimes called so.

Lov. What! Mr. Dalton, the merchant?

Sponge. I do speculate a little now and then.

Lov. (to Dalton.) He's too much for us. I see how it is.

Dal. (C.) Be quiet; he's a character.

Lov. (L.) Yes, and I fear a very bad one.

Dal. (aside.) No matter; we'll amuse ourselves with him.

Sponge. May I hope, gentlemen, that, now you know something of me, you'll not refuse. The dinner is a slight one: soups, a fowl, a beefsteak, a few tarts and a dessert.

Dal. (to Lovell.) Why, zounds! it's our own dinner he's inviting us to.

Sponge. Really, gentlemen, I can take no denial. Come, let us sit down; we shall soon forget that we have not been longer acquainted.

Dal. Well, since it must be so, we accept your invitation.

Sponge. Gentlemen, you honor me. Landlord, my two friends have arrived, and you may serve the dinner immediately.

Fee. (without.) Coming directly, sir. *(Two waiters bring a table, three chairs, etc., from* R., *and, with Feedwell, prepare dinner. During the time of setting the dinner, Dalton approaches Sponge.)*

Dal. Mr. Dalton, I have accepted your invitation; but it is on one condition, which is, that to-morrow, Tuesday, you honor me with your company to dinner, at the manor-house, on the hill.

Sponge. My dear sir, with the greatest pleasure.

Lov. (crosses to Sponge.) And I hope, Mr. Dalton, that, on the day after, you will likewise oblige me.

Sponge, (putting his hand on his stomach.) My dear sir, I have not the power of refusing you. *(Aside.)* Thank fortune, I have dinners provided for two days to come, at least. *(Dalton and Lovell seat themselves at the table, which is placed on* R. *of stage; as Sponge is going toward the table, enter several villagers, who crowd around him, apparently congratulating him.)* What does all this mean?

Fee. It's only the boys of the village, who, hearing of their landlord's arrival, have come to pay their respects to you.

Sponge. It's all very well, but the dinner's cooling.

Dal. Thank goodness, he's receiving their compliments instead of me.

Sponge. They're attacking the soup without mercy,— enough, enough! *(Looking at table.)* Now they're attacking the beefsteaks. Oh, the gluttons! *(To the villagers.)* Pray, less ceremony— another time. Here, landlord! waiter! take these people away!

Fee. Neighbors, retire awhile,— Mr. Dalton's busy now.

Dor. (coming from L. *in a hurry.)* In the name of goodness, what does all this mean!

Fee. Why it's Mr. Dalton, the rich merchant, who is going to do me the honor of dining at my house.

(The villagers exit, R.*)*

Dor. Can it be possible! why, that's the very man who acted so strangely with my son-in-law; but they said he was eccentric! A pretty business I've made of it! I must apologize. *(Sponge is about to seat himself at the table.)* Mr. Dalton! Mr. Dalton!

Sponge. Another interruption!

Dor. One word.

Sponge. One mouthful! I have no time.

Dor. You must excuse me,— but I can not permit you to leave me, until you suffer me to apologize for my rudeness this morning.

Sponge. My dear sir, apologize another time. *(Enter* MEASURETON *from* L., *with a napkin and spoon in his hand.)*

Mea. Why, father-in-law, how strangely you leave us.

Dor. (making signs with his hands for him to retire.) Directly. *(To Sponge, whom he still holds.)* No, no, you must not escape; and after all, you absolutely must take a family dinner with us.

Sponge. My dear sir, I would dine with you with the greatest pleasure, but, *(looking at the table,)* at this moment, I have invited two friends — two particular friends,—whom I could not leave for the world. *(Looking at table.)* Ah! there goes the last of the beefsteak.

Dor. (still holding him.) To-morrow, Mr. Dalton.

Sponge. To-morrow I'm engaged.

Dor. Then the day after.

Sponge. I'm engaged.

Dor. May I hope on Thursday, then?

Sponge. On Thursday, I'm yours. I shall attend, and with a good appetite. *(Aside.)* But in this moment of dreadful suspense —

Dor. It's agreed, then,—I shall expect you. *(Exit Doric,* L. *Measureton runs to Sponge, and seizes him by the button-hole.)*

Mea. My dear sir, pray pardon the freedom I made use of this morning; but, in truth, I did not know you.

Sponge. (R.) My dear sir, don't mention it; but have the kindness to leave me. *(Aside.)* There goes the merrythought.

Mea. No, no; you are engaged for Thursday, but I hope that on Friday—

Sponge. On Friday, be it,—and let that settle it. Ah! the fowl's all gone. *(Takes his hat off, and putting it on Measureton's head, presses it over his eyes. As Measureton exits* L. *Sponge goes to table.)* It appears you have not been idle, gentlemen. Fortunately, I am accustomed to quick eating, and I shall soon overtake you.

Enter GAMMON, L.

Gammon. Pray, is there one Mr. Dalton any where here? *(Dalton* R. *points to Sponge* L.*)* I beg your pardon, *(to Sponge,)* but I wish to speak a word with you, if you please, on an affair of the greatest importance.

Sponge. My dear fellow, another time, another time; at the present moment it's impossible. *(To Dalton, who is again helping himself.)* Sir, sir, you'll die of an indigestion. *(To Gammon, who is growing impatient.)* Now, now, don't be troublesome,—don't you see the dinner?

Gam. Yes, and the business I've come about is concerning the dinner.

Sponge. What can your business have to do with my dinner?

Gam. You'll know that soon enough.

Sponge, *(calling.)* Waiter, send more beefsteak! *(Gammon pulls Sponge by the sleeve.)* Why, in the name of famine, have you such an objection to my putting a bit of any thing in my mouth?

Gam. Explanation is unnecessary. I have orders to take your person. I shall be sorry to employ force; but if necessary, I have assistance at hand.

Sponge. This comes of taking people's names we know nothing of. *(Aside.)*

Gam. Come, come, I must take you to prison.

Sponge. Only wait until I get a bit of dinner, and you may take me any where. *(Gammon is pulling him away.)* This will never do; I think it will be more prudent to declare the truth—a word in your ear. *(Whispers in Gammon's ear.)*

Gam. (L.) What! then, after all, you're not Mr. Dalton?

Sponge. (R.) No, my name is Sponge, at your service,—happy to dine with you any day, after Friday. I'm not the rich man, upon my honor; but you ought to have known that by my appetite.

Gam. Sir, I have to ask you a thousand pardons. It's true, I was to arrest Mr. Dalton; but, bless your soul! it was all a sham; I'm no officer,—I was only employed to force him to dine at the manor-house, with his wife and friends. You see they had laid a wager—

Dal. (jumping up.) Which they have lost, for my dinner's ended. *(All start.)* Yes, my name's Dalton, and my dinner's ended!

Sponge. Your name Dalton! who then am I? I'm nobody.

Dal. However, we will repair home *(crosses to* L.*)* for the dessert, and regale our friends with the adventures of the morning. Waiter, toothpicks! *(The waiter gives them toothpicks.)* As for you, my dear Amphitryon, we heartily thank you for your kind invitation, and we hope you'll not forget ours. *(Exeunt Dalton and Lovell,* L.*)*

Sponge. You may depend upon me. I shall get no dinner till then, that's clear. *(As Sponge is musing, the waiter comes and offers him a toothpick; the other waiters clear the table.)* What is this?

Waiter. (R.) A toothpick?

Sponge. (L.) A toothpick! *(Kicks the waiter off* R.) This is the height of derision! Then it appears that every body has dined but me. By the event, however, I have made a good week of it; let me see, there are dinners for *(counting on his fingers,)* Tuesday, Wednesday, Thursday, and Friday; but nothing as yet decisive for to-day! *(Looks toward the table.)* They have cleared away the things, *(feeling his pockets,)* and I have not the means of enticing them to a second appearance. But if there should be, among all my friends present, any one who dines late,—very late,—and who has the least intention of inviting me home with him, I beg he will not put himself out of the way on my account—I am perfectly at any one's service; but if I should not be happy enough to meet with an invitation for to-day, I hope I shall be more fortunate when I next start "A Race for a Dinner."

Disposition of characters at fall of curtain:

R. C. L.

SPONGE.

HOB AND NOB.

A ROMANCE OF REAL LIFE, IN ONE ACT.

BY MADISON MORTON.

DRAMATIS PERSONÆ.

JOHN NOB, A journeyman printer.
JAMES HOB, A journeyman hatter.
MR. BOUNCER, A lodging-house keeper.

COSTUMES.

NOB, A small swallow-tailed black coat, short buff waistcoat, light trousers — short, turned up at bottom,— black stockings, shoes, cotton neckcloth, and shabby black hat.

HOB, A brown coat, long white waistcoat, dark trousers, boots, white hat, and black stock.

MR. BOUNCER, A waistcoat, nankeen trousers, and white apron.

REMARKS. The parts of Hob and Nob should be played in a manner bordering on burlesque; the more extravagant they can be made, the nearer will they be represented as the author intended, providing, always, that the bounds of gentlemanly conduct are not passed by the personators.

SCENE. *A Room. At* C., *a bed with curtains closed; at* L. C., *a door; at* L. H., *a door; a chest of drawers,* L. H.*; at back* R. H., *a window; a door* R. H*; below the door* R. H., *a fireplace with a mantle over it; table and chairs* R. C.; *a box of matches on the mantle-piece; a gridiron hanging by the side of the fireplace.* HOB, *dressed, with the exception of his coat, is discovered looking at himself in a small looking-glass, which he holds in his hands. Hob should wear a close-cropped, light-colored wig.*

Hob. I've half a mind to register an oath, that I'll never have my hair cut again! I look as if I had just been cropped for the militia! And I was particularly emphatic in my directions to the hair-dresser, only to cut the ends off. He must have thought I meant the other ends! Never mind— I shan't meet any body to care about so early. Eight o'clock, I declare! I haven't a moment to lose. Fate has placed me with the most punctual, particular, and peremptory of hatters, and I must fulfill my destiny. *(Knock,* L.*)* Open locks, whoever knocks.

Enter MR. BOUNCER.

Mr. B. Good-morning, Mr. Hob, I hope you slept comfortably, Mr. Hob?

Hob. I can't say I did, Mr. B. I should feel obliged to you, if you would induce Mrs. B. to accommodate me with a more protuberant bolster, Mr. B. The one I've got now, seems to me to have about a handful and a half of feathers at each end, and nothing whatever in the middle.

Mr. B. Any thing to accommodate you, Mr. Hob. Mrs. B. has gone into the country for a day or two, leaving me to attend to the wishes of her respected lodger.

Hob. Thank you; then, perhaps, you'll be good enough to hold this glass while I finish my toilet.

Mr. B. Certainly. *(Holding glass before Hob, who ties on his cravat.)* Why, I do declare, you've had your hair cut!

Hob. Cut? It strikes me I've had it mowed! It's very kind of you to mention it; but I'm sufficiently conscious of the absurdity of my personal appearance already. *(Puts on his coat.)* Now for my hat. *(Puts on his hat, which comes down over his eyes.)* That's the effect of having one's hair cut! This hat fitted me quite tight before. Luckily, I've got two or three more. *(Goes off* L., *and returns with three hats of different shapes, and puts them on one after the other, all of which are too big for him.)* This is pleasant!

Never mind,—this one appears to wabble about rather less than the others. *(Puts on a hat.)* And now I'm off! By the-bye, Mr. Bouncer, I wish to call your attention to a fact that has been evident to me for some time past,—and that is, that the coals go remarkably fast.

Mr. B. Lor, Mr. Hob!

Hob. It's not only the case with the coals, Mr. Bouncer, but I've lately observed a gradual and steady increase of evaporation among my candles, wood, sugar, and lucifer matches.

Mr. B. Lor, Mr. Hob! you surely don't suspect me?

Hob. I don't say I do, Mr. B.; only I wish you distinctly to understand, that I don't believe it's the cat.

Mr. B. Is there any thing else you've got to grumble about, sir?

Hob. Grumble! Mr. Bouncer, do you possess such a thing as a dictionary?

Mr. B. No sir.

Hob. Then I'll lend you one—and if you turn to the letter G you'll find "Grumble, verb neuter—to complain without a cause." Now that's not my case, Mr. B. And now that we are upon the subject, I wish to know how it is that I frequently find my apartment full of smoke?

Mr. B. Why, I suppose the chimney—

Hob. The chimney doesn't smoke tobacco; I'm speaking of tobacco smoke, Mr. B. I hope, Mr. B., your wife is not guilty of cheroots or Cubas?

Mr. B. Not she, indeed, Mr. Hob.

Hob. Nor partial to a pipe?

Mr. B. No, sir.

Hob. Then how is it that—

Mr. B. (confused.) Why—I suppose—yes that must be it.

Hob. At present, I am entirely of your opinion; because I haven't the most distant particle of an idea what you mean.

Mr. B. Why, the gentleman who has got the attics is hardly ever without a pipe in his mouth — and there he sits with his feet on the mantle-piece —

Hob. The mantle-piece! that strikes me as being a considerable stretch, either of your imagination, Mr. B., or the gentleman's legs. I presume you mean the fender, or the hob.

Mr. B. Sometimes one, sometimes t'other. Well, there he sits for hours, and puffs away into the fireplace.

Hob. Ah! then you mean to say, that this gentleman's smoke, instead of imitating the example of all other sorts of smoke, and going up the chimney, thinks proper to effect a singularity by taking the contrary direction?

Mr. B. Why—

Hob. Then, I suppose, the gentleman you are speaking of is the same individual that I invariably meet coming up stairs when I'm going down, and going down stairs when I'm coming up?

Mr. B. Why—yes—I—

Hob. From the appearance of his outward man, I should unhesitatingly set him down as a gentleman connected with the printing interest.

Mr. B. Yes sir; and a very respectable young gentleman he is.

Hob. Well, good-morning, Mr. Bouncer.

Mr. B. You'll be back at your usual time, I suppose, sir?

Hob. Yes, nine o'clock. You need n't light my fire in future, Mr. B.; I'll do it myself. Do n't forget the bolster. *(Going — stops.)* A half-penny-worth of milk, Mr. Bouncer, and be good enough to let it stand,—I wish the cream to accumulate. *(Exit* L.*)*

Mr. B. He's gone at last! I declare I was all in a tremble for fear Mr. Nob should come in before Mr. Hob went out! Luckily, they've never met yet, and, what's more, they're not very likely to do so, for Mr. Nob is hard at work at a newspaper office all night, and does n't come home till morning; and Mr. Hob is busy making hats all day long, and does n't come home till night; so that I'm getting double rent for my room, and neither of my lodgers is any the wiser for it. It was a capital idea of mine, that it was! But as Mrs. Bouncer has left me to attend to the domestic affairs, I have n't an instant to lose. First of all, let me put Mr. Hob's things out of Mr. Nob's way. *(Takes the three hats, Hob's dressing gown and slippers, and puts them away* R. H.*)* I really must beg Mr. Nob not to smoke so much; I was so dreadfully puzzled to know what to say, when Mr. Hob spoke about it. Now, then, to make the bed,—and I must n't forget what Mrs. Bouncer told me: the head of the bed for Mr. Hob becomes the foot of the bed for Mr. Nob—people's tastes do differ so. *(Goes behind the curtain of the bed, and seems to be making it; then appears with a very thin bolster in his hands.)* The idea of Mr. Hob presuming to complain of such a bolster as this! *(Disappears again behind curtain.)*

Nob, (without.) Why do n't you keep your own side of the staircase, sir? *(Enters* L.*, then puts his head out at door again, shouting.)* It was as much your fault as mine, sir! I say, sir, it was as much your fault as mine, sir!

Mr. B. (emerging from behind the curtains of bed.) Sir, Mr. Nob, what's the matter?

Nob. None of your business, Mr. Bouncer!

Mr. B. Dear, dear Mr. Nob, what a temper you are in, to be sure! I declare, you're quite pale in the face.

Nob. What color would you have a man to be, who has been setting up long leaders for a daily paper all night?

Mr. B. But then you've all the day to yourself.

Nob, (looking significantly at Mr. Bouncer.) So it seems! Far be it from me, Bouncer, to hurry your movements; but I think it right to acquaint you with my immediate intention of divesting myself of my garments, and going to bed.

Mr. B. Very well, Mr. Nob.

Nob. Stop! Can you inform me who the individual is that I invariably encounter going down stairs when I'm coming up, and coming up stairs when I'm going down?

Mr. B. (confused.) Oh—yes—the gentleman in the attic, sir.

Nob. There's nothing particularly remarkable about him except his hats. I meet him in all sorts of hats—white hats, and black hats,—hats with broad brims, and hats with narrow brims,—hats with naps and hats without naps;—in short, I've come to the conclusion that he must be, individually and professionally, connected with the hatting interest.

Mr. B. Yes, sir; and, by the bye, Mr. Nob, he begged me to request of you, as a particular favor, that you would not smoke quite so much.

Nob. Did he? Then you may tell the gentle hatter, with my compliments, that if he objects to the effluvia of tobacco, he had better domesticate himself in some adjoining parish.

Mr. B. Oh, Mr. Nob! You surely would'nt deprive me of a lodger. *(Pathetically.)*

Nob. It would come to precisely the same thing, Bouncer; because, if I detect the slightest attempt to put my pipe out, I at once give you warning, that I shall give you warning at once.

Mr. B. Well, Mr. Nob, do you want any thing more of me?

Nob. On the contrary, I've had quite enough of you!

Mr. B. Well, if I ever! What next, I wonder? *(Goes out* L., *angrily.)*

Nob. It's quite extraordinary the troubles I always have to get rid of Bouncer, and that venerable female he calls his wife! She knows I'm up all night; and yet she seems to set her face against my indulging in a horizontal position by day. Now, let me see,—shall I take my nap before I swallow my breakfast, or shall I take my breakfast before I swallow my nap? I mean, shall I swallow my nap—no—never mind! I've got a rasher of bacon somewhere. *(Feeling in his pockets.)* I've the most distinct and vivid recollection of having purchased a rasher of bacon? Oh! here it is, *(produces it, wrapped in paper, and places it on the table,)* and a penny roll. The next thing is to light the fire. Where are my lucifers? *(Looking on mantle-piece, and, taking a box, opens it.)* Now, 'pon my life, this is too bad of Bouncer—by several degrees—too bad! I had a whole box full three days ago, and now there's only one! I'm perfectly aware that she purloins my coals, and my candles, and my sugar; but I did think that my lucifers would be sacred. *(Takes candlestick off mantle-piece, in which there is a very small end of a candle.)* Now, I should like to ask any unprejudiced person or persons their opinion touching this candle! In the first place, a candle is an article that I don't require, because I'm only at home in the day time—and I bought this candle on the first of May, calculating that it would last me three months; and here's one week not half over, and the candle three parts gone! *(Lights the fire, then takes down the gridiron.)* Bouncer has been using my gridiron! The last article of consumption that I cooked upon it was a pork-chop, and now it is powerfully impregnated with the odor of red herrings. *(Places gridiron on fire; then, with a fork, lays rasher of bacon on the gridiron.)* How sleepy I am, to be sure! I'd indulge myself with a nap, if there was any body here to superintend the turning of my bacon. *(Yawns.)* Perhaps it will turn itself. I must lie down—so here goes. *(He lies down on the bed, closing the curtains around him, after a short pause,)*

Enter HOB, *hurriedly*, L.

Hob. Well, wonders will never cease! Conscious of

being eleven minutes and a half behind time, I was sneaking into the shop in a state of considerable excitement, when my venerable employer, with a smile of extreme benevolence on his aged countenance, said to me, "Hob, I shan't want you to-day; you can have a holiday." Thoughts of "Gravesend and back—fare one shilling," instantly suggested themselves, intermingled with visions of "Greenwich for four pence!" Then came the "two-penny omnibuses," and the "half-penny boats,"—in short, I'm quite bewildered! However, I must have my breakfast first,—that'll give me time to reflect. I've bought a mutton-chop, so I shan't want any dinner. *(Puts chop on table.)* Good gracious! I've forgot the bread. Halloa! what's this? A roll, I declare. Come, that's lucky! Now, then, to light the fire. Halloa! *(seeing the match box on table,)* who presumes to touch my box of lucifers? Why, it's empty! I left one in it, I'll take my oath I did. Hey day! why the fire *is* lighted! Where's the gridiron? *On* the fire, I declare. And what's that on it? Bacon? Bacon it is! Well, now, 'pon my life, there is a quiet coolness about Bouncer's proceedings that's almost amusing. He takes my last lucifer,—my coals and gridiron to cook his breakfast by! No, no—I can't stand this! Come out of that! *(Pokes fork into the bacon, and puts it on a plate on the table; then places his chop on the gridiron, which he puts on the fire.)* Now, then, for my breakfast things. *(Goes off* L. H.*)*

Nob, (suddenly showing his head from behind the curtains.) Come in! I wonder how long I've been asleep? *(suddenly recollecting.)* Goodness gracious—my bacon! *(Leaps off bed, and runs to fireplace.)* Halloa! what's this? A chop! Whose chop? Bouncer's I'll be bound. Bouncer thought to get a breakfast, whilst I was asleep,—with my coals, too—and my gridiron. Ha, ha! But where's my bacon? *(Seeing it on table.)* Here it is. Well, 'pon my life, Bouncer's going it! And shall I curb my indignation?

Shall I falter in my vengeance? No! *(Digs the fork into the chop, opens window, and throws chop out.)* So much for Bouncer's breakfast; and now for my own! *(Puts the bacon on the gridiron again.)* I may as well lay my breakfast things. *(Exit* R. H., *making a noise.)*

Hob, (coming in quickly, L.*)* Come in! come in! *(He has a small tray, on which are tea things, etc., which he places on drawers,* L. H., *and suddenly recollects.)* Oh, goodness! my chop. *(Running.)* Holloa! what's this? The bacon again! Oh, pooh! Zounds — confound it — dash it — I can't stand this! *(Pokes fork into bacon, and throws it out of the window; goes to drawers to get tea things; returning, he encounters Nob, coming with his tea things; they walk down* C. *of stage staring at each other.)* Who are you, sir?

Nob. If it comes to that — who are *you*?

Hob. What do you want here, sir?

Nob. If you come to that — what do *you* want?

Hob, (aside.) It's the Printer! *(Puts tea things on drawers.)*

Nob, (aside.) It's the hatter! *(Puts tea things on table.)*

Hob. Go to your attic, sir!

Nob. My attic, sir? *Your* attic, sir!

Hob. Printer, I shall do you a frightful injury, if you don't immediately leave my apartment.

Nob. Your apartment? You mean *my* apartment, you contemptible hatter, you!

Hob. Your apartment? Ha, ha! come, I like that! Look here, sir — *(Produces a paper out of his pocket,)* Bouncer's receipt for the last week's rent, sir,—

Nob, (produces a paper, and holds it close to Hob's face.) Ditto, sir!

Hob, (suddenly shouting.) Thieves!

Nob. Murder!

Hob and Nob. Mr. Bouncer! *(Each running to door* L. *and calling.)*

Mr. Bouncer *runs in at door* L.

Mr. B. What's the matter? *(Hob and Nob each seize him by an arm, and drag him foward.)*

Nob. Instantly remove that hatter!

Hob. Immediately turn out that printer!

Mr. B. Well—but, gentlemen—

Hob. Explain! *(Pulling him round to him.)*

Nob. Explain! *(Pulling him round to him.)*

Hob. Whose room is this?

Nob. Does'nt it belong to me?

Mr. B. No.

Hob. No!

Nob. There! you hear, sir—it belongs to me.

Mr. B. No—it belongs to both of you!

Hob and Nob. Both of us?

Mr. B. Gentlemen, don't be angry,—but you see this gentleman *(pointing to Nob,)* only being at home in the day-time, and that gentleman *(pointing to Hob,)* at night, I thought I might venture, until my little back second floor room was ready—

Hob and Nob, (eagerly.) When will your little back second floor room be ready?

Mr. B. Why, to-morrow—

Hob. I'll take it!

Nob. So will I.

Mr. B. Excuse me, gentlemen, but if you both take it, you may as well remain where you are.

Hob and Nob. True!

Nob. I spoke first, sir.

Hob. With all my heart, sir. The little back second floor room is yours, sir,—now go!

Nob. Go! Pooh—pooh!

Mr. B. Now don't quarrel, gentlemen. You see there used to be a partition here.

Hob and Nob. Then put it up!

Mr. B. Nay, I'll see if I can't get the other room ready this very day. Now *do* keep your tempers. *(Exit* L. *door.)*

Hob. What a disgusting position! *(Walking rapidly around the stage.)*

Nob, (sitting down on chair, at one side of table.) Will you allow me to observe, if you have not had any exercise to-day, you'd better go out and take it.

Hob. I shall not do any thing of the sort, sir. *(Seating himself at table opposite Nob.)*

Nob. Very well, sir.

Hob. Very well, sir! However, don't let me prevent *you* from going out.

Nob. Don't flatter yourself, sir. *(Hob is about to break a piece of the roll off.)* Holloa! that's my roll, sir. *(Snatches it away—puts a pipe in his mouth, and lights it—puffs smoke across table toward Hob.)*

Hob. Holloa! what are you about, sir?

Nob. What am I about? I'm about to smoke.

Hob. Wheugh! *(Goes to window and opens it.)*

Nob. Holloa! *(Turning round.)* Put down that window.

Hob. Then put your pipe out, sir?

Nob. There! *(Puts pipe on table.)*

Hob. There! *(Closes window and reseats himself.)*

Nob. I shall retire to my pillow. *(Gets up, takes off jacket, goes toward bed, and sits upon it.)*

Hob, (jumps up, goes to bed, and sits down on R. *of Nob.)* I beg your pardon, sir, I can not allow any one to rumple my bed. *(Both rising.)*

Nob. *Your* bed? Hark ye, sir,—Can you fight?

Hob. No, sir.

Nob. No! Then come on. *(Sparring at Hob.)*

Hob. Sit down, sir, or I'll instantly vociferate "Police!"

Nob, (seats himself; Hob does the same.) I say, sir—

Hob. Well, sir?

Nob. Although we are doomed to occupy the same room for a few hours longer, I don't see any necessity for our cutting each others throats, sir.

Hob. Not at all. It's an operation that I should decidedly object to.

Nob. And, after all, I've no violent animosity to you, sir.

Hob. Nor have I any rooted antipathy to you, sir.

Nob. Besides, it was all Bouncer's fault, sir.

Hob. Entirely, sir. *(Gradually approaching chairs.)*

Nob. Very well, sir!

Hob. Very well, sir! *(Pause.)*

Nob. Take a bit of roll, sir?

Hob. Thank ye, sir. *(Breaking a bit off—pause.)*

Nob. Do you sing, sir?

Hob. I sometimes join in a chorus.

Nob. Then give us a chorus. *(Pause.)* Have you seen the elephant yet?

Hob. No, sir,—my wife would n't let me.

Nob. Your wife!

Hob. That is—my *intended* wife.

Nob. Well, that's the same thing. I congratulate you. *(Shaking hands.)*

Hob, (with a deep sigh.) Thank ye. *(Seeing Nob about to get up.)* You need n't disturb yourself, sir. She won't come here.

Nob. Oh! I understand. You've got a snug little establishment of your own *here*, on the sly—cunning dog. *(Nudging Hob.)*

Hob, (drawing himself up.) No such thing, sir! I repeat, sir—no such thing, sir! But my wife—I mean, my *intended* wife — happens to be the proprietor of a considerable number of bathing machines.

Nob, (suddenly.) Ha! where? *(Grasping Hob's arm.)*

Hob. At a favorite watering-place. How curious you are!

Nob. Not at all, sir. Well?

Hob. Consequently, in the bathing season — which, luckily, is rather a long one — we see but little of each other; but as that is now over, I am daily indulging in the expectation of being blessed with the sight of my beloved. *(Very seriously.)* Are *you* married?

Nob. Me! Why, not exactly.

Hob. Ah! a happy bachelor?

Nob. Why, not precisely.

Hob. Oh! a widower?

Nob. No, not absolutely!

Hob. You'll excuse me, sir, but, at present, I don't exactly understand how you can help being one of the three.

Nob. Not help it, sir?

Hob. No, sir; not you, nor any other man alive!

Nob. Ah, that may be — but I'm not alive!

Hob, (pushing back his chair.) You'll excuse me, sir, but I don't like jesting upon such subjects.

Nob. I'm perfectly serious, sir: I've been defunct for the last three years!

Hob, (shouting.) Will you be quiet, sir?

Nob. If you won't believe me, I'll refer you to a very large, numerous, and respectable circle of disconsolate friends.

Hob. My dear sir — my *very* dear sir, if there does exist any ingenious contrivance whereby a man, on the eve of committing matrimony, can leave this world, and yet stop in it, I should n't be sorry to know it.

Nob. Oh! then I presume I'm not to set you down as being franticly attached to your intended?

Hob. Why, not exactly; and yet, at present, I'm only

aware of one obstacle to my doating upon her, and that is, that I can't abide her.

Nob. There's nothing more easy. Do as I did.

Hob, (eagerly.) I will! what was it?

Nob. Drown yourself!

Hob, (shouting again.) Will you be quiet, sir?

Nob. Listen to me. Three years ago, it was my misfortune to captivate the affections of a still blooming, though somewhat middle-aged widow, at Ramsgate.

Hob, (aside.) Singular enough! Just my case three months ago at Margate.

Nob. Well, sir, to escape her importunities, I came to the determination of enlisting into the Blue, or Life Guards.

Hob, (aside.) So did I. How very odd!

Nob. But they wouldn't have me — they actually had the affrontery to say that I was too short!

Hob, (aside.) And I wasn't tall enough.

Nob. So I was obliged to content myself with a marching regiment. I enlisted!

Hob, (aside.) So did I! Singular coincidence!

Nob. But I'd no sooner done so, than I was sorry for it.

Hob, (aside.) So was I!

Nob. My infatuated widow offered to purchase my discharge, on condition that I'd lead her to the altar.

Hob, (aside.) Just my case.

Nob. I hesitated,— at last I consented.

Hob. I consented at once.

Nob. Well, the day fixed for the happy ceremony at length drew near — in fact too near to be pleasant; so I suddenly discovered that I wasn't born to possess her, and I told her so; when, instead of being flattered by the compliment, she flew upon me like a tiger of the female gender. I rejoined; when suddenly something whizzed past me, within an inch of my ear, and shivered into a thousand fragments against the mantle-piece: it was the slop-basin. I retaliated with a tea-cup. We parted, and the next morning I was served with a notice of a breach of promise.

Hob. Well, sir?

Nob. Well, sir, ruin stared me in the face — the action proceeded against me with gigantic strides — I took a desperate resolution — I left my home early one morning, with one suit of clothes on my back and another tied up in a bundle — I arrived on the cliffs — opened my bundle, deposited the suit of clothes on the very verge of the precipice — took one look down in the yawning gulf beneath me, and walked off in the opposite direction.

Hob. Dear me! I think I begin to have some slight perception of your meaning. Ingenious creature! You disappeared — the suit of clothes were found —

Nob. Exactly; and in one of the pockets of the coat, or the waistcoat, or the pantaloons — I forget which — there was also found a piece of paper, with these affecting farewell words: "This is thy work, oh, Penelope Ann!"

Hob. Penelope Ann! *(Starts up, takes Nob by the arm, and leads him slowly to the front of the stage.)* Penelope Ann?

Nob. Penelope Ann!

Hob. Originally widow of William Wiggins?

Nob. Widow of William Wiggins!

Hob. Proprietor of bathing machines?

Nob. Proprietor of bathing machines!

Hob. At Margate?

Nob. And Ramsgate!

Hob. It must be she! And you, sir, you are Nob — the lamented, long lost Nob!

Nob. I am!

Hob. And I was about to marry the interesting creature you so cruelly deceived.

Nob. Ha! then you are Hob?

Hob. I am!

Nob. I heard of it; I congratulate you—I give you joy! And now I think I'll go and take a stroll. *(Going.)*

Hob. No you don't. *(Stopping him.)* I'll not lose sight of you till I've restored you to the arms of your intended.

Nob. *My* intended? You mean *your* intended.

Hob. No, sir,—yours.

Nob. How can she be my intended, now that I'm drowned.

Hob. You're no such thing, sir! and I prefer presenting you to Penelope Ann.

Nob. I've no wish to be introduced to your intended.

Hob. *My* intended? How can that be, sir? you proposed to her first.

Nob. What of that, sir? I came to an untimely end, and you popped the question afterward.

Hob. Very well, sir!

Nob. Very well, sir!

Hob. You are much more worthy of her than I am, sir. Permit me then to follow the generous impulse of my nature — I give her to you.

Nob. Benevolent being, I wouldn't rob you for the world! *(Going.)* Good morning, sir.

Hob, (seizing him.) Stop!

Nob. Unhand me, hatter, or I shall cast off the lamb and assume the lion!

Hob. Pooh! *(Snapping his fingers close to Nob's face.)*

Nob. An insult to my very face — under my very nose! *(Rubbing it.)* You know the consequences, sir,—instant satisfaction, sir!

Hob. With all my heart, sir. Mr. Bouncer!

Nob. Mr. Bouncer!

Mr. BOUNCER *enters* L.

Mr. B. What is it, gentlemen?

Nob. Pistols for two!

Mr. B. Yes, sir. (*Going.*)

Hob. Stop! You don't mean to say, thoughtless and imprudent man, that you keep loaded fire-arms in the house?

Mr. B. Oh, no — they're not loaded.

Hob. Then produce the murderous weapons instantly.

Exit Mr. BOUNCER L.

Nob. I say, sir,—

Hob. Well, sir?

Nob. What's your opinion of duelling, sir?

Hob. I think it's a barbarous practice, sir.

Nob. So do I, sir. To be sure I don't see much objection to it when the pistols are not loaded.

Hob. No; I dare say that *does* make some difference.

Nob. And yet, sir, on the other hand, doesn't it strike you as rather a waste of time, for two people to keep firing pistols at one another, with nothing in 'em?

Hob. No, sir, not more than any other harmless recreation.

Nob. Hark ye! Why do you object to marry Penelope Ann?

Hob. Because, as I've observed already, I can't abide her. You'll be very happy with her.

Nob. Happy! Me? With the consciousness that I have deprived you of such a treasure? No, no.

Hob. Don't think of me, Nob. I shall be sufficiently rewarded by the knowledge of my Nob's happiness.

Nob. Don't be absurd, sir!

Hob. Then don't you be ridiculous, sir.

Nob. I won't have her!

Hob. I won't have her!

Nob. I have it! Suppose we draw lots for the lady — eh, Mr. Hob?

Hob. That's fair enough, Mr. Nob.

Nob. Suppose we toss up for Penelope Ann?

Hob. The very thing I was going to propose. *(They each turn aside—take out some money.)*

Nob, (aside, examining money.) Where's my tossing shilling? Here it is! *(Selecting coin.)*

Hob, (aside, examining money.) Where's my lucky sixpence? I've got it!

Nob. Now then, sir, heads win?

Hob. Or tails lose—whichever you prefer.

Nob. It's the same to me, sir.

Hob. Very well, sir. Heads I win—tails you lose.

Nob. Yes—*(suddenly,)*—no. Heads win, sir.

Hob. Very well—go on! *(They are standing opposite to each other.)*

Nob, (tossing.) Heads!

Hob, (tossing.) Heads!

Nob, (tossing.) Heads!

Hob, (tossing.) Heads!

Nob. Ain't you rather tired of turning up heads, sir?

Hob. Could n't you vary the monotony of our proceedings by an occasional tail, sir?

Nob, (tossing.) Heads!

Hob, (tossing.) Heads!

Nob. Heads? Stop, sir! Will you permit me—*(taking Hob's sixpence.)* Holloa! your sixpence has got no tail, sir!

Hob, (seizing Nob's shilling.) And your shilling has got two heads, sir!

Nob. Cheat!

Hob. Swindler! *(They are about to rush upon each other; then retreat to some distance, and commence sparring, and striking fiercely at each other.)*

Enter Mr. Bouncer, L.

Hob and Nob. Is the little back second floor room ready?

Mr. B. Not quite, gentlemen. I can't find the pistols; but I've brought you a letter—it came by the general post, yesterday. I'm sure I do n't know how I forgot it, for I put it carefully in my pocket.

Hob. And you've kept it carefully in your pocket ever since?

Mr. B. Yes, sir. I hope you'll forgive me, sir. *(Going.)* By the by, I paid two pence for it.

Hob. Did you? Then I *do* forgive you. *(Exit Bouncer.)* *(Looking at letter.)* "Margate!" The postmark decidedly says "Margate!"

Nob. Oh! doubtless a tender epistle from Penelope Ann.

Hob. Then read it, sir. *(Handing letter to Nob.)*

Nob. Me, sir?

Hob. Of course. You do n't suppose I'm going to read a letter from your intended?

Nob. *My* intended? Pooh! it's addressed to you—H-O-B.

Hob. Do you think that's an H? It looks to me like an N.

Nob. Nonsense! Fracture the seal!

Hob, (opens letter—starts.) Goodness gracious!

Nob, (snatching letter—starts.) Gracious goodness!

Hob, (taking letter again.) "Margate, May the 4th. Sir: I hasten to convey to you the intelligence of a melancholy accident, which has bereft you of your intended wife." He means *your* intended!

Nob. No, *yours.* However, its perfectly immaterial—but she unquestionably was yours.

Hob. How can that be? you proposed to her first!

Nob. Yes, but then you—now do n't let us begin again. Go on.

Hob, (resuming letter.) "Poor Mrs. Wiggins went out for a short excursion in a sailing boat. A sudden and violent squall soon after took place, which, it is supposed, upset her, as she was found, two days afterward, keel upward!"

Nob. Poor woman!

Hob. The boat, sir! *(Reading.)* "As her man of business, I immediately proceeded to examine her papers, among which I soon discovered her will; the following extract from which, will, I doubt not, be satisfactory to you: 'I hereby bequeath my entire property to my intended husband.'" Excellent, but unhappy creature! *(Affected.)*

Nob. Generous, ill-fated being! *(Affected.)*

Hob. I'm sure, Mr. Nob, I can't sufficiently thank you for your sympathy.

Nob. And I'm sure, Mr. Hob, you could n't feel more, if she had been your own intended!

Hob. *If* she'd been *my own* intended? She *was* my own intended!

Nob. *Your* intended? Come, I like that! Did n't you very properly observe just now, sir, that I proposed to her first?

Hob. To which you very sensibly replied, that you'd come to an untimely end.

Nob. I deny it!

Hob. I say you have!

Nob. The fortune's mine!

Hob. Mine!

Nob. I'll have it!

Hob. So will I!

Nob. I'll go to law!

Hob. So will I!

Nob. Stop! A thought strikes me: instead of going to law about the property, suppose we divide it.

Hob. Equally?

Nob. Equally! I'll take two-thirds.

Hob. That's fair enough — and I'll take three-fourths.

Nob. That won't do: — half and half?

Hob. Agreed! There's my hand upon it.

Nob. And mine. *(About to shake hands — a knock is heard outside,* L.*)*

Hob. Holloa! That's the postman's knock.

Nob. Postman yesterday—postman to-day.

Enter MR. BOUNCER.

Mr. B. Another letter, Mr. Hob, two pence more.

Hob. I forgive you again. (*Taking letter. Exit Mr. Bouncer.*) Another trifle from Margate. (*Opens letter—starts.*) Goodness gracious!

Nob, (snatching letter—starts.) Gracious goodness!

Hob, (snatching letter again—reads.) "Happy to inform you—false alarm."

Nob, (overlooking.) "Sudden squall—boat upset—Mrs. Wiggins, your intended"—

Hob. "Picked up by a steamboat"—

Nob. "Carried into Boulogne"—

Hob. "Returned here this morning"—

Nob. "Will start by early train to-morrow."

Hob. "And be with you at ten o'clock, exact." (*Both simultaneously pull out their watches.*)

Nob. Hob, I congratulate you.

Hob. Nob, I give you joy.

Nob. I'm sorry that most important business at the Colonial Office will prevent my witnessing the truly happy meeting between you and your intended. Good-morning. (*Going.*)

Hob, (stopping him.) It's obviously for me to retire. Not for worlds would I disturb the rapturous meeting between you and your intended. Good-morning.

Nob. You'll excuse me, sir, but our last arrangement was that she was *your* intended.

Hob. No, yours!

Nob. Yours!

Hob and Nob. Yours! (*Ten o'clock strikes outside,* L.; *noise as if of a carriage.*)

Nob. Ha! what's that? A cab's drawn up at the door. (*Running to window.*)

Hob, *(leaning over Nob's shoulder.)* A lady's got out.

Nob. There's no mistaking that majestic person—it's Penelope Ann!

Hob. Your intended!

Nob. Yours!

Hob. Yours!

Nob. Hark! she's coming up stairs.

Mr. B. *(without.)* Mr. Hob! Mr. Hob!

Hob. I've just stepped out!

Nob. So have I.

Mr. B. *(entering* L.*)* It's only me—Mr. Bouncer.

Hob. Only you? Then where's the lady?

Mr. B. Gone,—and she's left a note for Mr. Hob.

Hob, *(taking it. Exit Mr. Bouncer.)* Goodness gracious!

Nob, *(snatching letter.)* Gracious goodness! *(Hob snatches letter and runs forward, followed by Nob.)*

Hob, *(reading.)* "Dear Mr. Hob, pardon my candor"—

Nob, *(looking over and reading.)* "But being convinced that our feelings, like our ages, do not reciprocate,"—

Hob. "I hasten to apprize you of my immediate union"—

Nob. "With Mr. Bob."

Hob. Huzza!

Nob. Three cheers for Bob! Ha, ha, ha!

Mr. B., *(putting his head in* L.*)* The little second floor back room is quite ready.

Hob. I don't want it.

Nob. No more do I.

Hob. What shall tear us asunder?

Nob. What shall part us?

Hob. Nob!

Nob. Hob! *(About to embrace; Nob stops, seizes Hob's hand, and looks eagerly in his face.)* You'll excuse the apparent insanity of the remark, but the more I gaze on your features, the more I'm convinced that you're my long lost brother.

Hob. The very observation I was going to make to you!

Nob. Ah! tell me, in mercy tell me! have you such a thing as a strawberry mark on your left arm?

Hob. No!

Nob. Then it is he! *(They rush into each others arms.)*

Hob. Of course, we stop where we are.

Nob. Of course.

Hob. For, between you and me, I'm rather partial to this house.

Nob. So am I. I begin to feel quite at home in it.

Hob. Then we'll stop here.

Nob. Agreed. There's my hand upon it; *(to audience,)* join but yours, agree that the house is big enough to hold us both, then Nob—

Hob. And Hob—

Hob and Nob. Are satisfied.

LOVE IN HUMBLE LIFE.

A PETITE COMEDY, IN ONE ACT

BY JOHN HOWARD PAYNE.

DRAMATIS PERSONÆ.

RENSLAUS, A soldier.	BRANDT, A waiter.
CARLITZ, A peasant.	CHRISTINE, A peasant girl.

COSTUMES.

RENSLAUS, The uniform of a Polish serjeant.	CARLITZ, BRANDT, CHRISTINE,	Rustic Polish dresses.

REMARKS. The part of Carlitz should be performed in a serio-comic manner; that of Renslaus gruffly, in the style of a soldier long used to move and speak with trained precision; Brandt has but to take a waiter at a country inn for his model. The part of Christine requires great delicacy in personation. It is presumed that but few females are incapable of understanding the feelings of a young maiden in her situation, and consequently there will be but little difficulty in finding a competent personator.

SCENE. *A Garden. On* R. H., *a post with a sign upon it, "Good Entertainment for Man and Horse;" a table and two chairs on stage at back, in* C. *As curtain rises,* BRANDT *comes from* R. *and busies himself arranging table.*

Renslaus, (speaking outside.) March on to the barracks, comrades! I shall halt here. *(Enters, carrying a musket and knapsack.)* Where's the landlord, waiter? Why do n't he run out to catch customers, as he's in duty bound to do? Hey, lad! how dare he send such a ninny as you to represent his dignity?

Brandt. There's no landlord, sir, and mistress is busy with a party.

Rens. So much the better for her. Attention! Bring me an excellent breakfast; and send me your mistress for company: I've something to say to her.

Brandt. I beg your honor's pardon; but perhaps mistress would like to know your honor's name.

Rens. Renslaus, the soldier.

Brandt. No more, your honor?

Rens. What more would you have? The name of soldier and a countryman should be a passport any where. Quick step! forward! march! *(Exit Brandt* R., *Renslaus giving him a tap with the butt of his gun.)* No bar maid? No! My heart beats! ay, ten chances to one but poor little Christine's gone! At any rate, the landlady can give me some clue. Ouf! tolerable marching this. Ten leagues before breakfast over the mountains! But we've no right to complain: the enemy we pursue keeps ahead of us for all that; and though we gave 'em now and then a few shots, by way of "how are you to-day," the unmannerly knaves would n't so much as turn to say, "Very well, I thank you." *(Takes off his knapsack, and sets it away one side.)* For the first time in my life, my luggage seems heavy. Those villainous bank-notes, no doubt; such things never before straggled into my knapsack. Poor Colonel! I think I see him yet, stretched wounded upon the field of battle! "Renslaus," exclaimed he, "I have long been alone in the world I'm now quitting, and I must n't make the foe my heir. Take this pocket-book! Zounds! these bits of paper are not what I stand in need of; but cartridges, boy, cartridges!" From that hour, I've never fired a cartridge at the enemy; but I told 'em, "Here, you scoundrels, here's a *billet-döux* from my poor dead Colonel!" Well, well! though the weight of cash is rather new to me, yet I get on under it more gaily than ever; for I now meet the unfortunate with a different feeling from what I used to have, conscious that I possess not only a sword for their protection, but a purse for their miseries.

Enter CHRISTINE *from* R., *speaking as she enters.*

Chris. Renslaus, did he say? Renslaus, the soldier? Bless my heart! Where? where?

Rens. Ay, come at last. 'Twas almost time. *(Turns.)* I say, land—*(starting.)* Christine!

Chris. (running to him.) Oh, Renslaus! how glad I am to see you.

Rens. (faltering.) Christine! *(Turns aside.)* Zounds! what ails my eyes? *(Aloud.)* Christine? *(Aside.)* Where's my voice? I can't, I can't— *(Runs up and shakes hands with her.)* How are you, Christine?

Chris. When they told me your regiment was coming across the country, I said to myself, I'm sure we shall see him, or have a letter, at least, I'm sure. I hope you mean to stop awhile?

Rens. *Two hours,* at most—only to take breath. Then buckle on your knapsacks, shoulder your muskets, and away! We soldiers are obliged to forget our friendship at the roll of the drum, and to force as much love as we can into the little time we get between marches. Then comes the drum—'rum—'rum! Good-by to love! farewell to friendship, and off we go.

Chris. Don't your wound trouble you in these forced marches?

Rens. Not in the least, pet. You took too good care to cure it for me. I should have been obliged to quit the post but for you, Christine; and when I remember how, for one whole month—

Chris. Nonsense! nonsense! No more of that. Your being here at that time saved us from many a trouble. But for you, our house might have been burnt down; and I, who was only waiting-maid, perhaps should not now have been mistress.

Rens. Hey! What! *you* mistress, Christine? *You?*

Chris. Oh, it's a story worth hearing: I'll tell you all about it. The inn, the garden, the farm, all belong to me. You can't think how happy it makes me to receive you in *my* house, Renslaus! Will you take a turn round *my* grounds, Renslaus? But you are hungry, I know — I will prepare you something to eat.

Rens. First bring me something to drink,— water.

Chris. Water?

Rens. Ay, pure and sparkling water. I have long been a soldier, Christine, and never, though marching beneath a blazing sun, or over snow and ice, have I needed any beverage better than that which, gushing from every mountain, flowing in every valley, invites the thirsty to partake and be refreshed; yes, Christine,

> "Water, cold water, cold water for me,
> Give wine, give wine to the debauchee."

Chris. (calling R.*)* Some water, Brandt. *(Enter* BRANDT *with a pitcher of water and a tumbler, which he sets on the table, and exit* R. *Renslaus pours out a tumbler of water, and comes toward Christine.)*

Rens. Well, lassie, while I drink, you must tell me the whole affair.

Chris. You know how unhappy I was — a poor orphan, and obliged to be dependent on the old landlady, Madam Donderspank, that cross, ill-tempered —

Rens. (setting down his glass on table.) She that cooked us such bad dinners? I always hated that woman.

Chris. Well, about four months after you went away, a soldier, returning home on leave of absence, called here, and took me aside; "Miss," says he, "I have two thousand crowns to give you, from a friend, who only prays that you may be happy. Farewell!" He was gone before I had time to speak.

Rens. Right! right! *(Exultingly.)* I knew that hussar was an honest dog.

Chris. Hey! what hussar? Who told you his uniform?

Rens. (embarrassed.) Didn't you yourself?

Chris. Not I. I said a soldier, not hussar. I see now— I see you know more of this than I do, Renslaus. Who is my benefactor? You hesitate. Now I know who it is. There's nobody but you could have done so generous an action.

Rens. I, indeed! I? Pshaw, child! pshaw!

Chris. Renslaus, I have not been ashamed to accept your services, and yet you are ashamed to own you have bestowed them.

Rens. No, girl, I glory in it—I glory in it; but 'tis n't I, 'tis my Colonel. His pocket-book, which he gave me when dying, contained four thousand crowns, which I determined to divide thus: two thousand for you, and two thousand for my father,—half to him who gave me life, and half to her who preserved it. That was no more than just, you know. I charged one of my comrades with your share, and the other half I have lately been carrying with myself; but my father—a veteran—an invalid—

Chris. Well—

Rens. Had no longer need of it. He had left the service; he had gone there— *(pointing upward,)* to receive his pay. *(Wipes his eyes, pauses a moment.)* This is as it should be: you deserve to be very happy.

Chris. (sighing.) Happy!

Rens. Yes, and you must be; *(timidly and fidgeting,)* for—he—on whom—you may—deign to bestow your hand—can not help making such an—angel— *(seems greatly embarrassed, approaches her, as if to take her hand, once or twice, then recedes; aside.)* Zounds, Renslaus! courage, old boy! Do n't stand shilly-shally. *(Rallying—aloud.)* Hear me, Christine. For one whole year, you have been my file-leader, and you were always by my side, whether stretched on the cold sod after a hard march, or in the midst of whizzing bullets from the hot fire of the enemy. I have money that I do n't know what to do with; I've a heart which has not been given, and a hand which was never raised unworthily. All are at your service, and here I offer them. *(With forced resolution.)* Will you have me?

Chris. Mr.—Mr. Renslaus!—can it be—that—

Rens. Will you marry me? Out with it!—I've only two hours allowed, and there's no time to lose. *(All this is given awkwardly, with great fidgetness, a sort of sheepish manner, seen through the abruptness.)*

Chris. I do n't know how to express my gratitude; but I—what you propose is—impossible!—I—one—one ought, at least—you know—one should have time—to—to—love.

Rens. Hey! What? Do n't you love me, then?

Chris. Why—why—

Rens. Do you love me—yes or no?

Chris. Pray—in mercy—Mr.—

Rens. "Mr., Mr." Come, I hate beating about the bush. It 's a plain question: answer in one word—yes, or no!

Chris. Well, then—n—n—no!

Rens. No! not love me!—me? Can't be, Christine. Why I 'm your brother, your friend; I'd plunge for your sake into the cannon's mouth. I'd do more for you than for my poor Colonel; and for what living reason should n't you love me? I love you—and yet you treat me harder than ever German corporal treated a recruit.

Chris. I feel what you have done for me deeply—yes,

deeply! I shall never forget it, never! But I am not worthy of your kindness, and you must let me give it all back.

Rens. Give it all back! Hang it! There was only that stroke wanting. This girl will make me die of a broken heart!

Chris. Nay, pray — pray, only hear!

Rens. *(pacing violently.)* I 'll hear nothing.

Chris. Renslaus! — Renslaus!

Rens. Nothing!

Chris. Dear Renslaus!

Rens. (R.) Hey? Go on, Christine, go on.

Chris. If it should happen that I am not mistress of my choice — if, before I ever saw you, it should so chance that I loved another?

Rens. Another? True — true — I never thought of that! Ay—well — so — you loved another?

Chris. Suppose I tell you — suppose it were so, what would you say?

Rens. What would I say? I 'd say, let him take care of himself — let him keep out of the way. If I should once get hold of him —

Chris. What would you do?

Rens. Kill him!

Chris. And why would you kill him?

Rens. For having the impudence to love you. *(Crosses to L.)*

Chris. And if he did not love me?

Rens. Not love you! Who can help loving you? I should like to catch the scoundrel that did not love you.

Chris. And if you did, you 'd kill him too, would you not?

Rens. Why — no, no, — I — But come — this attachment! Now be frank — tell me — I 'm not angry — tell me —

Chris. Three years ago, I left in my native place, a cousin who had been my companion from infancy. In parting, he plighted his faith, and I believed him, for we readily believe what we wish. I have not heard from him since. He did not love me, though he said so; but I loved him, though I said nothing.

Rens. What! you never told him —

Chris. Never. I was too poor, and so was he, to think of marrying. But when — thanks to your bounty! — I had enough to live on of my own, I wrote to him to come and share it with me, and to make haste and marry me.

Rens. And he —

Chris. He never came, and yet he got the letter — oh! I 'm sure he got the letter. That was the time I bought the inn.

Rens. Now you see you 've nothing to expect from him; what are you waiting for, in order to be happy?

Chris. Alas! I only wait to feel I no longer love him.

Rens. Christine, you are an honest girl; you would not deceive me. I see, I see it 's all over. *(Clapping his hand on his heart.)* You have it there, girl, there — and what 's once there, sticks fast—fast—fast! *(Emphatically, turning away.)*

Chris. (sighs.) Ay!

Rens. Right,— right! I 'll come this way a few months hence. I— *(Going, stops short, and returns.)* Only promise me, Christine, that if you forget your cousin, you 'll think of me.

Chris. Oh! with all my heart, I promise.

Rens. Good! one day you 'll be Mrs. Renslaus. *(Laughing and voices heard on the* R, *calling, "Waiter! Landlady! Ha, ha, ha!")*

Chris. They 're calling; I must run. You 're at home here, remember, you 're quite at home. *(Exit Christine,* R.*)*

Rens. (looking after her.) Would I were indeed at home!

Enter CARLITZ, *whistling lazily,* L., *with a bundle across his shoulder, at the end of a stick. Renslaus still gazing after Christine.*

Carl. Beg pardon, Mr. —— for coming upon you so; but if you can only tell me the nearest road to the next town, you 'll oblige me very much, Mr. Soldier.

Rens. (turning.) Hallo; I know that voice! Bless my heart! 't is poor Carlitz! Do n't you remember me, lad? Do n't you remember me a month ago, at the farm in the forest, thirty leagues off? *(Holding out his hand to him.)*

Carl. (shaking hands awkwardly.) Ah! yes. You belong to that regiment that drove off the enemy the day of the battle, near our farm. Ay, a hot day's work. I fought, too, that day, with a pitchfork; and when the General saw me, he laughed, and named me "soldier," on the field. But nothing came of the nomination; for, like many a brave fellow, I had only a smile for my service, and then was straight forgotten. *(Casting down his bundle and stick* L.*)*

Rens. So it seems you 've left the farm.

Carl. Yes, Mr. Soldier; I 'm no longer a plow-jogger — I 'm an officer.

Rens. An officer!

Carl. Civil, Mr. Soldier — a civil officer: I 've a place under government. I got it by patronage; 't was Peter Linski, town clerk, that got me named Horse-post, for two leagues round our village.

Rens. Yes, one would take you for a post.

Carl. Horse, if you please — horse-post! — that is, till I lost my horse; for last night a party of the enemy's troops fell in with me,— or fell out with me, I should say — for, after parading me a few leagues, blind-fold, they set me down in the middle of the wood, gave me a cuff by the side of the head, and rode off with my horse and bags, leaving me nothing but what you see: so I 've been trudging it on foot ever since, not knowing where I was, more than the child unborn.

Rens. Then you 've had no breakfast?

Carl. Not a morsel. This is the first house I've come across; and one's feelings, on encountering a tavern sign, depend very much on the state of one's pocket, you know. I dare n't go in. So I've only ventured here to ask —

Rens. What, lad! hungry, and tired too! Here! *(taking him to table,)* here you shall eat, and drink, and be joyful! Do n't be afraid — I pay all.

Carl. What, you? No! you do n't say so? *You* pay all?

Rens. That seems to astonish you.

Carl. Not at all, 'T would astonish me a great deal more to pay for it myself. But I don't like you should spend your money for me though.

Rens. Come, no flinching, I'm at home here. Hollo! waiter? But they're all busy. I'll go myself. One's always quicker served to help one's self. Rest yourself there. You need rest — I'll come back presently — rest, rest. *(Exit Renslaus* R.*)*

Carl. I wasn't over and above pleased to meet this soldier; for he's a terrible fellow — as surly as a pioneer — and he uses his sabre with as little ceremony as I use my spurs; but he's a good fellow at heart, for he stands treat, and I could n't have kept up much longer. *(Casting himself down by his bundle.)* One finds friends where one least expects. Just as we fancy it's all over with us, something pops up unlooked for, to show that Providence never forgets us, as long as we do n't forget ourselves. When I'm rich, I'll make it up to this soldier. And I shall be rich — ay, ay, I shall work my way in the world, I am sure I shall. Peter Linski was in the right. It's foolish to get married; for then all great projects stop — one comes to a dead stand — and yet something makes me so uncomfortable — something weighs whenever I think of her. Nonsense! I can't help it though. My heart's as heavy as my eyes! I should like to see her again. Ay, that I should — I should — I — I — *(Sleeps.)*

Enter CHRISTINE *and* BRANDT, *with plates, table, cloth, napkins, etc.*

Chris. Come, lay the cloth there; brisk! brisk! mind that nothing's wanted — see that all's in order — all the best. *(Laying cloth on table.)* *(Exit Brandt* R.*)*

Carl. (dreaming.) Poor dear! Poor Christine! Chris — ris —

Chris. (starting) Who calls? *(Turns and sees Carlitz.)* Gracious me! 'tis he! 'Tis Garlitz! *(Runs to him, and checks herself, seeing Renslaus enter* R. *with a plate in each hand.)*

Rens. Victory! I see you have the table set already. *(Christine's eyes are riveted on Carlitz. Renslaus goes up to her and takes her hand.)* What's the matter, Christine? Your hand trembles.

Chris. (her eyes on Carlitz.) N — n — nothing; n — nothing.

Rens. Nothing? 't is something, I'm sure. It's what I've been saying, is n't it Christine? Ah! so much the better — that's a good sign — ay, ay — I'm glad to see that. Come, you shall sit down there, and keep us company.

Chris. No, no, no! Oh, no! I'm wanted within. The waiter will stay with you — and I — while you're at table, I'll be in and out, to see there's nothing forgot.

(Exit Christine still looking, as she goes, at Carlitz.)

Rens. As you please. *(Slaps Carlitz on the shoulder.)* Comrade! to your post!

Carl. (starting up.) I've nothing more, soldiers! You've got all I had. *(Rubbing his eyes.)* Hey? *(Looking around, recovers, and then bursts into a laugh.)* Ha, ha, ha! Well, if I did n't think I was caught by the enemy again.

Rens. No, not the enemy; but the best friend in the world, to a hungry traveler — a breakfast for a general.

Carl. Ah! what a pity! *(Sighing.)*

Rens. What a pity?

Carl. Yes! just as you waked me I was deputy post-master of the village, and from my house window I saw myself riding in a one-horse chaise, to a smoking dinner at the justice's. *(They sit at the table, Renslaus* R., *Carlitz opposite.)*

Rens. Your dreams end in smoke, do they? I'm for the solid. Come, set to. Now I should sooner have thought that a young-looking lad like you, would have dreampt of riding to see some fair dulcine — some village beauty. I'm sure you have some one in a corner thereabouts. *(Christine returns with some plates, and sets them on table at back. She remains in, her eyes riveted on Carlitz, and from time to time recedes or advances, as the conversation more or less excites her interest. Pouring out water.)* Drink my toast: "Here's to the girl of my heart." *(Drinks.)*

Carl. "Here's to the girl of my heart." *(Drinks.)* That's all right. *(Eating.)* But then, you see, Mr. Soldier, in my situation, one never ought to dream of marrying.

Chris. (aside.) Indeed!

Carl. I'm not exactly my own master. True, there was somebody of our parts that I did promise to marry.

Rens. You did promise! and why did n't you keep your promise?

Carl. Oh! family reasons, *(still eating,)* family reasons.

Rens. That's another matter — that's no business of mine. Your health, Mr. Post-horse.

Carl. I could n't have a nicer girl, because — though 't is a long time since I saw her, yet she was so gentle, so pretty, — I did love her so! but just as I was making up my mind, I thought how I should manage to get on in the world. Then I thought what a fine thing it was to be a man of consequence; and these ideas, you know, drive out the others.

Rens. A promise to a woman is like a promise to a

colonel, and ought to be held sacred. Though fortune disappoint or exceed our hopes, 't is all the same. Every thing else may change, but plighted vows never. Your honor once given, you have no right to flinch.

Chris. (aside.) Honest heart!

Carl. But then, Mr. Soldier, if it should so happen that I should not, by keeping my promise, make her happy? *(Christine starts forward.)*

Rens. That alters the case. Then you should tell her so at once, and not keep the poor girl in the fidgets. You should write the truth to her thus: *(Takes his knife and seems to write with the point of it on the plate, as he repeats slowly.)* "Miss: I take up my pen to make it known unto you, that I do n't love you any more, and so you have no need to wait any longer, and you are free to marry any body else as soon as you like. This from your loving husband that *was to be.* Carlitz." That 's the way delicate and feeling people do, when they 've had a good education.

Carl. Very well; but then I'll never write that to her.

Rens. You wo n't? *(Sternly.)* What! you wo n't?

Carl. I did n't say I would n't write — no, I will write; but then I 'll phrase it in another sort of way. I 'm willing to tell her, "Miss, I do n't love you any more"— but then I ca n't say, "Miss, you may love somebody else." She 's a treasure, I know; and though I 'm content not to take the treasure to myself, I should n't like to see it in another man's keeping.

Rens. What do you mean by that? Do you want to make a fool of the girl? Write, I tell you. Waiter! *(Enter* BRANDT *from* R.*)* Pen, ink, and paper!

Brandt. You 'll find 'em all in the room at the side there where mistress makes out her bills. *(Exit Brandt,* R.*)*

Carl. (rises.) I will write, as you insist upon it; for, after the breakfast you have given me, Mr. Soldier, 't would be ungrateful not to oblige you; but then I'll turn it my own way.

Rens. Turn it as you please, but write.

Carl. I'll go and write directly. You shall see. Yes, I will write.

Rens. Then why do n't you?

Carl. Yes, I will—I will. *(Renslaus pushes him off* R. CHRISTINE *comes down* L., *looks after Carlitz, and bursts into tears.)*

Rens. These young chaps! it's so hard to bring 'em to their senses! Perhaps the poor girl is fretting like Christine! *(Turns and sees her.)* Zounds, Christine! what's all this?

Chris. Do n't mind me; do n't mind me—it's over, it's over. *(Aside.)* But I'll have firmness; I'll have courage. *(Aloud.)* Renslaus, do you love me.

Rens. Do I love you? By the great cannons, I love you more than fighting!

Chris. Well, then—I—I should so like to be revenged on him! *(Aside.)* Renslaus, I almost *think* I love you, but I won't answer for it.

Rens. No matter. The first plunge is all.

Chris. Awhile ago, you offered me your hand—

Rens. Which you now accept?

Chris. No, no not instantly; because you are going away, you know. But never, never, without your leave shall it be given to another. I promise, never without your leave. In a month, or when you come back—then—not—not just now—I—I—I'll marry you, Renslaus.

Rens. You promise?

Chris. Yes, I promise, on one condition.

Rens. Nonsense! always making conditions! Well, well, speak! what conditions?

Chris. That from this moment you *call* yourself my husband.

Rens. Hey!

Chris. Yes, never speak of me but as your wife.

Rens. For what reason?

Chris. I can't tell—I— Oh! you are welcome to refuse. Is it so hard for you to consent to let me wear your name?

Rens. Hard? No Christine; but when I would give my life for you, it seems too little merely to give you my name! However, have your own way; 't is yours! Though but an humble name, it is at least a pure one; and that is an advantage which many an one much better born ca n't bring with him to the altar. *(Carlitz is heard without,* R.*)*

Carl. I've done it.

Chris. So! here he comes. *(Aside.)*

Carl. (entering with the letter.) I've done it, Mr. Soldier, and I'm sure it will please you a great deal better than your own. You'll be astonished at me, *that* you will, when you read it. *(Sees Chris.)* What—what—Christine! Hey! ha, ha, ha! Christine!

Chris. (feigning astonishment.) Why, bless me! if that is n't Carlitz!

Rens. (C.) And how came you to know him, hey?

Chris. (R.) He's a relation of mine, that I've not seen for a long, long while. Well, now, who would have thought of seeing *you* here, Carlitz?

Carl. (L. *aside.)* She's prettier than ever! *(Puts up the letter.)* How queer I do feel!

Chris. (aside.) My heart beats so, I can hardly stand. *(Aloud.)* You ca n't think how pleased we are both—both, to see you here, Carlitz.

Carl. "Both?" what does she mean by "both?" *(Aside.)*

Rens. "Both!" *(Aside exultingly.)* That word gives me such a fluttering! "Both!" *(Aloud.)* Ay, lad, both; for my wife's relations are always welcome to her husband.

Carl. (aside.) Wife! husband!

Chris. What's the matter, Carlitz? you seem dull. Nothing to say, after three years' absence? How does all go on in our village? Do your affairs prosper? Your sweethearts in the village, how are they all, hey?

Carl. (sulkily.) All goes on well enough—well enough, miss.

Rens. Miss! You don't call my wife a miss?

Carl. Beg pardon, madam. *(Aside.)* Zounds! that word kills my heart. *(Staggers against table.)*

Chris. What ails you, Carlitz? ain't you well? *(Crosses to him.)*

Carl. (aside.) Ay, ay! 'twere better I should be off. *(Aloud.)* Christine, I should only wish to say a few words to you, about family affairs, before I go.

Rens. Well, lad, talk away. No ceremony—we'll hear you.

Carl. Yes; but then—

Chris. Perhaps he would rather it should only be between us *alone!*

Rens. (aside to her.) I'd rather stay.

Chris. (aside to him.) Yes, but I wouldn't like he should go and say I had a husband that wasn't accommodating.

Rens. (aside to her.) Oh! for that—so then, husbands must—

Chris. Yes.

Rens. Oh! *(bows,)* since I'm in that regiment, I must obey the countersigns. I'm off! *(Renslaus retires a little* R. *Carlitz, who has been standing by the table, with his back to Christine, turns ill-humoredly, and exclaims with emphasis.)*

Carl. As you were married, miss, for what reason?—*(Renslaus starts, returns, looks at him, walks to Christine, and says in a low tone.)*

Rens. I leave you, Christine, without fear; because I have your promise you'll be mine, or you'll be no other man's without my leave; so I'm easy. For a moment, then, adieu!

(Looks sternly at Carlitz, and then exits R.*)*

Chris. We're by ourselves, now. Well, Carlitz, and those family affairs you had to speak about?

Carl. There's no family affairs. I only wanted to make you my compliments on your constancy, and did n't dare before him.

Chris. What do you mean by my constancy? Was I bound to stay single all my lifetime, because it pleased my gentleman not to answer my letter?

Carl. Who could have guessed you would have been in such a hurry? and you must have been in a great hurry to have taken such a fellow for a husband.

Chris. And pray, sir, what is there about him so bad?

Carl. You need n't bawl so — every body knows what soldiers are; and this fellow is a jealous dog, and a brute into the bargain.

Chris. Brute or no brute, he loves me, and he is right; for I return it, and heartily too! yes, heartily, Mr. Carlitz! I love him! I adore him! and I'm never happy without him! So, sir, there! *(Crosses to* R.*)*

Carl. Wow, wow, wow! It's all very well! exceedingly well! Do n't fancy I'm jealous. I might have cared, indeed, if it had been any decent, well-mannered man. But *(with a vexed laugh,)* for such a spitfire! ha, ha! a fellow that I am sure will make you miserable, ha, ha, ha! that's all right! that's as it should be! Yes, miserable! that's what will please me. Then, then, at least, I shall — I shall — ha, ha, ha! — I shall be revenged.

Chris. Revenged!

Carl. I shall be revenged!

Chris. What, Carlitz, revenged? What harm did I ever do you? Is it my fault that you refused me? you, to whom, as soon as I got a little fortune, I offered my hand and heart,— you? "We shan't be, just at first, very rich," said I to myself; "but then we'll work hard, and be very saving; and Carlitz, who always had lofty notions, will be pleased to find himself master of the head inn of the province; and he'll think how much better it is to command in his own house, than to be commanded in another man's. We'll work hard all day, and have little parties of our friends in the evening; and hear the neighbors, as we pass along to church on Sunday, dressed in our best clothes, saying to one another, with a smile, 'There goes honest Carlitz, and his happy wife, Christine.'" This, Carlitz, is the plan of happiness I had formed for you; and it is for this, Carlitz, that you now wish to be revenged!

Carl. (thumping his hand on the table.) What a poor, unhappy fellow I am! and what I've lost! Oh, what I've lost! But perhaps you could n't wait any longer! Oh, I hate him more than ever, for having robbed me of the treasure of such a heart as yours.

Chris. Did n't you refuse it? only a moment ago, did n't you write to refuse? That very letter —

Carl. That letter! what of that letter? Come, now, if you knew all — if you could guess — my — my — secret.

Chris. Hey! what! a secret? have you a secret?

Carl. Yes; but I mus n't tell it to you — you're married.

Chris. Come, now, there's only one proof you can give me, that your vows were ever sincere. Tell me the secret.

Carl. Take — read — read! My secret is in that letter; and when you've read it, I go — I leave you! I'll walk to the world's end. *(Gives the letter.)*

Chris. (reading.) "Loving Miss: I look high in the world; but I'm no rascal. An honest chap has just proven unto me that if I do n't love you any more, I'm in duty bound to say so; accordingly I take up my pen to tell you, that —" Well! the next lines are scratched out.

Carl. (sobbing.) Read on, read on.

Chris. Ah! "to tell you that *(rapidly,)* I love you as much as ever; and I could n't write the other word for the soul of me, because I feel now 't would be a lie!" *(Christine stops and sobs.)*

Carl. (sobbing.) Read on, read on.

Chris. (reading.) "Yes, my loving cousin, it is Peter Linski and his counsels that have turned me out of the straight road, by promising to make me a great man; but I never stopped loving you, and I always will love you, and I 'll marry you as soon as you like. Your loving cousin, and expected husband, that is to be, Carlitz." *(Carlitz takes his hat.)*

Carl. Good-by, good-by!

Chris. What! won't you stop here?

Carl. (stopping short.) How can you have the heart to keep me here by you, after what you 've read? You see, Mrs. Renslaus, I love you yet — you see that. Good-by, cousin, good-by! *(Going toward* R. *meets Renslaus, who turns him back.)*

Chris. Renslaus! *(Runs off* L.*)*

Rens. Where are you going to, comrade?

Carl. Can't you see? I 'm going — I 'm going —

Rens. It seems *you* can't see, lad! Where are your eyes? Your road's that way. *(Pointing toward the back of the stage.)*

Carl. Right — right. There 's something in my eyes that — *(Aside.)* She 's no longer there! I shall never see her again!

Rens. So, lad, you 've said "good-by," and had your parting kiss.

Carl. No, no, no! That — I forgot that.

Rens. It 's all one — I 'll take it for you. There 's your path: *(pointing off,)* it 's a fine road. Pleasant journey: — good-by, kinsman, good-by. What! not gone yet?

Carl. Ay — ay — I was — Before I go, I have a favor to ask.

Rens. (aside.) What does all this mean? He seems extremely loath to go. *(Loud and coarsely.)* Well, out with it! I hear you.

Carl. Why — 'tis — you see — I was thinking —

Rens. You talk too slow, lad. Quick time! forward!

Carl. (very quick.) Well! I say, if you'd only have the kindness just to give me a place in the inn, only as a waiter, you'd be satisfied with me — I know you'd be satisfied; and I only ask my living and my lodging — that's all; and I'll serve you without any wages — without any wages.

Rens. (gloomily.) Indeed! we'll think of that — we'll see — we'll see; ay, you *shall* come, on *trial;* and though you offer to come without wages — *(Clapping him on the shoulder. Carlitz trembles.)* You *shall* have wages, do you hear? You shall have wages, I *promise* you.

Carl. Thank ye, Mr. Soldier; thank ye! but you say that with such a tone! I'm sure I wouldn't put you out of the way, not I, to give me wages; and if the plan don't happen, Mr. Soldier, to suit you —

Rens. It suits me well enough, well enough; but I must first see if it suits my wife. *(Going* R., *Carlitz runs after him.)*

Carl. Oh! 'twill suit her, I know — I know 'twill suit her.

Rens. (turns abruptly.) How do you know that, sir?

Carl. Oh! she — she, herself — she said she'd like — I'd stop.

Rens. She! she'd like? *(Aside.)* Can Christine mean to play upon me — to deceive me? Impossible! impossible! and as for him! — *(Aloud.)* Hear me! *(Crosses to him.)* I'll see my wife, and come to an understanding with her; Meantime, you may stop on one condition.

Carl. (eagerly.) Well?

Rens. Never to speak one word to Christine. You hear?

Carl. Oh yes, I hear.

Rens. And if you should chance to catch any whipper-snapper fluttering about her, and trying to get a word with her, you must tell me, and I'll teach the butterfly what my sabre's made of. You can take a hint? *(Exit Renslaus,* R.*)*

CHRISTINE *peeps in* L.

Christine. No, Renslaus is not there. *(Comes down.)* Ah, Carlitz, not gone! *(Carlitz makes a sign.)* What's the matter? Dumb! Is the man crazy? *(Carlitz takes a napkin, and motions that he is to be a waiter.)* No! what? to stay here as— Well, now! And your high notions—your plans of greatness?

Carl. Yes, Christine, I've given up greatness; and here I'll stick. But then, Christine, sure you'll not be angry if I ask one favor—it's the last.

Chris. What favor?

Carl. Only one kiss — one kiss, to say it's all over, Carlitz.

Chris. A kiss! What would Renslaus say?

Carl. Zounds! what do I care? The rascal! What, Christine, is there no way — none — no way that can be hit on, lawfully, to let me love you?

Chris. Why, yes, there may be one.

Carl. May there? Ha, ha, ha! What is it, Christine? Hey! what is it?

Chris. To get his leave.

Carl. (receding.) His leave!

Chris. Yes, it depends entirely upon him; and if he gives you leave — But you must ask him *yourself.*

Carl. I ask! He'd murder me on the spot.

Chris. Then you don't love me well enough to ask?

Carl. Don't I? Indeed, whether I die by his rage, or my own fretting, it amounts to the same thing at last; so I'll—I'll—

Rens. (without, violently.) Christine! Christine!

Carl. Blessed Saint Diggory! Look! he's coming now— now — *(rallying.)* I feel all my courage *(relapsing, turns.)* going.

Enter RENSLAUS, R.

Renslaus. Christine, I say! Christine! So I've found you at last. But I did n't *(low to her)* expect to find you here with *him.* What, Christine! can it be you have secrets from me? By the great cannon! if I thought so I'd— *(Aside.)* Hang it! I forgot I'm only a husband on trial. Forgive me, Christine, and as a pledge of peace — come, kiss and be friends. *(Approaching to kiss her, sees the letter in her bosom, and starts.)* Zounds! what letter's that?

Carl. (shuddering.) O, dear! O, dear!

Chris. That! that's — a — love-letter!

Rens. A love-letter!

Chris. Yes, I've just received it; and as I've no concealments from you, there, *(holding out the letter,)* read it!

Rens. (taking it.) A love-letter!

Carl. He'll guess it's I, and then my game's up. O, dear! O, dear!

Chris. Now go and ask him; this is the happy moment. *(Pushing him forward.)*

Carl. (aside, trembling.) Ay, mighty happy!

Rens. (aside, his eyes riveted on the letter.) Can it be? What! *(Looks at him.)* That booby! can he be the cousin she was pining after? *(Turns again to the letter.)* Confound it! there's real love here! *(Christine pushes Carlitz forward.)*

Carl. (stammering.) M — M — Mr. S — S — Soldier.

Rens. (without turning.) Well, what do you want of me?

Carl. M — Mr. Soldier, I — do n't know how to get about it — to — tell you — or rather, Mr. Soldier,— to ask you —

Rens. Let's have it at once. *(Listening with his back turned toward him.)*

Carl. Well, then, Mr. Renslaus, it's no fault of mine, you know — so, you know, you wo n't get in a — passion, Mr. Soldier; but it strikes me — I — I — I love your wife.

Rens. *(coldly.)* I know you do.

Carl. Then — then Mr. Soldier — I only wanted to — ask you — if it's all one to you — no, that's not what I mean — I mean — it can't be all one to you — I know that very well; but for all that, if you would be so good as to allow that in return, your wife —

Rens. Well!

Carl. M — m — might — love me!

Rens. *(starting round, with a violent gesture.)* Ha!

Carl. *(dropping on his knees.)* A little — only a little — no more. *(Rens. turns away.)* Why — why — bless my soul, he do n't fly into a rage!

Rens. *(very loud, and without turning.)* Come here! *(Carlitz totters across to him.)* And who was it that bade you ask me?

Carl. (C.) Hey! *(Aside to Christine.)* Must I tell?

Chris. (L. *aside, to him.)* Yes, yes.

Carl. Christine herself. She said it depended on you; and without your leave there was no way.

Rens. (R. *to himself.)* Right! That's well — that's very well! *(Crosses to* C.*)* So, *(faltering,)* Christine, 'tis you.

Chris. Yes, 'tis I. But remember, you have the right to refuse. My promise has been given — my word is sacred; and whatever you may command, I obey without a murmur.

Rens. Without a murmur! No, Christine, you are too tender for the school of anguish; but an old soldier is used to hard rubs, and knows how to suffer and be silent. *(To Carlitz.)* You ask leave to love Christine: do you promise to make her happy?

Carl. *(aside.)* What an odd question for a husband! *(Aloud.)* Well, Mr. Soldier, I'll promise to do the best I can.

Rens. Still, you have nothing and Christine is rich.

Carl. Rich; ay, so she is! I never thought of that.

Rens. Then take this pocket-book; go, offer it to Christine—'tis yours. And now, Carlitz, now you may marry her. *(Agitated, crosses to* R. *corner.)*

Carl. Marry your wife!

Rens. She is not my wife; that treasure Heaven never meant for me. But of this, at least, I'm master; and in making it the source of happiness to the virtuous, I pay the noblest tribute to his memory who gave it. I only ask, in return, that you never let the poor soldier leave your door unsuccored; but tell him, as he departs rejoicing on his way, "*Take this for the sake of poor Renslaus.*" My duty calls. *(Clasping their hands.)* Farewell! God bless you! God bless you both!

Disposition of Characters at fall of Curtain:

R.	C.	L.
CARLITZ.	RENSLAUS.	CHRISTINE.

THREE ERAS
IN THE
LIFE OF A FARMER'S SON.

A DOMESTIC DRAMA, IN THREE ACTS.

BY P. A. FITZGERALD.

DRAMATIS PERSONÆ.

FARMER CONTENT. | GEORGE, Farmer's son. | 2d BOY.
DAME CONTENT. | 1st BOY. | JOHN.
ELLEN, the Farmer's daughter. Boys, Girls, etc.

COSTUMES, MODERN.

ACT I.*

SCENE. *A kitchen in Farmer Content's house. Supper table set: on one side is seated the Farmer, Ellen and George on the other, Mrs. Content at the head.*

Farmer. (L.) Well, wife, once again — thanks to the bounty of that Providence to which we are so much indebted! — we are seated around our family board with appetites sharpened by honest labor. It is given us to partake; and with grateful hearts, thinking of those, who, being poor, have not the means of satisfying their hunger; of the sick who pine in their dreary chambers, let us now thankfully attack the viands which your skill has made so tempting.

*A year is supposed to elapse between each Act.

Ellen. (R.) Dear father, you are so happy always that it seems impossible for you to be otherwise. Tell us, father, how is it that you are so?

Far. I will tell you. I would have George listen, too; for if possible, I would have him overcome the desire he has to become a resident of the metropolis, rather than remain upon the farm.

George. (R.) I confess, father, that I am tired of the country; it is so dull.

Far. My son, years ago, I was a youth like you; but unlike you, I had no happy home,—no mother, father or sister to take an interest in my welfare. I had no friend, save the hope of youth, nothing to trust to, save a will that scorned all opposition. Lacking in education,—then we knew not, as the children of this generation know, the blessings of a system of instruction favoring equally the wealthy and proud, the poor and humble,—I worked. There was ahead of me a star whose light lured me on to struggle, and I did struggle. I have ever been a hard-working man; but I have also been a happy man. To the labor of these hands am I indebted for the comforts that now, in my age, surround me. To be an honest, independent farmer, was my desire; and the summit of my ambition being attained, why should I not be happy? You, George, know what comforts surround the industrious farmer; you know that his pursuit is an honorable one; and yet, on this evening, you leave us to tempt the dangers of a sphere of life with which you are entirely unacquianted.

George. What you say is true, father; but a farmer's life is too much of an every-day affair. I want something exciting.

Far. Well, George, I have said upon the subject all that I think necessary. If you are determined to forsake the parental roof in the vague hope of acquiring riches, you must e'en take your own course. But remember the honor of the name you bear. No stains rest on that your father proudly writes, and should you, yielding to the numerous temptations that will doubtless assail you, bring disgrace upon it, you will have planted a thorn in your parent's heart, that to eradicate I fear would be impossible.

Dame Content. And, George, don't, as you value the blessings of Heaven, forget the lessons your mother has taught you. You have been a child of many prayers, forget not that.

George. I will not, mother:

Enter JOHN, L.

John. Master, what are we to do with that old brindle? she's been playing her tricks with the fence again. That's the worst old cow I ever did see!

Far. We'll attend to her soon, John.

John. So, master George, you are going to the city, eh!

George. When the stage arrives I shall start.

John. Well, every one to his taste; but I would rather stay in the country and breathe the fresh air, than be cooped up in the dusty city.

Far. I fear John, nothing but painful experience will turn him to your way of thinking; yet should the trials for which he may be destined show him how fallacious are the hopes of man, they will be blessed to a useful end.

Ellen. Your trunks are in the hall, are they not, George?

George. Yes; when the stage arrives, John will assist me to carry them out to the road, will you not, John?

John. Certainly, master George. (*Exit* L.)

Far. (*all rise and come forward.*) Now, George, as you are determined not to listen to my advice in this matter,—though you are proceeding contrary to what I could desire,—yet would I say that which it behooves a son to listen to as coming from a father, and a father to speak, when parting from one who will soon be surrounded by other associations than those to which he has been accustomed.

Dame. (L.) I hope George will continue virtuous, for the sake of his old mother.

Far. (R. C.) And for the sake of that feeling which accompanies the practice of virtue.

George, (R.) But why, father, do you fear for me? I have never yet failed in filial duty, in loving those who are bound to me by the ties of kindred and affection.

Far. Very true, my son; yet you are but young, and youth is impressible. Town vices are gaily gilt, rank in growth.

George. But, there are thousands in our large cities who deserve respect for their virtue, for all the qualities that enrich, ennoble man.

Far. Ay, were it not so, what would save our towns and cities from the fate of the now silent Dead Sea city? There are many benevolent, Christian residents in our cities; but the majority of their population is composed of those who regard not the laws of morality as strictly as they should. It is the example of the bad that is to be feared, for evil is ever present. Our natures, debased originally, seek that excitement in the pursuit of worldly pleasures which, indulged in to an undue extent, is too apt to claim alliance with wickedness.

George. Well, father, your forebodings with respect to my career will prove groundless. I will ever remain worthy your regard.

Far. Fervently do I hope so. To see you become a good man, a worthy citizen, has been, and will continue to be, my never ceasing prayer. If the expectations thus formed should be disappointed, the hope of years will be extinguished.

Enter JOHN, L.

John. The stage is in sight.

Far. Well, John, get the trunks out to the road: George will be ready in a few minutes. *(Exit John, L.)*

Dame. Oh, I wish you would give up this idea, George, Now that you are about to say "farewell," I feel how hard it is for a mother to part from her child. But you will not, I am sure, forget us,—you will write often—tell us everything; but, above all, be a good boy. When tempted to wrong, let your thoughts turn to us;—think of your mother, father, sister!—

George. There, there, don't take on so! I will, as you desire, be all that a respectable young man should be.

Ellen. (L. C.) That I am sure he will! George can never forget us, for where will he find others to love him half as fervently as we do?

George. I will strive, sister, to follow good; but you must not blame me for desiring to leave the country. I do not feel that I am qualified for a farmer's life, and I am certain that mercantile pursuits will prove more consonant with the abilities I possess.

Far. My son, ere you leave us I have one thing more to say to you: "Virtue is its own reward." Remember that—practice the lesson it teaches—and the fears I have expressed relative to your welfare will certainly prove groundless. Now, take with you a father's blessing, and this "Holy Book." *(Giving Bible.)* The Bible, well studied, will furnish you with infallible rules of conduct—its contents, my son, fell from the lips of God, or those of his inspired prophets and apostles. Study them, then. Let no day or night pass without a few minutes' perusal of its pages—adhere strictly to the teachings therein contained, and you will be proof against the assaults of evil. Value it as your parents' gift; but more, in that it contains the exposition of your Creator's holy will.

John, (entering L.*)* The stage is waiting.

Far. Farewell, boy, farewell! and may heaven be with you! *(Shakes his hand, then retires up.)*

Dame, (embracing him.) So prays your mother, boy. There, go—go—and forget not those you leave behind.

George. Good-by! I shall return to prove how well your counsel has been remembered. Good-by, sister. *(Embracing her.)* Farewell, all! *(Exit George.* L.*)*

Far. Farewell, my son, farewell! *(Farmer falls into a chair,* C; *Dame kneels one side of him,* R., *Ellen the other,* L.*)*

ACT II.

SCENE. *Kitchen in Farmer Content's house as before; work-table, and Basket,* C.; *chairs, etc. Farmer and Dame discovered, at Table.*

Far. (L.) Just one year ago to-day since our boy left us! Alas, wife, I fear that all is not right with him! I long for his return, yet dread to meet him.

Dame, (L.) Nay, husband, George was too good a boy to be easily led astray. I am certain all is as it should be. Here comes Ellen.

Enter ELLEN, L.

Far. Well, rosebud, what say the lads and lasses, eh?

Ellen. George's friends are collecting. In a few minutes he will be here.

Enter JOHN, L.

John. The young folks are here, sir, inquiring if master George has yet arrived.

Far. (rising.) Bid them welcome! *(Exit John,* L.*)* Ellen, my dear, prepare some refreshments for the young folks. *(Enter several young people of both sexes.)* You are welcome, lads and lasses. George will be delighted at finding so many of his former companions ready to meet and welcome him.

1st Boy. Yes, but if George has got to be a city man, he won't be much pleased with our homespun clothes and country breeding, I am afraid.

2nd Boy. George was always a little proud, to be sure but he never will slight his old playmates, merely because they are more coarsely habited than are your fine city folks. Our faces may be browned by the sun, because we are exposed to his rays while engaged in honest labor; yet what of that? If the sun does paint our skin a little dark, it does n't take from our worth, nor should we blush to look an honest mirror in the face.

Far. Well said, my lad! no man need blush at being called a working-man. Labor's scars are honorable, for labor was ordained man's lot by a decree of the world's great Master. The shame is for those who, thinking labor not genteel, despise it; while the only qualifications they possess are those that should bring them into disrepute with every honest man.

Enter JOHN, L.

John. The stage has turned the brow of the hill; in five minutes more it will be here.

Dame, (down R. H.*)* Oh, how I long to see the boy! Only think, how for one whole year he has been a stranger to his childhood's home — one year! an age to parents who love their children.

Far. And where, Dame, will we find those who do not? It is a holy feeling,— natural to all. But see! the coach has stopped, and here comes our boy. *(Enter* GEORGE, L., *dressed very foppishly.)* My dear boy, welcome back to your father's house! There, embrace your mother and sister! then do not forget your young friends, who have assembled to greet you.

George, (in an affected manner, crossing to C.*)* Ah, governor!

Far. (surprised.) Governor!

George, (drawlingly.) Or father. Governor is a term made use of by us in the city,—it is synonymous with the word father, but more expressive; father being too old-fogyish for us of the city to admire.

Dame. Why, George, it strikes me that the term governor is an irreverent one.

George. Not at all, not at all. We of the city have a very high idea of the excellence of family ties; but we are progressive—father is ancient, so we discard the term for one more expressive of goaheaditiveness.

Ellen, (L.; boys and girls are ranged behind.) How altered you are in appearance, brother, you do not look as healthy as you were before you left us.

George. Aw, sis.,—excuse my abbreviation of the term; it is a fashion in vogue with us of the city—you are quite mistaken: I was never better in all my life, I assure you! 'pon honor. But what can it be that operates so intensely upon my sense of smell since my arrival? The odor of a barn-yard seems to pervade the entire atmosphere. *(Applying his handkerchief to his nose.)*

Far. Why, boy, I suppose you have been so used to the delicate *air* of a fashionable store, that ours is too healthy for your endurance. But, now that I look at you again, I perceive a marked change in your appearance,—you look weak, and—nay! that can not be—as if suffering from the effects of dissipation and late hours.

George. Well, to tell the truth, I have been somewhat nocturnal in my pleasures. We find but little time during the day for participation in the sports going on, so we take night. Quite natural, you know, and the way with city folks.

Dame. Alas! alas!

George. Halloo! how's this? you seem to look upon me as if there was something wrong. What is it, eh? Tell me, sis., what's the matter with the governor, and the old woman?

Ellen. George, George, I am ashamed of you! That you should speak so irreverently of those to whom you are bound by the strongest ties of relationship; of those whom you should love and reverence, fills me with wonder. It is wrong, George, wrong!

George. Another lecturer in feminine attire. Sis., your education has been neglected; you should come to the city, leave these vulgar people, and mingle with those who are refined.

Ellen. Vulgar people! why, our neighbors are all respectable, honest tillers of the soil — men of intelligence, and women of worth: what would you more?

George. Well, there is a certain air that is only to be acquired by intercourse with us of the city. It is impossible for people who do nothing but dig in the ground, cut grass, hoe potatoes and corn, and participate in such other laborious and plebeian occupations, to acquire the manner *distingué*, as the French say — to become like us people of the *ton.*

Far. Do you not see, George, that your young friends wonder to hear such sentiments advanced by one who was born and reared amongst those whom he now affects to despise!

George. Why, yes, gov.— I mean father — they do certainly seem somewhat surprised; but then it 's the way with us of the city never to notice any thing of the kind. They are, of course, ignorant of the rules that govern good society, and I can, therefore, excuse them.

Dame. I am afraid, my son, that your education in the ways of the city has hardened your heart — done evil to its former virtues.

Far. *(apologetically.)* Nay, nay, Dame, our boy is merely playing upon his friends. It can not be that one single year could change him from a warm-hearted boy to one familiar with worldliness. Are you so changed, my boy?

Ellen. Say no, my brother. Tell us that this singular

conduct is foreign to your nature; that the sentiments you utter are equally so, to the ones you really hold.

George. Why, what a fuss you are kicking up, to be sure, merely because I wear the appearance of a man of fashion, and have independence enough to differ with my friends and acquaintances as to the pleasure of a country life—the expediency of the course I have taken for success in the future. *(Ellen throws her arms around his neck.)* I beg your pardon, sis., but if you'll take the trouble to look, you'll find that you are disarranging my linen, by your plebeian manner of embracing. Pray, have some feeling for my laundress.

Far. Leave him, Ellen, leave him; the caresses of a sister are dear to him no more. Come with your mother and me, for our nightly rendering of thanks to the Power that preserves us is yet to be made. George, as you were about to leave us, I placed in your hand a copy of God's *Holy Bible*—much, I fear, my son, you have not read it.

George. Why, as to that, I think I have looked into it on several occasions; but it's not the book for us of the city; so, in fact, I—I have not perused it very extensively.

Ellen. Those, George, who speak as you have spoken, must be strangers to the lessons taught them in that book of books, which you speak so lightly of. Deeply, brother, do I deplore that you ever left your quiet country home, to mingle with those to whom virtue is a jest—the debased, to whom purity is unknown,—the worldly-minded, the wicked, who, forgetful of their duty to man, to Heaven, spurn the teachings of religion; and so doing, prove themselves foolish, even to the destruction of their souls.

George. You are certainly right, sis., but I can't, as I'm alive, discover the reason for this singular conversation. Make yourself comfortable, sis., I shan't come either to the prison or the gallows,—but I must be allowed to remark that your observations are certainly ancient and out of keeping with the spirit of the age. *(Ellen is going* R.*)* You are going, eh? Well, *au revoir*, sis.

Far. George, the day is indeed fraught with sorrow The prodigal son has returned, but not repentant. Dame, Ellen, come — our family circle must not be forgotten, nor in our prayers, will be my wayward son.

(Exeunt Dame, Farmer, and Ellen, R.*)*

George. What antiquated beings they are! Well, boys and girls, here I am at last. I've come like a good missionary, to clear your benighted minds — to show you a sample of "Young America."

1*st Boy.* Why, what a fine gentleman you have got to be?

2*d Boy, (aside to the others.)* Yes, "fine feathers," they say, "make fine birds."

1*st Boy.* Tell us something about the city, George.

George. Listen, then. *(Places a chair* C.*, and stands upon it.)* Be this my rostrum. Fellow citizens, though you live in the country, removed from the center of civilization, I think you have sense enough to comprehend what I am about to say. In the first place, then, you must know that man was made for society; and it is a false feeling, the offspring of necessity alone, that binds him to inhabit where solitude is the monarch — where there is nothing to be seen but fields and woods, nothing to be heard save the lowing of cattle, the cackling of hens, or the squealing of hogs. What, my friends, are the advantages of a city life? I will tell you. There you can study man and manners — obtain a knowledge of the great world — there you have a chance of becoming famous, for *progress* is the word! Young America there plumes himself for a returnless flight. So, hurrah for the city! *(All shout except 2d Boy.)*

2*d Boy, (aside.)*

"How much a dunce that has been sent to Rome,
Excels a dunce that has been kept at home."

George. That is right—and now I move we adjourn.

1st Boy. Yes let's adjourn.

George. Well said, my little one. I suppose the governor is anxious to have some talk with me, and as I do not wish to rouse the old gent.'s prejudices, I must allow him the opportunity.

All. Right, so good-night.

George. Or, as we say in the city, "*bon soir.*" *(All exit* L.) Ha, ha, ha! my return has kicked up considerable of a dust, and no mistake. If the governor knew the liabilities I have to pay, I should not escape a huge torrent of parental exhortation. However, this is too dull for me; to-morrow, and ho! for the city again! *(Exit* R.*)*

ACT III.

SCENE. *Same as in the last Act. Enter* ELLEN, *reading a letter,* R.

Ellen. How shall I break the news to my poor parents? Oh, George! brother so much loved, son so dear, how could you thus destroy all the hopes that have so clung around your career? *(Reads.)* "Dear Sister:—I have brought disgrace upon you all; I am now a criminal, fleeing before the officers of justice. In an evil hour, tempted beyond forbearance, I abstracted from my employer's till a small sum of money. The crime was soon discovered, and I, the criminal, forced to flee in shame and disgrace from the sight of those who knew me!"

Enter JOHN, L.

John. Oh, Miss Ellen, such news! Old Deacon Perry

has just returned from a visit to his son, and he says he met with master George on the way, looking —

Ellen. Hush, John, for mercy's sake! I fear Deacon Perry was not mistaken; but the news he brings must not be allowed to spread.

John. That's what I told the deacon, and he said that no one should learn of the matter from him. The Deacon is a man of his word, so the secret is a safe one. But what in the world could have induced Master George to this course?

Ellen. That which has ruined thousands, ere he fell — the influence of a city life upon one reared in the country.

John. Thank goodness, Miss Ellen, I am content to remain in the country, content

> "To plough, and sow, and reap, and mow,
> And be a farmer's boy."

Ellen. You will be happier for the disposition. Ah! I hear the sound of a wagon — father and mother are returning.

John. Well, I'll away, to take care of the horses.

(Exit L.*)*

Ellen. A faithful heart concealed beneath the roughness of an uncouth exterior. They come.

Enter FARMER *and* DAME, L.

Far. A chair, Ellen, for the poor old farmer, and his grief-bowed wife. *(Sits.)* Lo! this is rest for the wearied limbs; but where shall we look to find rest for our wearied hearts!

Dame, (by the farmer, L., *pointing up.)* There! we can look for consolation to Him who hath often, ere this, soothed our sorrows. Remember "there is balm in Gilead, there is a physician there."

Far. True, true! else would we fall beneath the weighty woe that hath come upon us.

Ellen, (aside.) Can it be they have learned the news? *(Aloud.)* Father, what ails you? you look unwell.

Far. My boy, my boy! Your brother, Ellen!

Ellen. You have heard — ?

Far. (weeping.) Too much, too much! I have just seen Deacon Perry, and — alas! that these old eyes should ever dim in weeping over a son's downfall.

Ellen. But he has repented, father.

Far. What repentance can restore to him the feelings of his youth ere lured from home? He left us to fall, fall, fall! *(Weeps.)*

Dame. What letter have you there, Ellen?

Ellen. 'T is from George.

Far. From George! give it me. *(Takes letter and reads.)* Poor misguided youth! we must go to him; he shall again return to his home! Tell John to get the wagon ready. Dame, you are too much exhausted, I fear, to accompany me. I will, alone, go and seek my misguided boy.

(Ellen exit L.*)*

Dame. No, I will go with you. I could not remain behind, suffering from the suspense that I now feel.

Re-enter ELLEN, L.

Ellen. Surely, mother, you need some refreshment ere you depart — some rest.

Far. Rest! rest for this old body, while a loved son is trembling on the verge of a precipice, whose frowning brow looks ever over a gulf of sorrow, woe, despair? No rest for me, until George is again restored to us. Come, Dame, hand in hand, trusting to Heaven for strength, together let us on.

(Exeunt Farmer and Dame, L.*)*

Ellen. Poor father, poor mother! would I could alleviate their sorrows. I can but weep with them. *(Exit* R.*)*

John, (entering L.*)* Miss Ellen! Miss Ellen! *(calling.)* Where can she be gone to? *(Looks off* L.*)* Halloo! there's a straggler in the yard; I must look to him. Master is gone, so vigilance is my duty. *(Exit* L.*)*

Ellen, (entering R.*)* I thought I heard John's voice. I must send for Deacon Perry, and learn from him how my poor brother seemed. I'll write a note to him, and John shall carry it. *(Exit* R.*)*

Enter GEORGE, L., *looking sick, and dressed in tattered clothes.*

George. No one here to welcome me — me, the houseless wanderer, the young in years, the old in sin and folly. Could I have foreseen my fate, how gladly would I have availed myself of the privileges a rural life affords, instead of wasting time within the cramped confines of a city. I am sick — sick in body, sick in heart. Oh, home, home! sweet, sweet home! The prospect of my parents' forgiveness, the hope that, forgetful of my past follies, I may be permitted to pass my future years amid the hallowed scenes of childhood, conspire to give me strength, to keep me from falling. A heart-crushed beggar, upon the hearth-stone of my father's house — the home of that mother, whose prayers have so often gone up to heaven in behalf of her erring son — that sister, whose pure love I slighted in my pride, but which now I feel will be a solace beyond price. *(Enter Ellen,* R.*)* Sister!

Ellen. George! *(They rush into each other's arms.)*

George. Ay, George! the prodigal son, the erring brother, returned to seek forgiveness of those he has so deeply wronged; to die, if needs be, where the music of a mother's voice is heard in softly whispered words of comfort — where familiar scenes grow more beautiful, more dear, as life, fleeting on its journey, bids adieu to the clay-cold tenement it joys to leave.

Ellen. Nay, brother, cheer. There is one who can forgive — to him appeal, and all your sorrows shall be forgotten. Happiness will weave for you her amaranthine chaplet — fond friends will smile upon you,—your own heart made joyous.

will exult in the bliss it possesses, and all, henceforward, will be bright and beautiful.

George. My sweet sister! Oh, how I have wronged the love of those to whom I am so much indebted.

Ellen. Our parents, George!

George. John, whom I met just ere I came in, told me of their errand. I immediately dispatched him to inform them of my arrival. They will soon be here — too soon, if the dread I have of meeting them should prove prophetic.

Ellen. Fear not, 'twill be to them ecstacy to pronounce your forgiveness.

George. Let me regain their love, and years, years of devotion to all that is good, all that will yield them pleasure, shall repay them for their kindness and love. The son hath sorrowed for his sins; "the lost is truly found!"

Far. (outside, L.*)* Where, where is my boy? *(Enters* L., *followed by the Dame.)*

George. Father! mother! *(Rushing to, and embracing them.)*

Far. My son! my son!

Dame, (embracing him.) My darling! Repentant, too! Oh, yes, yes! I read it in your countenance!

George, (C.) Is it possible that you can forgive me?

Far. (R.) The culprit upon the cross appealed not in vain to his Heavenly Father. Shall I, an earthly one, hesitate to follow my Master's example. Come to my arms, for thou art forgiven.

Enter JOHN, L.

John. Here come George's friends. I could n't keep 'em back.

Enter the boys and girls. They shake hands with George.

George. How can I thank you, friends, for your generous kindness, better than by owning the error of my ways? Henceforth, in the calm pursuit of one who tills the soil, I

6*

will rest my happiness, and *(taking out the Bible from his breast,)* from this book, too long neglected, will I learn the true duty of man to his God, and his fellows. Therefore, oh my father, and you, my mother! bless the prodigal son who now kneels to thee a penitent, resolved to be henceforth worthy thy love. *(Kneels* C., *Dame on one side, Ellen on the other; behind them the Farmer, with his hands raised in blessing; the others ranged at back.)*

Disposition of Characters at fall of Curtain:

BOYS AND GIRLS. FARMER. BOYS AND GIRLS.

DAME. GEORGE. ELLEN. JOHN.

SCENES FROM

SHAKSPEARE AND OTHER STANDARD AUTHORS,

WITH REMARKS, DESCRIPTION OF COSTUMES, ETC.

BY P. A. FITZGERALD.

SCENES FROM HAMLET.

COSTUMES.

HAMLET. The proper, or the costume which is usually worn for Hamlet in this scene, consists of a black velvet tunic, trimmed with black bugles, black tights, and shoes. Order on breast, cross-hilted sword.

GHOST. Complete suit of armor, and helmet.

In school exhibitions, it will be sufficient if the speakers are dressed in suits of black, frock coats, pants, etc.

No. 1. HAMLET AND THE GHOST.

REMARKS. The character of Hamlet, in Shakspeare's sublime tragedy of that name, is that of a philosopher devoid of resolution. He can conceive but not execute. At one instant he is determined, the next vacillating. Imaginative and studious, he can reason, yet, in a moment, doubts the justness of his conclusions. Naturally of a melancholy temperament, he takes no pleasure in the allurements of royalty. "The glass of fashion and the mould of form," he is content to forsake the court for the "academic hall," and is only prevented therefrom by the entreaties of his mother. Urged to avenge the murder of a parent by the appeal of that parent, who is permitted to assume the form in which the "Majesty of buried Denmark did sometimes walk," that he may tell the fearful story of his death, he vows that, at once, he will rid the world of the fratricide, his uncle, then "palls in resolution." "assumes an antic disposition," and allows himself to become the very slave of circumstances. Not until, through the means of poison, intended for himself by the king, he sees his mother fall a corpse at his feet, and maddened by the consciousness that in his own system rankles a deadly poison, drawn from the envenomed sword of his adversary,

Laertes, as it entered his bosom, does he complete his mission, and send "the murderous Dane" to follow his mother. His knowledge of the world is beautifully developed in his "Advice to the Players," and his speech to Horatio, his intimate and much-loved friend. The address made by the "ghost," is one of the grandest that imagination ever conceived.

The language of this scene, or that portion of it given to the ghost, affords an excellent chance for elocutionary display in the management of the monotone. The ghost should deliver his lines in a hollow, sepulchral voice, somewhat tremulous in tone, when speaking of his own fearful condition; but sonorous and authoritative when charging Hamlet to revenge his murder. By proper change of inflection in the monotone, a judicious speaker can produce a very fine effect in the delivery of this address. In speaking the last line, "Adieu, adieu!" etc., the voice should be permitted to die away in a solemn whisper, like that described by Virginius in his madness, when thinking he hears his daughter's voice, he exclaims:

> "I hear a sound so fine that nothing lives
> 'Twixt it and silence."

Positions on Stage at rise of Curtain:

HAMLET.

GHOST.

R.--L.

FRONT OF STAGE.

HAMLET *and* GHOST *discovered.*

Hamlet, (C.) Whither wilt thou lead me? speak!
I'll go no further.

Ghost, (L. C.) Mark me.

Ham. (R. C.) I will.

Ghost. My hour is almost come
When I to sulph'rous and tormenting flames
Must render up myself.

Ham. Alas, poor ghost!

Ghost. Pity me not; but lend thy serious hearing
To what I shall unfold.

Ham. Speak, I am bound to hear.
Ghost. So art thou to revenge, when thou shalt hear!
Ham. What?
Ghost. I am thy father's spirit:
Doomed for a certain term to walk the night;
And, for the day, confined to fast in fires,
Till the foul crimes, done in my days of nature,
Are burnt and purged away. But that I am forbid
To tell the secrets of my prison-house,
I could a tale unfold, whose lightest word
Would harrow up thy soul; freeze thy young blood;
Make thy two eyes, like stars, start from their spheres,
Thy knotted and combined locks to part,
And each particular hair to stand on end,
Like quills upon the fretful porcupine:
But this eternal blazon must not be
To ears of flesh and blood: List, list, oh, list!—
If thou didst ever thy dear father love—
Ham. Oh, heaven!
Ghost. Revenge his foul and most unnatural murder.
Ham. Murder!
Ghost. Murder most foul, as in the best it is;
But this most foul, strange, and unnatural.
Ham. Haste me to know it, that I, with wings as swift
As meditation, or the thoughts of love,
May sweep to my revenge.
Ghost. I find thee apt.
Now, Hamlet, hear:
'Tis given out, that, sleeping in my orchard,
A serpent stung me; so that the whole ear of Denmark
Is, by a forged process of my death,
Rankly abused: but know, thou noble youth,
The serpent that did sting thy father's life
Now wears his crown.

Ham. Oh, my prophetic soul! my uncle?

Ghost. Ay, that incestuous, that adulterate beast,
With witchcraft of his wit, with traitorous gifts,
Won to his shameful lust
The will of my most seeming-virtuous queen:
Oh, Hamlet, what a falling off was there!
From me, whose love was that of dignity,
That it went hand in hand, even with the vow
I made to her in marriage; and to decline
Upon a wretch, whose natural gifts were poor
To those of mine! —
But, soft, methinks I scent the morning air —
Brief let me be: — sleeping within mine orchard,
My custom always of the afternoon,
Upon my secure hour thy uncle stole,
With juice of cursed hebenon in a phial,
And in the porches of mine ears did pour
The leperous distillment: whose effect
Holds such an enmity with blood of man,
That swift as quicksilver it courses through
The natural gates and alleys of the body;
So it did mine.
Thus was I, sleeping, by a brother's hand,
Of life, of crown, of queen, at once despatched!
Cut off, even in the blossoms of my sin,
No reck'ning made, but sent to my account
With all my imperfections on my head.

Ham. Oh, horrible! Oh, horrible! most horrible!

Ghost. If thou hast nature in thee, bear it not;
Let not the royal bed of Denmark be
A couch for luxury and damned incest,
But, howsoever thou pursu'st this act,
Taint not thy mind, nor let thy soul contrive
Against thy mother aught; leave her to Heaven,

And to those thorns that in her bosom lodge,
To goad and sting her. Fare thee well at once!
The glow-worm shows the matin to be near,
And 'gins to pale his uneffectual fire.
Adieu, adieu, adieu! remember me. *(Vanishes,* L. C.*)*

Ham. (R.) Hold, hold, my heart;
And you, my sinews, grow not instant old,
But bear me stiffly up. (C.) Remember thee?
Ay, thou poor ghost, while memory holds a seat
In this distracted globe. Remember thee?
Yea, from the table of my memory
I'll wipe away all forms, all pressures past,
And thy commandment all alone shall live
Within the book and volume of my brain,
Unmixed with baser matter; yes, by heaven,
I have sworn it.

No. 2. HAMLET'S ADVICE TO THE PLAYERS.

REMARKS. The worth of these instructions has been recognized by all who have given them the attentive perusal they merit. Faults in delivery and action are commented on in language at once explicit and forcible. The student will do well to remember these instructions whenever he has occasion to appear before the public in the capacity of a speaker.

Positions on Stage at rise of Curtain:

HAMLET.

PLAYER.

R.--L.

FRONT OF STAGE.

HAMLET *and* PLAYER *discovered.*

Hamlet. Speak the speech, I pray you, as I pronounced it to you, trippingly on the tongue; but if you mouth it, as many of our players do, I had as lieve the town-crier spoke my lines. Nor do not saw the air too much with your hand thus; but use all gently: for in the very torrent, tempest, and, as I may say, whirlwind of your passion, you must acquire and beget a temperance that may give it smoothness. Oh, it offends me to the soul, to hear a robustious, periwig-pated fellow tear a passion to tatters, to very rags, to split the ears of the groundlings; who, for the most part, are capable of nothing but inexplicable dumb shows, and noise! I would have such a fellow whipped for o'erdoing Termagant; it out-herods Herod: pray you avoid it.

1*st Act.* (R.) I warrant your honor.

Ham. Be not too tame, neither; but let your own discretion be your tutor: suit the action to the word, and the word to the action; with this special observance, that you o'er step not the modesty of nature: for any thing so overdone is from the purpose of playing, whose end, both at the first, and now, was and is, to hold, as 'twere, the mirror up to nature; to show virtue her own feature, scorn her own image, and the very age and body of the time, his form and pressure. Now this, over done, or come tardy off, though it make the unskillful laugh, can not but make the judicious grieve; the censure of which one, must, in your allowance, o'erweigh a whole theater of others. Oh, there be players that I have seen play—and heard others praise, and that highly—not to speak it profanely, that neither having the accent of Christians, nor the gait of Christian, Pagan, or man, have so strutted, and bellowed, that I have thought some of nature's journeymen had made men, and not made them well, they imitated humanity so abominably.

1*st Act.* I hope we have reformed that indifferently with us.

Ham. (C.) Oh, reform it altogether. And let those that play your clowns speak no more than is set down for them: for there be of them that will themselves laugh, to set on some quantity of barren spectators to laugh too; though, in the mean time, some necessary question of the play be then to be considered: that's villainous; and shows a most pitiful ambition in the fool that uses it. Go, make you ready. Horatio! *(Exit 1st Actor, L.)*

Enter HORATIO, R.

Horatio, (R.) Here, sweet lord, at your service.

Ham. Horatio, thou art e'en as just a man
As e'er my conversation coped withal.

Hor. Oh, my dear lord!—

Ham. Nay, do not think I flatter:
For what advancement may I hope from thee,
That no revenue hast, but thy good spirits,
To feed and clothe thee? Why should the poor be flattered?
No, let the candid tongue lick absurd pomp,
And crook the pregnant hinges of the knee,
Where thrift may follow fawning. Dost thou hear?
Since my dear soul was mistress of her choice,
And could of men distinguish her election,
She hath sealed thee for herself; for thou hast been
As one, in suffering all, that suffers nothing;
A man, that fortune's buffets and rewards
Hast ta'en with equal thanks: and blessed are those
Whose blood and judgment are so well commingled,
That they are not a pipe for fortune's finger
To sound what stop she please; give me that man
That is not passion's slave, and I will wear him
In my heart's core, ay, in my heart of heart,
As I do thee. Something too much of this.
There is a play to-night before the king:
One scene of it comes near the circumstance
Which I have told thee of my father's death.
I pr'y thee, when thou see'st that act afoot,
Even with the very comment of thy soul
Observe my uncle; if his occulted guilt
Do not itself unkennel in one speech,

It is a damnèd ghost that we have seen;
And my imaginations are as foul
As Vulcan's stithy; give him heedful note:
For I mine eyes will rivet to his face;
And, after, we will both our judgments join
In censure of his seeming.

Hor. Well, my lord. *(Exit* R.*)*

Ham. They are coming to the play; I must be idle.
Get you a place. *(Goes and stands,* R.*)*

SCENE FROM RICHARD III.

COSTUMES.

Duke of Gloster. Crimson velvet shirt, edged with sable fur, gold waistcoat with black velvet sleeves puffed with gold coming through the hanging sleeve of the shirt, gold waist-belt carrying a cross-hilted sword and dagger, purple stockings, order of Garter under left knee, gold collar of suns and roses, black velvet cap with jewel, high riding boots and spurs, and gauntlets.

Lieutenant of the Tower. Puce velvet shirt with hanging sleeves.

King Henry VI. Long black velvet gown with hanging sleeves and ermine cape, black velvet cap with jewel, and black velvet pointed shoes.

In this as in the other pieces the costumes may be modern.

MURDER OF KING HENRY.

Remarks. The crook-backed tyrant — the Duke of Gloster, afterward Richard III.— is represented by Shakspeare, and Colley Cibber, the compiler of the stage edition of that tragedy in the most odious light. He was a man of the most fertile genius, unscrupulous, murderous in his disposition, turbulent in his pretensions to meekness and simplicity, adroit and versatile. His villainy was smooth and smiling; he rejoiced at the turpitude of his crimes, and boasted of having a "tongue that could wheedle with the devil."

A hypocrite of the most finished character,

> "He could murder while he smiled,
> And cry content to that which grieved his heart
> And wet his cheeks with artificial tears,
> And frame his face to all occasions."

The following scene is supposed to occur in the Tower of London, after the murder of King Henry's son, by Gloster, Clarence, and others, adherents of the house of York. Gloster visits the Tower with the intention of murdering Henry, who accelerates his fate by the reproaches he heaps upon his bloody-minded visitor. Angered, he plunges his sword into the body of the imprisoned monarch. To be sure that he is dead, repeats the stab, and in a voice of fiendish exultation, as if the act committed was one entitling him to the regard of the arch-demon himself, exclaims,

> "Down, down to hell, and say I sent thee thither—
> I, that have neither pity, love, nor fear."

This scene affords peculiar opportunities for facial acting. The various emotions of rage, exultation, and deep and terrible hate, are to be exhibited by the personator of Gloster while writhing under Henry's stinging reproaches. The unhappy monarch, made desperate by the imprisonment of his queen, the murder of his son, and his own hard fate, forgets his habitual mildness, and seemingly, as if to woo his own death at the hands of the man who had already made his heart desolate, repeats to him the omens which, attending his birth, proclaimed him to have been born to "massacre mankind."

Positions on Stage at rise of Curtain:

HENRY, *asleep on Couch.*

R.--L.

HENRY, *discovered sleeping.* *Enter* LIEUTENANT, R.

Lieutenant. Asleep so soon! but sorrow minds no seasons,
The morning, noon, and night, with her's the same;
She's fond of any hour that yields repose.

King H., (waking.) Who's there! Lieutenant, is it you?
Come hither!

Lieut. You shake, my lord, and look affrighted.

King H. Oh! I have had the fearful'st dream! such sights,
That, as I live,
I would not pass another hour so dreadful,

Though 'twere to buy a world of happy days.
Reach me a book: I'll try if reading can
Divert these melancholy thoughts. *(Lieut. gives him a book.)*

Enter GLOSTER, R.

Gloster. Good-day, my lord; what, at your book so hard?
I disturb you.

King H. You do, indeed.

Glos. (to Lieut.) Friend, leave us to ourselves, we must confer. *(Exit Lieut.* R.*)*

King H. What bloody scene has Roscius now to act?

Glos. Suspicion always haunts the guilty mind;—
The thief does fear each bush an officer.

King H. Where thieves without controlment rob and kill,
The traveler does fear each bush a thief:
The poor bird that has been already limed,
With trembling wings misdoubts of every bush:
And I, the hapless mate of one sweet bird,
Have now the fatal object in my eye,
By whom my young one bled, was caught, and killed.

Glos. Why, what a peevish fool was that of Crete,
That taught his son the office of a fowl!
And yet, for all his wings, the fool was drowned;
Thou should'st have taught thy boy his prayers alone,
And then he had not broke his neck with climbing.

King H. Ah! kill me with thy weapon, not thy words;
My breast can better brook thy dagger's point,
Than can my ears that piercing story;
But wherefore dost thou come? Is't for my life?

Glos. Think'st thou I am an executioner?

King H. If murdering innocents be executing,
Then thou'rt the worst of executioners.

Glos. Thy son I killed for his presumption.

King H. Had'st thou been kill'd when first thou didst presume,

Thou hadst not lived to kill a son of mine;
But thou wert born to massacre mankind.
How many old men's sighs, and widow's moans;
How many orphans' water-standing eyes;
Men for their sons', wives for their husbands' fate,
And children for their parents' timeless death,
Will rue the hour that ever thou wert born?
The owl shriek'd at thy birth, an evil sign!
The night-crow cry'd, forboding luckless times;
Dogs howl'd, and hideous tempests shook down trees;
The raven rook'd her on the chimney top,
And chattering pies in dismal discord sung;
Teeth hadst thou in thy head when thou wert born,
Which plainly said, thou cam'st to bite mankind;
And if the rest be true which I have heard,
Thou cam'st—

Glos. I'll hear no more;—die, prophet, in thy speech:
For this, among the rest, was I ordained. *(Stabs him.)*

King H. Oh! and for much more slaughter after this:
Just heav'n forgive my sins, and pardon thee! *(Dies.)*

Glos. What! will the aspiring blood of Lancaster
Sink in the ground? I thought it would have mounted.
See how my sword weeps for the poor king's death.
Oh, may such purple tears be always shed
From those that wish the downfall of our house!
If any spark of life be yet remaining,
Down, down to hell, and say I sent thee thither—
(Stabs him.)
I, that have neither pity, love, nor fear.
Indeed, 'tis true what Henry told me of;
Then since the heav'ns have shaped my body so,
Let hell make crook'd my mind to answer it!
I have no brother, and am like no brother—
Let this word love, which grey-beards call divine,

Be resident in men like one another,
And not in me;—I am—myself alone.
Clarence, beware, thou keep'st me from the light;
But if I fail not in my deep intent,
Thou'st not another day to live; which done,
Heaven take the weak king Edward to his mercy,
And leave the world for me to bustle in.
But soft;—I'm sharing spoil before the field is won.
Clarence still breathes, Edward still lives and reigns,—
When they are gone, then I must count my gains. (*Exit* R.)

SCENE FROM THE PLAY OF LOVE.

BY SHERIDAN KNOWLES.

COSTUMES.

HUON. A dark-colored blouse, and black belt.

COUNTESS. A handsome, white silk, satin, or muslin dress.

REMARKS. The lowly in station, though possessed in mind of all that ennobles, are too often compelled to feel their inferiority, as recognized by the arbitrary laws which govern society, to those, who, perhaps, by the aid of adventitious circumstances alone, rank amongst the rich, the noble. The serf may be in all respects, so far as his manhood is concerned, his master's superior; but to the world he is known only as that master's vassal. He may love one, who, in rank, towers far above him, with a holy love, but death awaits him if he but breathes a hint of his passion; he may be loved in return; but what high-born dame would dare stoop to an alliance with one of lowly birth and vulgar lineage? Vulgar only by the laws of heraldry, not by the laws of God. Such is the situation of the characters in the play—the Countess, and Huon, the serf—from which the following scene is taken. As yet, the Countess is not represented as loving the serf: she feels an interest in his welfare, which her pride will not allow her to acknowledge to herself; nothing more. Huon, reasoning from the poet's text, that station should not build up itself as a barrier between two souls destined for each other, and loving her with whom he reasons, speaks the very language of his soul; hesitates not in pointing out her duty to his mistress; to her, whose power could, without being for an instant questioned, doom him to a vassal's death. The language of the scene will, to the careful reader, suggest the manner in which the characters should be represented.

Positions on the rising of the Curtain:

COUNTESS, *sitting.*

HUON, *standing, a book in his hand.*

R.--L.

FRONT OF STAGE.

The COUNTESS *discovered,* R. C. HUON *reading to her,* L.

Countess. Give o'er! I hate the poet's argument!
'Tis falsehood—'tis offence. A noble maid
Stoop to a peasant!—Ancestry, sire, dam,
Kindred and all, of perfect blood, despised
For love!

Huon. The peasant, though of humble stock,
High nature did ennoble—

Coun. What was that?
Mean you to justify it? But go on.

Huon. Not to offend— *(Rises and comes forward.)*

Coun. Offend!—No fear of that,
I hope, 'twixt thee and me! I pray you, sir,
To recollect yourself, and be at ease,
And as I bid you, do. Go on.

Huon. Descent,
You'll grant, is not alone nobility,
Will you not? Never yet was line so long,
But it beginning had: and that was found
In rarity of nature, giving one
Advantage over many; aptitude

For arms, for counsel, so superlative
As baffled all competitors, and made
The many glad to follow him as guide
Or safeguard: "and with title to endow him,
For his high honor, or to gain some end
Supposed propitious to the general weal,
On those who should descend from him entailed."
Not in descent alone, then, lies degree,
Which from descent to nature may be traced,
Its proper fount? And that which nature did,
You'll grant she may be like to do again;
And in a very peasant, yea, a slave,
Enlodge the worth that roots the noble tree.

(The Countess eyes him.)

I trust I seem not bold, to argue so.

Coun. Sir, when to me it matters what you seem,
Make question on't. If you have more to say,
Proceed — yet mark you how the poet mocks
Himself your advocacy; in the sequel
His hero is a hind in masquerade!
He proves to be a lord.

Huon. The poet sinned
Against himself in that! He should have known
A better trick, who had at hand his own
Excelling nature to admonish him,
Than the low cunning of the common craft.
A hind, his hero, won the lady's love:
He had worth enough for that! Her heart was his.
Wedlock joins nothing, if it joins not hearts.
Marriage was never meant for coats of arms.
Heraldry flourishes on metal, silk,
Or wood. Examine as you will the blood,
No painting on't, is there? — as red, as warm,
The peasant's as the noble's!

Coun. Dost thou know
Thou speak'st to me?
Huon. 'T is therefore so I speak.
Coun. And know'st thy duty to me?
Huon. Yes.
Coun. And see'st
My station, and thine own?
Huon. I see my own.
Coun. Not mine?
Huon. I can not, for the fair
O'er topping height before.
Coun. What height?
Huon. Thyself,
That towerest 'bove thy station!—Pardon me!
Oh, would'st thou set thy rank before thyself?
Would'st thou be honored for thyself, or that?
Rank that excels its wearer, doth degrade;
Riches impoverish, that divide respect.
Oh, to be cherished for oneself alone!
To owe the love that cleaves to us to naught
Which fortune's summer—winter—gives or takes!
To know that while we wear the heart and mind,
Feature and form, high heaven endowed us with,
Let the storm pelt us, or fair weather warm,
We shall be loved! Kings, from their thrones cast down,
Have blessed their fate, that they were valued for
Themselves, and not their stations, when some knee,
That hardly bowed to them in plenitude,
Has kissed the dust before them stripped of all!
Coun. (confused.) I nothing see that's relative in this,
That bears upon the argument.
Huon. Oh, much,
Durst but my heart explain.
Coun. Hast thou a heart?

I thought thou wast a serf; and, as a serf,
Had'st thought and will none other than my lord's,
And so no heart—that is, no heart of thine own.
But since thou say'st thou hast a heart, 't is well,
Keep it a secret; let me not suspect
What, were it e'en suspicion, were thy death. (*Huon smiles.*)
Sir, did I name a banquet to thee now,
Thou lookedst so?

Huon. To die for thee were such.

Coun. Sir?

Huon. For his master oft a serf has died,
And thought it sweet; and may not, then, a serf
Say, for his mistress 't were a feast to die?

Coun. Thou art presumptuous—very—so, no wonder
If I misunderstood thee. Thou 'dst do well
To be thyself, and nothing more.

Huon. Myself!

Coun. Why, art thou not a serf? What right hast thou
To set thy person off with such a bearing?
And move with such a gait? to give thy brow
The set of noble's, and thy tongue his phrase?
Thy better's clothes sit fairer upon thee
Than on themselves, "and they were made for them."
I have no patience with thee—can't abide thee!
There are no bounds to thy ambition, none!
How durst thou e'er adventure to bestride
The war-horse—sitting him, that people say
Thou, not the knight, appear'st his proper load?
How durst thou touch the lance, the battle-axe,
And wheel the flaming falchion round thy head,
As thou would'st blaze the sun of chivalry?
I know! my father found thy aptitude,
And humored it, to boast thee off! He may chance
To rue it; and no wonder if he should,

If others' eyes see that they should not see,
Shown to them by his own.
Huon. Oh, lady —
Coun. What?
Huon. Heard I aright?
Coun. Aright — what heard'st thou, then?
I would not think thee so presumptuous
As through thy pride to misinterpret me.
It were not for thy health,— yea, for thy life!
Beware, sir. It would set my quiet blood,
On haste for mischief to thee, rushing through
My veins, did I believe! — Thou art not mad;
Knowing thy vanity, I aggravate it.
Thou know'st 't were shame, the lowest free-woman
That follows in my train should think of thee!
Huon. I know it, lady.
Coun. That I meant to say,
No more. Do n't read such books to me again,
I would you had not learned to read so well,
I had been spared your annotations.
For the future, no reply when I remark.
Hear, but do n't speak — unless you're told — and then
No more than you are told; what makes the answer up,
No syllable beyond. *(Huon retires up, c.)*
My falconer! *(crosses and looks off* L.*)* So,
An hour I 'll fly my hawk. A noble bird
Knows his bells, is proud of them, yet
They are no portion of his excellence,
It is his own! 'T is not by them he makes
His ample wheel; mounts up, and up, and up,
In spiry rings, piercing the firmament,
Till he o'ertops his prey; then gives his stoop,
More fleet and sure than ever arrow sped!
How nature fashioned him for his bold trade!

Gave him his stars of eyes to range abroad,
His wings of glorious spread to mow the air,
And breast of might to use them! I delight
To fly my hawk. The hawk's a glorious bird;
(Huon advances, R.)
Obedient—yet a daring, dauntless bird!
You may be useful, sir: wait upon me. *(Exeunt* L.)

SCENE FROM THE COMEDY OF MONEY.

BY BULWER.

COSTUMES.

EVELYN, Fashionable suit.
GRAVES, Black dress coat, pants, and vest.
SHARP, Black frock coat, pants, and vest.

REMARKS. The political huckster, who stands ready to barter his conscience—if he ever possessed a commodity so valuable—will find himself faithfully mirrored in the characters of Glossmore and Stout, in the following scene from Bulwer's comedy of Money. No less true to nature is that of Evelyn, who, becoming suddenly rich, after having been a poor dependent, a "hanger-on," imagines his disposition to have become soured, his generous nature warped, when in truth the most noble impulses sit,

"Crowned monarchs o'er his heart."

A charitable cynic, he sneers at the idea of there being any honesty in mankind, calls them "fools, knaves, hypocrites," "rails at all the world in good set terms," and then dispatches his man of business with £100 to the relief of a poor bricklayer. Graves is one of the nondescripts of society, wears black, mourns the loss of his "Sainted Maria," yet is ready to fall in love, and marry again as soon as that "monstrous fine woman," Lady Franklin, will afford him the opportunity. Man is, in truth, a being made up of the most contradictory materials.

Arrangement of Stage:

TABLE *and* CHAIRS. DESK, *for* SHARP.

R.———————————— ————L.

FRONT OF STAGE.

EVELYN *discovered at table reading a newspaper.* SHARP *at desk looking over accounts.*

Enter STOUT, R.

Eve. Stout, you look heated!

Stout. I hear you have just bought the great Groginhole property.

Eve. It is true. Sharp says it's a bargain.

Stout. Well, my dear friend Hopkins, member for Groginhole, can't live another month — but the interests of mankind forbid regret for individuals! The patriot Popkins intends to start for the boro' the instant Hopkins is dead! — your interest will secure his election! — now is your time! — put yourself forward in the march of enlightenment. By all that is bigoted, here comes Glossmore! [*Crosses to* L.

Enter GLOSSMORE, R.; SHARP *still at his desk.*

Gloss. So lucky to find you at home! Hopkins, of Groginhole, is not long for this world. Popkins the brewer, is already canvassing underhand — so very ungentlemanly-like! Keep your interest for young Lord Cipher — a valuable candidate. this is an awful moment — the *Constitution* depends on his return! Vote for Cipher!

Stout. Popkins is your man!

Eve. (*musingly.*) Cipher and Popkins — Popkins and Cipher! Enlightenment and Popkins — Cipher and the Constitution! I *am* puzzled! Stout, I am not known at Groginhole.

Stout. Your *property's* known there!

Eve. But purity of election — independence of votes —

Stout. To be sure: Cipher bribes *abominably.* Frustrate his schemes — preserve the liberties of the borough — turn every man out of his house who votes against enlightenment and Popkins!

Eve. Right! Down with those who take the liberty to admire any liberty except *our* liberty! That *is* liberty!

Gloss. Cipher has a stake in the country — will have £50,000 a year — Cipher will never give a vote without considering beforehand how people of £50,000 a year will be affected by the motion.

Eve. Right: for as without law there would be no property, so to be the law for property is the only proper property of law! That *is* law!

Stout. Popkins is all for economy — there 's a sad waste of the public money — they give the Speaker £5,000 a year, when I 've a brother-in-law who takes the chair at the vestry, and who assures me confidentially he 'd consent to be Speaker for half the money!

Gloss. Enough, Mr. Stout. Mr. Evelyn has too much at stake for a leveller.

Stout. And too much sense for a bigot.

Eve. Mr. Evelyn has no politics at all! Did you ever play at *battledore?*

Both. Battledore!

Eve. Battledore! — that is a contest between two parties: both parties knock about something with singular skill — something is kept up — high — low — here — there — everywhere — nowhere! How grave are the players! how anxious the bystanders! how noisy the battledores! But when this something falls to the ground, only fancy — it's nothing but cork and feather! Go, and play by yourselves — I'm no hand at it! (*Crosses*, L.)

Stout. (*aside.*) Sad ignorance! Aristocrat!

Gloss. Heartless principles! Parvenu.

Stout. Then you don't go *against* us? — I'll bring Popkins to-morrow.

Gloss. Keep yourself free till I present Cipher to you.

Stout. I must go to inquire after Hopkins. The return of Popkins will be an era in history. (*Exit,* R.)

Gloss. I must be off to the Club — the eyes of the country are upon Groginhole. If Cipher fail, the Constitution is gone! (*Exit,* R.)

Eve. (*At table,* R.) Sharp, come here, (*Sharp advances,*) let me look at you! You are my agent, my lawyer, my man of business, I believe you honest; but what *is* honesty? — where does it exist? — in what part of us?

Sharp. In the heart, I suppose.

Eve. Mr. Sharp, it exists in the pocket! Observe! I lay this piece of yellow earth on the table — I contemplate you both; the man there — the gold here! Now, there is many a man in yonder streets, honest as you are, who moves, thinks, feels, and reasons as well as we do; excellent in form — imperishable in soul; who, if his pockets were three days empty, would sell thought, reason, body, and soul too, for that little coin! Is that the fault of the man? — No! it is the fault of mankind! God made man — Sir, behold what mankind have made a god! When I was poor I hated the world; now I am rich I despise it. (*Rises.*) Fools — knaves — hypocrites! By the by, Sharp, send £100 to the poor bricklayer whose house was burnt down yesterday.

Enter GRAVES, R.

Ah, Graves, my dear friend! what a world this is!

Graves. It is an atrocious world! — it will be set on fire one day — and that's some comfort!

Eve. Every hour brings its gloomy lesson — the temper sours — the affections wither — the heart hardens into stone! Zounds! Sharp! what do you stand gaping there for? — have You no bowels? — why don't you go and see to the bricklayer? (*Exit Sharp,* R.)

Eve. Graves, of all my new friends — and their name is Legion — you are the only one I esteem ; there is sympathy between us — we take the same views of life. I am cordially glad to see you.

Graves, (groaning.) Ah! why should you be glad to see a man so miserable?

Eve. (sighs.) Because I am miserable myself!

Graves. You? Pshaw! *you* have not been condemned to lose a wife?

Eve. But, plague on it, man, I may be condemned to take one! Sit down and listen. *(They seat themselves.)* I want a confident. Left fatherless when yet a boy, my mother grudged herself food, to give me education. Some one had told her that learning was better than house and land — that's a lie, Graves.

Graves. A scandalous lie, Evelyn.

Eve. On the strength of that lie I was put to school — sent to college, a sizar. Do you know what a sizar is? In pride he is a gentleman, in knowledge a scholar, and he crawls about, amidst gentlemen and scholars, with the livery of a pauper on his back. I carried off the great prizes — I became distinguished — I looked to a high degree, leading to a fellowship; that is, an independence for myself — a home for my mother. One day a young lord insulted me — I retorted — he struck me — refused apology — refused redress. I was a sizar! a Pariah — a thing to *be* struck! Sir, I was at least a man, and I horsewhipped him in the hall, before the eyes of the whole college! A few days, and the lord's chastisement was forgotten. The next day the sizar was expelled — the career of a life blasted. That is the difference between rich and poor: it takes a whirlwind to move the one, a breath may uproot the other. I arrived at London. As long as my mother lived, I had one to toil for; and I did toil, did hope, did struggle to be something yet. She died! and then, somehow, my spirit broke. I resigned my spirit to my fate — I ceased to care what became of me. At last I submitted to be the poor relation — the hanger-on and gentleman-lackey of Sir John Vesey. But I had an object in that: here was one in that house whom I had loved at the first sight.

Graves. And were you loved again?

Eve. I fancied it, and was deceived. Not an hour before I inherited this mighty wealth, I confessed my love, and was rejected because I was poor. Now, mark: you remember the letter which Sharp gave me when the will was read?

Graves. Perfectly: what were the contents?

Eve. After hints, cautions and admonitions — half in irony, half in earnest, (ah, poor Mordaunt had known the world!) it proceeded — but I'll read it to you: "*Having selected you as my heir, because I think money a trust to be placed where it seems likely to be best employed, I now, not impose a condition, but ask a favor. If you have formed no other and insuperable attachment, I could wish to suggest your choice: my two nearest female relations are my niece Georgina, and my third cousin Clara Douglas, the daughter of a once dear friend. If you could see in either of these one whom you could make your wife, such would be a marriage that, if I live long enough to return to England, I would seek to bring about before I die.*" My friend, this is not a legal condition: the fortune does not *rest* on it; yet need I say, that my gratitude considers it a moral obligation? Several months have elapsed since thus called upon — I ought now to decide: you hear the names — Clara Douglas is the woman who rejected me!

Graves. But now she would accept you.

Eve. And do you think I am so base a slave to passion, that I would owe to my gold what was denied to my affection?

Graves. But you must choose one in common gratitude; you *ought* to do so; yes, there you are right.

Eve. Of the two, then, I would rather marry where I should exact the least. A marriage to which each can bring sober esteem and calm regard may not be happiness, but it may be content; but to marry one whom you could adore, and whose heart is closed to you — to yearn for the treasure, and only to claim the casket — to worship the statue that you may never warm to life — oh! such a marriage would be a hell the more terrible because Paradise was in sight.

Graves. Georgina is pretty, but vain and frivolous. *(Aside.)* But he has no right to be fastidious — he has never known Maria! *(Aloud.)* Yes, my dear friend, now I think on it, you *will* be as wretched as myself: when you are married, we will mingle our groans together.

Eve. You may misjudge Georgina; she may have a nobler nature than appears on the surface. On the day, but before the hour in which the will was read, a letter, in a strange or disguised hand, "*From an unknown Friend to Alfred Evelyn*," and enclosing what to a girl would have been a considerable sum, was sent to a poor woman for whom I had implored charity, and whose address I had given only to Georgina.

Graves. Why not assure yourself?

Eve. Because I have not dared. For sometimes, against my reason, I have hoped that it might be Clara! *(Taking a letter from his bosom and looking at it.)* No, I can't recognize the hand. Graves, I detest that girl! *(Rises.)*

Graves. Who, Georgina!

Eve. No; but I've already, thank heaven, taken some revenge upon her. Come nearer. *(Whispers.)* I've bribed Sharp to say that Mordaunt's letter to me contained a codicil leaving Clara Douglas £20,000.

Graves. And didn't it?

Eve. Not a farthing! But I'm glad of it — I've paid the money — she 's no more a dependant. No one can insult her now. She owes it all to me, and does not guess it man, does not guess! owes it to me whom she rejected — me, the poor scholar! Ha, ha! there's some spite in that, eh?

Graves. You're a fine fellow, Evelyn, and we understand each other. Perhaps Clara may have seen the address, and dictated this letter, after all.

Eve. Do you think so? I'll go to the house this instant. (R.)

Graves. Eh? Humph! then I'll go with you. That Lady Franklin is a fine woman. If she were not so gay, I think — I could —

Eve. No, no; do n't think any such thing: women are even worse than men.

Graves. True; to love is a boy's madness.

Eve. To feel is to suffer.

Graves. To hope is to be deceived.

Eve. I have done with romance.

Graves. Mine is buried with Maria.

Eve. If Clara did but write this —

Graves. Make haste, or Lady Franklin will be out! A vale of tears — a vale of tears!

Eve. A vale of tears, indeed! (*Exeunt*, R.)

Re-enter GRAVES *for his hat.*

Graves. And I left my hat behind me! Just like my luck! If I had been bred a hatter, little boys would have come into the world without heads. (*Exit*, R.)

SCENE FROM LOVE'S MARTYR.

A DIALOGUE, BY MAYNE REID.

REMARKS. Casimir, a noble soldier, wedded to a young maiden, discovers her love for Basil, a foster-brother. After witnessing a parting interview between his wife and the youth, he determines that they shall be made happy in the possession of each other, though at the cost of his own life. He thus breaks to his wife the knowledge he had gained of her love, by the interview just mentioned. This extract offers a fine scope for elocutionary display.

On the rise of Curtain, MARINELLA *discovered sitting.*

Enter CASIMIR.

Casimer. Marinella!

Marinella. My lord?

Cas. Why do you start?

Mar. Your voice, my lord, was sudden—
I knew not you were here.

Cas. Marinella,—

Mar. My lord?

Cas. I have a tale for you.

Mar. What is 't, my lord? *(They sit.)*

Cas. Far from the echoes of a troubled world,
Within the soft embrace of vine-clad hills,
There lay a sunny vale, in whose warm lap
Had art divine, and nature, more divine,
Poured out their wealth for very wantonness!
A valley of bright fields and emerald groves,
Above whose glowing foliage lordly towers
Rose to the sapphire sky! upon the ear

There fell no sounds that were not musical—
The songs of birds, and bees, and falling waters,
The voice of Nature's God, as soft and sweet
As when it thrilled through Earth's first Paradise!
The winds were never rude—no storms came there,—
Alone the breeze from the blue Appenines,
Stole softly down among the perfumed trees,
Filling the air with incense!
It was indeed a scene of loveliness;
And over all
Hung a rich canopy of blue and gold,
The sky of Italy!

Mar. Oh! sweet, sweet scene, how like our own dear home!

Cas. Within this vale
A maid of noble lineage had been reared;
She was indeed the ideal of her sex,—
The bright embodiment of love itself!
Of form so lovely, so divine a face,
It seemed as if the spirit of the place
Had gendered her from out its glowing flowers,
To make the picture perfect.

Mar. How beautiful!

Cas. This maiden had a brother, a brave youth;
Her father, too, still lived, a good old man,
The sole possessor of all these fair scenes,
'Midst which they dwelt in innocence and peace,
Unclouded as their skies!
A stranger came from a far distant land,
And sought this quiet vale—he soon became
Its owner's welcome guest—companion of
The maiden and her brother:
He was their elder, yet had never loved,
For his young days had been all rudely spent
Within the camp, or on the battle-field.

But the rare beauty of this glowing maid,
Soon made its image on his yielding heart;
And he did love as only they can love,
Whose youth's and manhood's flame have both been blent
Into one burning passion!
He was not skilled in love's diplomacy,
And knew not even how to woo the maid,—
He told the good old father of his love,
Who wooed and won her for him.
They were wed.
She then was but a child, and ill could know
The nature of her vow; but the old lord,
Fearing a malady that vexed him much,
Desired thus soon to see his daughter wedded.
Close on the bridal morn the father died
So suddenly, that there was no one near,
Save his confessor, whom he gave in charge
Confession, that the youth whom all the world
Supposed his son, and brother of the maid,
Was not his son, nor yet the maiden's brother.
Mar. How strange, my lord, how like —
Cas. Nay, hear me, Marinella, to the end —
This sad confusion was made known to all,
The stranger lord, the maiden, and the youth;
But they had grown together, three such friends,
They would not part, but lived like as before,
In the sweet commune of the common hearth!
Now grows my tale more sad:
In time, the maiden found within her heart,
A feeling undefined, which never yet
Had centered there, or only as a dream:
It soon became developed — it was love!
Love not for him whom she had vowed to love,
But for the foster-brother!

The youth, too, loved the maid: Nature had placed
The germ within their hearts where it had lain
Amidst the darkness of an erring fate.
Till Nature called it forth to bud and bloom —
Each sorrowed for this love; each struggled hard
To stifle it — when they had striven in vain,
Lest that their friend should suffer from the thing,
Each then resolved to see the other one
No more on earth; — they met at length to part;
'T was then that first they knew each other's love
Confessed at parting — parting when confessed
And without even a kiss, they spoke the sad,
Sad word, farewell!
Meanwhile the husband from some circumstance
Had grown suspicious of his young wife's love;
He was admonished when this parting scene
Was to take place;
And leaving for a moment, honor's path, became
A witness to it all. It broke his heart!

(Marinella faints on Casimir's breast.)

Cold as the marble from Carrara's mine,
Sweet — sweet — and cold! *(Kissing her.)* Mine is a poor right
To these cold kisses now.

DIALOGUE

ON THE SUBJECT OF EXHIBITION DAY.

BY P. A. FITZGERALD.

IN WHICH THE NAMES OF TEACHER, SUPERINTENDENT, SCHOLARS, MEMBERS OF THE BOARD OF EDUCATION, AND CITIZENS OF THE DISTRICT, ARE MENTIONED.

The parties in the Dialogue should address each other by their proper names.

John. Good-evening, William. I am glad to see that you are true to your appointment; you know you promised to meet me here, to discuss the propriety of school exhibitions.

William. Yes, I did; and I think I shall be able to make you acknowledge the truth and force of my arguments.

John. Truth is mighty and must prevail; but I fear you will prove a sorry champion for the cause you are to defend.

Will. I do n't think so. There's a man in the poor-house, who told me last week, that it was very foolish for us to waste our time in studying how to speak in public, because, when we get to be statesmen, lawyers, or ministers, it will all come natural to us. He said no one ever caught him studying such nonsense.

John. Very likely; nor anything else, I presume?

Will. I do n't know; he does seem a little ignorant, still he may be a very sensible man.

John. I can't agree with you. I call Mr. ——, *(one of the Board,)* a sensible man, and his sentiments differ somewhat from those of your friend's in the poor-house.

Will. A little, I'll allow; still, I can't see why Mr. ——

(the teacher,) has got up this parade and show. For my part, I don't like it. Here we have to stand, and be criticised and cat-hauled by half the people in the district.

John. If you had applied yourself as closely to your studies as some of us, you would be able to see the utility of what you are opposing, and be glad to have our friends come and see what we can do. There 's Mr. —— *(superintendent,)* who superintends all the schools — he wants to see that we have learned something, and can tell what we have learned.

Will. O, yes; you are a favorite of Mr. ——'s, *(superintendent,)* I presume. You want to get into his good graces, so that if you should apply for the situation of a teacher, he may pass you without a strict examination.

John. I am afraid that if you were to apply, you would not be favored with an examination at all.

Will. You seem to think that all the great people are on your side.

John. I know they are; for they are the friends of education. Ask the Rev. Mr. ——, *(minister,)* and see if he do n't agree with me.

Will. Is the art of public speaking a branch of education?

John. I think it is. How would you get along if you were called upon to make a stump speech.

Will. Why I 'd take my position, and then — then I'd — I'd — talk!

John. But suppose you knew nothing of oratory? you would probably come off second-best in your dispute with your opponent.

Will. Not if I had the best side.

John. You would have to make it appear the best to some who did not think it so, and failing to win them would be a loss.

Will. But I never expect to make a stump speech.

John. I confess you do not give any great promise of distinction as an orator, at present; but I remember a time when you spoke in quite a persuasive manner.

Will. When was that?

John. The other day, when Mr. ——, *(the teacher,)* called you up to his desk, and began to look around for his ruler, you cried, "O Mr. ——, *(the teacher,)* do n't, if you please; I won't do so again!" If never before, you had something a little *smart* about you then — you need n't try to hide your hand — I expect it feels a little curious yet.

Will. I was n't trying to hide my hand, and there 's no use in your attempting to make the people believe that —

John. You were ever subjected to contact with a ferule! But I won't expose you any more, for as Miss —— *(some girl)* is present, I know your feelings must be the opposite of pleasant.

Will. Miss —— has too much good sense to be influenced by your raillery; besides, you would n't have mentioned her name, if you had n't been jealous, because she would n't let you see her home from school the other day.

John. Indeed! Now suppose you were old enough to marry, and Miss —— favored you, how would you, unless you were fluent of speech, unembarrassed for want of language, pop the question?

Will. I'd make out; I'd — I'd do as Mr. —— *(some person present,)* did.

John. How did he proceed?

Will. He said, "I want to marry you, miss, and I want you to want to marry me!"

John. A novel proceeding, surely. Now I would proceed like Mr. ——. *(Some other person present.)* He entered the room, conscious that the question he was about to propound was a most important one. Very earnestly, yet with diffidence, he plead his suit — spoke eloquently — vowed that existence would be a blank, unless shared with the object of his adoration, and, gracefully kneeling, tremblingly implored to hear the little "yes," for which he sighed. He made love like a gentleman and an orator, and in the spirit and with the voice of an orator. Mrs. —— *(name of person's wife,)* answered "Yes!" Did n't she, Mr. ——? *(Appealing to the person.)*

Will. Well, it may be very well to study the art of oratory for an occasion like that; but over there, in District No. ——, they never make any such fusses.

John. No, they never show their hands in that district. I expect they are afraid. But, William, there are many occasions when a man may be called on to express his views, and he should be prepared, as far as study can prepare, to do himself and his cause honor. Few are so gifted but they can borrow advantages from education.

Will. You can talk better than I can, John; but there is no use in your standing there and trying to convince the people that I am in earnest in opposing school exhibitions.

John. Not in earnest? You espouse the unpopular side of a question just for fun? You are more self-sacrificing than Mr. —— *(name of some town officer,)* was, when he run for office the last time.

Will. I did it in order to give you an opportunity to talk. Unless you have an opponent, how are you to dispute?

John. I do n't know what to think about your being in fun. You said you were not in earnest when Mr. —— *(teacher,)* caught you burning his willow wand. You thought he intended to use it for your benefit, and not as a pointer for the black-board. Were you in fun that time, eh?

Will. I acknowledge that — I — we have all been guilty of little deviations from the strict line of duty.

John. I hope that none of us have been guilty of doing wrong, and that as often as exhibition day comes, we may be recognized as having been attentive to our teacher and our duties. Good-by, William.

Will. Good-by, John. Remember how Miss —— gave you the mitten, and don't try it again.

John. I won't — good-by.

NOTE. To make it amusing, the names to be used in this dialogue should not be made known previous to the exhibition. The names of persons present should be fixed upon, if possible.

CATILINE TO HIS FRIENDS,

AFTER FAILING IN HIS ELECTION TO THE CONSULSHIP.

REV. GEORGE CROLY.

Are there not times, Patricians, when great States
Rush to their ruin? Rome is no more like Rome,
Than a foul dungeon's like the glorious sky.
What is she now? Degenerate, gross, defiled;
The tainted haunt, the gorged receptacle
Of every slave and vagabond of earth:
A mighty grave that luxury has dug,
To rid the other realms of pestilence!
Ye wait to hail me Consul?
Consul! Look on me — on this brow — these hands;
Look on this bosom, black with early wounds;
Have I not served the state from boyhood up,
Scattered my blood for her, labored for, loved her?
I had no chance; wherefore should *I* be Consul?
No, Cicero still is master of the crowd.
Why not? He's made for them, and they for him;

They want a sycophant, and *he* wants slaves.
Well, let him have them!
  Patricians! they have pushed me to the gulf;
I have worn down my heart, wasted my means,
Humbled my birth, bartered my ancient name
For the rank favor of the senseless mass,
That frets and festers in your Commonwealth,—
And now —
The very men with whom I walked through life,
Nay, till within this hour, in all the bonds
Of courtesy, and high companionship,
This day, as if the heavens had stamped me black,
Turned on their heel, just at the point of fate,
Left me a mockery in the rabble's midst,
And followed their plebeian consul, Cicero!
This was the day to which I looked through life,
And it has failed me,— vanished from my grasp,
Like air!
Roman no more! The rabble of the streets
Have seen me humbled; slaves may gibe at me!
For all the ills
That chance or nature lays upon our heads
In chance or nature, there is found a cure!
But *self-abasement* is beyond all cure!
The brand is here, burned in the living flesh,
That bears its mark to the grave; that dagger's plunged
Into the central pulses of the heart;
The act is the mind's suicide, for which
There is no after-health, no hope, no pardon!

CATILINE'S DEFIANCE.

REV. GEORGE CROLY.

Banished from Rome! What's banished, but set free
From daily contact of the things I loathe?
"Tried and convicted traitor!" Who says this?
Who'll prove it, at his peril on my head?
Banished? I thank you for 't. It breaks my chain!
I held some slack allegiance till this hour;
But *now* my sword's my own. Smile on, my lords;
I scorn to count what feelings, withered hopes,
Strong provocation, bitter, burning wrongs,
I have within my heart's hot cells shut up,
To leave you in your lazy dignities.
But here I stand and scoff you! here I fling
Hatred and full defiance in your face!
Your Consul's merciful. For this all thanks: —
He *dares* not touch a hair of Catiline!
"Traitor!" I go; but I *return*. This — trial!
Here I devote your Senate! I've had wrongs
To stir a fever in the blood of age,
Or make the infant's sinews strong as steel.
This day's the birth of sorrow! This hour's work
Will breed proscriptions! Look to your hearths, my lords!
For there, henceforth, shall sit for household gods,
Shapes hot from Tartarus! — all shames and crimes; —
Wan Treachery, with his thirsty dagger drawn;
Suspicion poisoning his brother's cup;
Naked Rebellion, with the torch and ax,
Making his wild sport of your blazing thrones:
Till Anarchy comes down on you like Night,

And Massacre seals Rome's eternal grave.
I go; but not to leap the gulf alone.
I go; but when I come, 'twill be the burst
Of ocean in the earthquake, — rolling back
In swift and mountainous ruin. Fare you well!
You build my funeral-pile; but your best blood
Shall quench its flame!

REMORSE.

SHAKSPEARE.

O, my offense is rank, it smells to Heaven;
It hath the primal, eldest curse upon 't,
A brother's murder! Pray, can I not,
Though inclination be as sharp as will;
My stronger guilt defeats my strong intent;
And, like a man to double business bound,
I stand in pause where I shall first begin,
And, both neglect. What if this cursed hand
Were thicker than itself with brother's blood?
Is there not rain enough in the sweet heavens,
To wash it white as snow? Whereto serves mercy,
But to confront the visage of offense?
And what 's in prayer, but this two-fold force,—
To be forestalled, ere we come to fall,
Or pardoned, being down? Then I 'll look up;
My fault is past. But, O, what form of prayer
Can serve my turn? Forgive me my foul murder?
That can not be; since I am still possessed
Of those effects for which I did the murder,—

My crown, my own ambition, and my queen.
May one be pardoned, and retain the offense?
In the corrupted currents of this world,
Offense's gilded hand may shove by justice;
And oft 't is seen the wicked prize itself
Buys out the law. But 't is not so above;
There is no shuffling; there, the action lies
In his true nature; and we ourselves compelled,
Even to the teeth and forehead of our faults,
To give in evidence. What then? What rests?
Try what repentance can. What can it not?
Yet what can it, when one can not repent?
O wretched state! O bosom black as death!
O limed soul; that struggling to be free,
Art more engaged! Help, angels, make assay!
Bow, stubborn knees! and, heart, with strings of steel,
Be soft as sinews of the new-born babe;—
All may be well!

PART II.

TABLEAUX VIVANTS,

OR, LIVING PICTURES.

DESIGNED AND ARRANGED BY P. A. FITZGERALD.

TABLEAUX VIVANTS.

NO I. WASHINGTON'S DREAM OF LIBERTY.

DESIGNED FOR A FOURTH OF JULY, OR WASHINGTON'S BIRTH-DAY SCHOOL CELEBRATION.

BY P. A. FITZGERALD.

Enter BOY, *in front of Curtain.*

PROLOGUE TO TABLEAU NO. I.

Boy. When War, dread desolator, waves his blood-stained flag,
Till Havoc howls to know her feast is made.
To her, Carnage is beautiful. The agony-fraught groans
Of dying men, whose hearts are growing cold, the shrieks,
The tramp of wounded, rushing steeds, the clang
Of clashing steel, the imprecations dire
Of foes whose only thoughts are how to kill.
The sound of blood-drops pattering, music is to her
More sweet than breathings of the softest lute.
Fearful such sounds, such sights, yet tyrants proud,
Eager in thought to clasp their manacles,
Array and marshal forth their mighty hosts,
And bidding them on speed! the tocsin sound
They fain would make the knell of Liberty!
But He, the God of Hosts, within whose hand
The globe is held, who measures every man
With but a glance, whose fiat none can stay,
Bids ofttimes rise to stem the fierce onslaught,
A chosen champion of all "Human Rights."
Such was thy mission, Glorious Washington!

As such shall be thy fame. To thee in dreams
Thy course was shown: sweet Heaven-born Liberty
To thee appeared, and crowned thee, happy fate!
Thy country's sire — her brave deliverer.
Behold his vision! sons and daughters see
How sweet his smile, how grand his destiny. *(Exit.)*

The Curtain is then drawn to discover the proper position on the Stage, of the Characters forming the first Tableau.

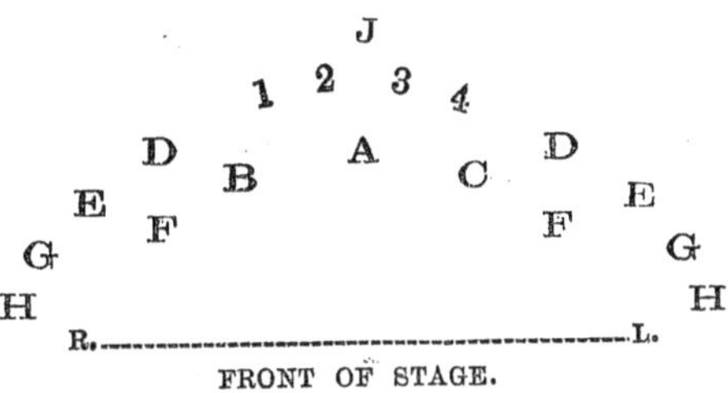

KEY TO TABLEAU NO. I.

A, Represents Washington, reclining on a couch.

B, Boy kneeling on left knee, and holding out an open Bible.

C, Boy kneeling on right knee, presenting a sword.

1, 2, 3, 4, Girls in white, holding wreaths over Washington.

J, Girl representing the Genius of Liberty — the cap of Liberty upon her head, and holding in her right hand a small American flag.

D, E, G, H, Young girls forming a line, with wreaths joined and raised a little above their heads, and extended over toward the figures represented by F.

F, Figures kneeling in an attitude of supplication, having chains in their hands, which they drop simultaneously as the boy who is presenting the sword utters the sentence: "*Ne'er sheath it till sweet liberty is won.*"

DIALOGUE SPOKEN DURING TABLEAU NO. I.

Genius of Liberty. We hail thee, Washington, Columbia's guardian! Be strong in heart, resolute in purpose, pure in thy aspirations! Then shall a world yield thee its acclamations — then shall thy name become great in the mouths of all men.

Boy with Bible, (reading.) "I will say of the Lord, he is my refuge and my fortress: my God; in him will I trust. Surely he shall deliver thee from the snare of the fowler; and from the noisome pestilence. He shall cover thee with his feathers, and under his wings shalt thou trust: his truth shall be thy shield and buckler."

Boy with Sword. This weapon thine, the cause a holy one. Ne'er sheathe it till sweet liberty is won!

Genius of Liberty, (as the chains fall.) Thus shall the captives' chains forsake their limbs!

All the Characters. And all the world shall hail thee "FATHER OF THY COUNTRY." *(Curtain drops.)*

NO. II. MARION AND THE BRITISH OFFICER.

AN HISTORICAL SCENE OF THE AMERICAN REVOLUTION.

Enter Boy in front of Curtain.

PROLOGUE TO TABLEAU NO. II.

Boy. The first of men, of patriots ye have seen;
Upon another and his trusty band, staunch
Yeomen all, ye'll look when drawn this screen.
Humble their meal, and scanty— strange to him
Who wears the costume of their country's foe.
What cares the patriot? He's no epicure,
The coarsest viands satisfy the men
Who fight to win the great, the priceless boon
Of Liberty; — the right to act, to speak
As honest freemen! The tyrant's minions gaze
With wonder on the band, yet feel how great

The hearts that beat beneath their worn attire.
"Our food," cries Marion. The ashes raked
Reveal the frugal meal; frugal, yet free!
Grown in and dug from out an earth whose sod
Our patriot fathers swore should never bear
The tread of tyrants! kept they then their oath?
Let this the nineteenth century reply! for ours
Is freedom's life! No crowns bedecked with gems,
Adorn their brows who rule our happy land.
A plain elected citizen, a man 'mongst men,
One by his peers there placed, a few short years
Sits in the chair of state. No tyrant, he
Performs his duty: rules;—to private life retires,
And yields again to those who gave it him
His brief authority. Say ye who now are here,
Shall this not always be? Ye answer, "Yes!"
Our prayer be this — "Heaven grant it ever so,"
And all our efforts, may they ever tend
To keep this land as our Creator meant
It should be kept,—the hope of the oppressed,
Freedom's Asylum, her eternal home! *(Exit.)*

The Curtain is then drawn to discover the proper position on the Stage of the Characters forming the second Tableau.

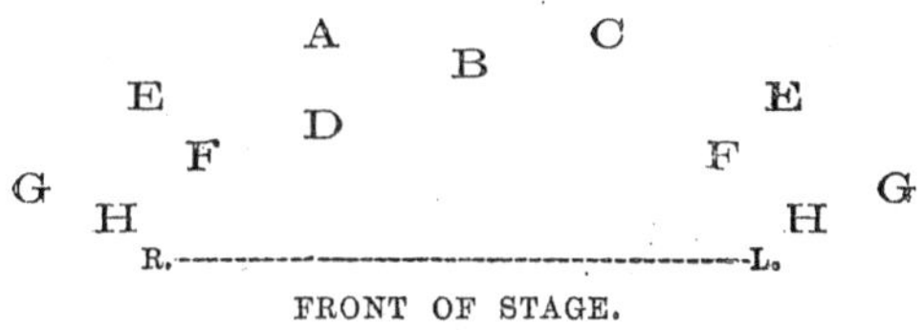

FRONT OF STAGE.

KEY TO TABLEAU NO. II.

A, British Officer, seated upon a small log.

B, Marion, partially reclining, his right elbow on a log, and leaning his head upon his hand.

C, British soldier standing; in his hand a flag of truce.

D, One of "Marion's Men," in his left hand a large potato, from which he is brushing the ashes with the right sleeve of his coat.

E, F, G, H, "Marion's Men" in various attitudes, some sleeping, others partially sitting up.

DIALOGUE, SPOKEN DURING TABLEAU NO. II.

British Officer. And is this the kind of food the country for which you are fighting furnishes you?

Marion. This, sir, is a holyday meal. Ofttimes we get but little even of this. But, sir, tell your king from us, that poorly as we are fed and clothed, we can not be conquered. A scanty meal is better to men who love freedom—more relished than would be the most gorgeous banquet ever presided over by the royal tyrant, whose crimson-clad armies are now battling in the cause of a despotism alike obnoxious to the Creator and to man. *(Curtain drops.)*

NO. III. YOUNG AMERICA:

A CHARACTERISTIC SCENE OF THE PRESENT DAY.

Enter Boy, *in front of Curtain.*

PROLOGUE TO TABLEAU NO. III.

Boy. I come, kind friends, as others have, to speak
You for your favor. We are yet but young,
And for your smiles look anxiously to find
If these our efforts please you. Progress is our word!
A motto good; who stops becomes a clog
Upon society. All races, men of every creed
Are up and doing;—yet be not too fast
Young men and women; stop sometimes for breath,

To ponder carefully, or perchance you'll miss
What you are striving for. "Not always he,"
So says authority, "the race will gain
Who at the first speeds fastest; nor those men
The battle win, whose guns the farthest shoot,"—
A homely verse, may be, but full of truth.
Our Young Americans would plume for flight
Ere time to leave the nest. Behold our youth;—
They lead the fashion; what a jaunty air
They carry with them! Consequential boys!
And so our sisters, not content to *bloom*
In costumes such as did their mothers wear,
They'd "*Bloomers*" be, and loudly talk of "Rights,"—
Throw down their needles, and take up their pens;
Study the "Art of Oratory," 'stead of that
Which teaches them to bake, and brew, and sew.
Well, well, they'll get the better yet of that,
And lose their foolish notions, as comes care
Along with rip'ning years. Then will our sisters find
A "woman's right" is that to cheer her home:
Our youth, that solid studies best engage
The mind that would expand. This age is one
That not alone of progress talks, but also of
Equality. No man is more than to his brother peer,
When all are honest, now that learning's halls
Are open kept for all who'd enter them;
But while I talk, our "Young Americans,"
And others too not born upon our soil,
Are waiting me. The Black—hot Afric's son—
The drawling Yankee, beef-fed Englishman,
The oatmeal-eating Scotchman, and the son
Of that "Green Isle," whose Emmet fell a prey
To laws with more of blood than justice in them,
Long to express their sentiments, and force,

If so they can, you into their belief,—
So draw the curtain! Hold! when I am off,
And give our friends a glimpse of "Young America." *(Exit.)*

The Curtain is then drawn to discover the proper position on the Stage, of the Characters forming the third Tableau.

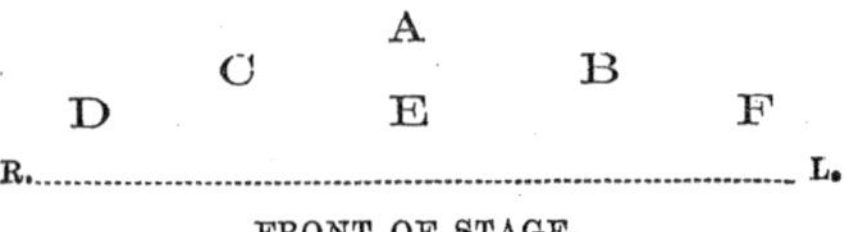

FRONT OF STAGE.

KEY TO TABLEAU NO. III.

A, Girl dressed in Bloomer costume, shouldering a gun.

B, Boy representing "Young America," having his hat cocked upon one side of his head, a cigar in his mouth, his hands in his pockets, and his pants rolled up.

C, Boy sitting on a stool, nursing a baby, and looking very much ashamed.

D, Boy dressed like an Irishman, standing in an attitude of grotesque alarm at the appearance of the "Bloomer."

E, A ragged Negro, sitting upon the Stage, engaged in blacking a pair of boots — one boot upon his hand, the other lying by his side.

F, A boy with a woman's apron on; a parasol in one hand, and carrying a bandbox in the other.

DIALOGUE SPOKEN DURING TABLEAU NO. III.

The Bloomer. We women are the boys! *(To the boy holding baby.)* Husband, take care of that child, or I'll show you that one of the "*Rights*" of my sex is to handle a broomstick for the correction of fractious husbands.

Boy with Child. Hush, baby dear! Mamma is obliged to leave you, as she has been called upon to address an audience of the "Strong-minded," at a Woman's Rights Convention.

Irishman. Ow! murther, murther! Look at the clothes

of her! It 's short they are, intirely! By the sod of ould Ireland, I 'm blushing down to my very toes at the sight of the cratur. And is it a "Bloomer," ye 'z are?

Negro. Yes sah, she 's a "Bloomer," sah—a regular Bloomer! Yah, yah, yah!

Young America. Yes, sir, she 's a "Bloomer" gal, and I 'm a "Bloomer" boy—both regular specimens of "Young America." *(Curtain drops.)*

NO. IV. A CLASSICAL TABLEAU

OF DEITIES FAMOUS IN ANCIENT MYTHOLOGY, DESIGNED EXPRESSLY FOR YOUNG LADIES.

Justice, Purity, Beauty, Plenty, Liberty.

PROLOGUE TO TABLEAU NO. IV.

Believing that the great object of education is to invest us with a love of the traits personified in the characters we are about to present to you, let me, for your assistance in understanding their excellencies, as I am delegated for that purpose, make a few remarks.

"A thing of beauty is a joy forever," wrote the poet. There is no less of truth than poetry in the sentence; for whatever presents to the mind an image calculated to act upon, to arouse its finer impulses, must aid in strengthening and refining them.

We are easily impelled to admire, when the object presented is one upon which the eye is enabled to dwell with pleasure; and though but indicated when personified, who who does not feel that Purity should be loved, Beauty admired, and Liberty and Justice worshipped?

LIBERTAS. VESTA.

COSTUMES FOR CLASSICAL MYTHOLOGICAL TABLEAUX.

The traits which distinguish him who, honoring Liberty, will defend her cause; being a votary of Justice, will see that her scales are ever equally poised; a lover of Purity, that her maxims are extended, studied, and followed; an admirer of Beauty, that no plague spot be allowed to mar the exquisiteness of her fair exterior, are such as make the honest-hearted, free-thoughted man, whom all should be delighted to honor.

To some has been given an intuitive longing for the reign of Right. The Maker of all things has blessed the fair portion of his creation, to whom 'tis given

"To soothe our griefs, our woes allay,"

with so exquisite an appreciation of all that refines, that only by the long continuance of debasing influences, can they be brought to forget how high was their intended destiny, how lovable the surroundings, amongst which they were created to exist. Be it theirs, then, to remember that, as all most worthy of admiration has been personified in the female form, the world has been taught to look upon them as the possessors and lovers of the most amiable qualities. May their reputation, as such, continue for aye! and the sisters, wives, and mothers of our land, be ever adored for their purity, venerated for their love of justice and liberty, honored for their wisdom, and loved for their beauty;—and let their brothers, husbands, and sons, remember that where Justice and Liberty are recognized as worthy worship, there will Plenty and Purity be found: there will bloom the domain of Beauty.

Directions to be followed in arranging the Tableau.

The costumes and positions of the characters forming it, should correspond with those represented in the accompanying engraving, as they are accurately designed from the best authorities.

That full effect may be given to the tableau, the figures

should be elevated upon pedestals of various heights, as per the following illustration:—

Pedestal, 2½ feet high.
JUNO.

Pedestal, 2 feet.
VESTA.

Pedestal, 2 feet.
CERES.

Pedestal, 1½ feet.
JUSTICE.

Pedestal, 1½ feet.
LIBERTY.

NOTE. In order that a promiscuous audience may understand the characters represented, the names of each should be painted in large sized letters, and placed underneath on the pedestals, as in Tableaux Vivants, or living pictures, it is difficult to maintain the same position for any great length of time, they must never be allowed to continue more than three minutes. By the end of that time the curtain should be closed. If a repetition is desired, sufficient time should be allowed the characters to rest before they again resume their positions for the encore. As the labor of getting up the tableau is considerable, that the audience may be led fully to understand its teachings, it should be repeated several times in the course of the exhibition.

NO. V. A CLASSICAL TABLEAU,

ADVERSE TO THE PRECEDING, AND DESIGNED TO BE REPRESENTED BY BOYS.

Oppression, Vice, Impurity, Famine, Despotism.

PROLOGUE TO TABLEAU NO. V.

When mankind forget the great principles involved in the love of Liberty, of Justice, Servility follows. They cringe beneath Oppression, bow to Vice, waste beneath the clasp of Impurity, pine in the clutches of Famine, and offer willing limbs to the chains, willing hearts to the service of Despotism. Look on the two pictures, O; ye youth! Admire the beauty of the one, shudder at the deformity of the other, and taking a lesson from both, so live, that after your mission has been accomplished, they who read your epitaph may be led to exclaim, "Here lie the remains of one who lived as a Christian should live, who died, as only a Christian can die, 'in the full hope of a blessed immortality.'"

The Curtain is then drawn to discover the proper position on the Stage of the Characters forming the fifth Tableau.

3
IMPURITY.

2 VICE. 4 FAMINE.

1
OPPRESSION. DESPOTISM.

R.--L.

FRONT OF STAGE.

KEY TO TABLEAU NO. V.

1, Oppression is represented by a figure having its back toward Vice. The right hand, holding a whip, is elevated as if to strike, while the left foot is placed upon an open book.

2, Vice — a bloated figure; a glass filled with liquor in its right hand, in its left a dagger. Attitude as if about to drink.

3, Impurity — a crouching figure, having the representation of a serpent coiled about its neck.

4, Famine — a gaunt, aged form, somewhat bent; over its eyes a green blind; in the left hand a crust of bread, the right is extended as if soliciting charity.

5, Despotism — a figure kneeling upon the left knee; chains upon the limbs; its head bowed, and right hand laid upon the heart.

NOTE. The adjuncts to the two foregoing tableaux should correspond with their character. Everything connected with the first must wear an appearance of cheerfulness, while wretchedness should characterize the appointments and surroundings of the second.

NO. VI. THE REWARD OF MERIT.

DESIGNED FOR THE CLOSE OF AN EXHIBITION.

The Characters — the teacher, and such of his, or her, pupils, as may be deemed most deserving of the reward.

For a hint as to the positions of Teacher and those to be rewarded, see engraving. To give a pleasing effect to the tableau, an evergreen arch, wreathed with flowers, should be sprung across the stage; and some of the pupils selected as judges. They may be arranged as follows:

TEACHER AND PUPILS TO BE REWARDED.

R.——————————————————L.

FRONT OF STAGE.

The Characters being in position, the Curtain is to be drawn, when the Teacher will thus address the Audience.

Teacher. For their physical triumphs, the victors in the "Olympian Games" were held worthy of public ovations — poets sang their praises, and the populace vied with each other in doing them honor. How much more worthy of such honors are they, who, contending in the arena of Mind, faint not, falter not; but with an unchangable determination, struggle on to the end, to victory! To win your favor, these, my pupils, have labored long, and earnestly; and for so doing we deem it but right, that, in your presence, and thus publicly, we should bear testimony to their worth — thus express how

CERES.

APHRODITE.

COSTUMES FOR CLASSICAL TABLEAUX.

highly gratifying to us has been their conduct. *(To the Pupils.)* And now, my pupils, a few words to you: You have proved yourselves worthy our regard in the strict attention you have paid to your duties as scholars—you have evinced a desire for improvement that entitles you to our consideration, and the speed of your advancement has been commensurate with the efforts you have made. But there are other reasons why we deem you worthy this public testimonial. We have reason to believe that you are dutiful to your parents—you have shown an appreciation of their kindness in placing you where knowledge is to be acquired; you have ever acted kindly toward your schoolmates, and shown, in all things, a determination to win the approbation of your teacher, your friends, and your parents. For so doing, receive this, your reward! and if, when grown to the estate of men and women, you maintain the reputation of your youth, your path through life will be a pleasant one, your existence undisturbedly happy! *(Having bestowed the Rewards, the Teacher will dismiss the Audience as follows:)* In the name of my pupils, and in behalf of myself, I thank you, friends, for your presence here. The interest you have taken in our exercises will spur us on to greater efforts in the furtherance of the cause of education. To please you has been our aim, and that acquired, we can only hope, that so long as our connection lasts, we may deserve and maintain an approbation, honorable to those who bestow it, and pleasing, most pleasing, to the gratified recipients, who unite with me in wishing you every happiness that existence can bestow.

PART III.

SENATORIAL.

SENATORIAL.

LIBERTY AND UNION.

WEBSTER.

I profess, sir, in my career hitherto, to have kept steadily in view the prosperity and honor of the whole country, and the preservation of our Federal Union. It is to that Union we owe our safety at home, and our consideration and dignity abroad. It is to that Union we are chiefly indebted for whatever makes us most proud of our country. That Union we reached only by the discipline of our virtues, in the severe school of adversity. It had its origin in the necessities of disordered finance, prostrate commerce, and ruined credit. Under its benign influences, these great interests immediately awoke, as from the dead, and sprang forth with newness of life. Every year of its duration has teemed with fresh proofs of its utility and its blessings: and although our territory has stretched out wider and wider, and our population spread further and further, they have not outran its protection or its benefits. It has been to us all a copious fountain of national, social, personal happiness. I have not allowed myself, sir, to look beyond the Union, to see what might lie hidden in the dark recess behind. I have not coolly weighed the chances of preserving liberty, when the bonds that unite us together shall be broken asunder. I have not accustomed myself to hang over the precipice of disunion, to see whether, with my short sight, I can fathom the depth of the abyss below; nor could I regard him as a safe counselor in the affairs of this Government, whose thoughts should be mainly bent on considering, not how the Union should be best preserved, but how tolerable might be the condition of the people when it shall be broken up and destroyed.

While the Union lasts, we have high, exciting, gratifying prospects spread out before us, for us and our children. Beyond that I seek not to penetrate the veil. God grant that in my day, at least, that curtain may not rise! God grant that on my vision never may be opened what lies behind! When my eyes shall be turned to behold, for the last time, the sun in heaven, may I not see him shining on the broken and dishonored fragments of a once glorious Union; on states severed, discordant, belligerent; or on a land rent with civil feuds, or drenched, it may be, in fraternal blood! Let their last feeble and lingering glance rather behold the gorgeous ensign of the Republic, now known and honored throughout the earth, still full high advanced, its arms and trophies streaming in their original luster, not a stripe erased or polluted, nor a single star obscured, bearing for its motto no such miserable interrogatory as "*What is all this worth?*"— nor those other words of delusion and folly, "*Liberty first, and Union afterward!*— but everywhere spread all over, in characters of living light, blazing on its ample folds as they float over the sea and over the land, and in every wind under the whole heavens, that other sentiment, dear to every true American heart — Liberty *and* Union, now and forever, one and inseparable!

PEACEABLE SECESSION.

WEBSTER.

Sir, he who sees these states now revolving around a common center, and expects to see them quit their places and fly off without convulsion, may look the next hour to see the heavenly bodies rush from their spheres, and jostle against each other in the realms of space, without causing the crush of the universe.

There can be no such thing as a peaceable secession. Peaceable secession is an utter impossibility. Is the great Constitution under which we live, covering the whole country, is it to be thawed and melted away by secession, as the snows on the mountain melt under the influence of a vernal sun, disappear almost unobserved, and run off? No, sir! No, sir! I will not state what might produce the disruption of the Union: but, sir, I see as plainly as I see the sun in heaven, what that disruption itself must produce; I see that it must produce war, and such a war as I will not describe, *in its two-fold character!*

Peaceable secession! peaceable secession! The concurrent agreement of all the members of this great Republic to separate! A voluntary separation, with alimony on one side and on the other. Why, what would be the result? Where is the line to be drawn? What states are to secede? What is to remain American? What am I to be? — an American no longer? Am I to become a sectional man — a local man, a separatist, with no country in common with the gentlemen who sit around me here, or who fill the other house of Congress? Heaven forbid! Where is the flag of the Republic to remain? Where is the eagle still to tower! — or is he to cower, and shrink, and fall to the ground? Why, sir, our ancestors — our fathers and our grandfathers, those of them that are yet living amongst us with prolonged lives — would rebuke and reproach us; and our children, and grandchildren, would cry out shame upon us, if we, of this generation, should dishonor these ensigns of the power of the Government, and the harmony of that Union, which is every day felt among us with so much joy and gratitude. What is to become of the army? What is to become of the navy? What is to become of the public lands? How is any one of the thirty states to defend itself?

Sir, we could not sit down here to-day, and draw a line of separation that would satisfy any five men in the country. There are natural causes that would keep and tie us together; and there are social and domestic relations which we could not break, if we would, and which we should not, if we could.

ON RECOGNIZING THE INDEPENDENCE OF GREECE.

HENRY CLAY.

Are we so low, so base, so despicable, that we may not express our horror, articulate our detestation, of the most brutal and atrocious war that ever stained earth, or shocked high heaven, with the ferocious deeds of a brutal soldiery, set on by the clergy and followers of a fanatical and inimical religion, rioting in excess of blood and butchery, at the mere details of which the heart sickens? If the great mass of Christendom can look coolly and calmly on, while all this is perpetrated on a Christian people, in their own vicinity, in their very presence, let us, at least, show that, in this distant extremity, there is still some sensibility and sympathy for Christian wrongs and sufferings; that there are still feelings which can kindle into indignation at the oppression of a people endeared to us by every modern tie. But, sir, it is not first and chiefly for Greece that I wish to see this measure adopted. It will give them but little aid — that aid purely of a moral kind. It is, indeed, soothing and solacing in distress to hear the accents of a friendly voice. We know this as a people. But, sir, it is principally and mainly for America herself, for the credit and character of our common country, that I hope to see this resolution pass — it is for our own unsullied name that I feel.

What appearance, sir, on the page of history, would a record like this make?—"In the month of January, in the year of our Lord and Saviour 1824, while all European Christendom beheld with cold, unfeeling apathy the unexampled wrongs and inexpressible misery of the Christian Greece, a proposition was made in the Congress of the United States—almost the sole, the last, the greatest repository of human hope and of human freedom, the representatives of a nation capable of bringing into the field a million bayonets—while the freemen of that nation were spontaneously expressing its deep-toned feeling, its fervent prayer, for Grecian success; while the whole continent was rising, by one simultaneous motion, solemnly and anxiously supplicating and invoking the aid of heaven to spare Greece, and to invigorate her arms; while temples and senate-houses were all resounding with one burst of generous sympathy;—in the year of our Lord and Saviour—that Saviour alike of Christian Greece and of us—a proposition was offered in the American Congress to send a messenger to Greece, to inquire into her state and condition, with an expression of our good wishes and our sympathies, and it was rejected!" Go home, if you dare—go home if you can to your constituents, and tell them you voted it down. Meet, if you dare, the appalling countenances of those who sent you here, and tell them that you shrank from the declaration of your own sentiments; that, you can not tell how, but that some unknown dread, some indescribable apprehension, some indefinable danger, affrighted you; that the spectres of cimeters, and crowns, and crescents, gleamed before you, and alarmed; and that you suppressed all the noble feelings, prompted by religion, by liberty, by liberty, by national independence, and by humanity! I can not bring myself to believe that such will be the feeling of a majority of this house.

EXTENT OF COUNTRY NO BAR TO UNION.

EDMUND RANDOLPH.

[*In the Virginia Convention on the Federal Constitution*, 1788.]

Extent of country, in my conception, ought to be no bar to the adoption of a good government. No extent on earth seems to me too great, provided the laws be wisely made and executed. The principles of representation and responsibility may pervade a large, as well as a small territory; and tyranny is as easily introduced into a small as into a large district. Union, Mr. Chairman, is the work of our salvation. Our safety, our political happiness, our existence, depend on the union of these states. Without union, the people of this and the other states will undergo the unspeakable calamities which discord, faction, turbulence, war, and bloodshed, have continually produced in other countries. Without union, we throw away all those blessings for which we have so earnestly fought. Without union, there is no peace, sir, in the land.

The American spirit ought to be mixed with American pride — pride to see the union magnificently triumph. Let that glorious pride which once defied the British thunder, reanimate you again. Let it not be recorded of Americans, that, after having performed the most gallant exploits, after having overcome the most astonishing difficulties, and after having gained the admiration of the world by their incomparable valor and policy, they lost their acquired reputation, lost their national consequence and happiness, by their own indiscretion. Let no future historian inform posterity that Americans wanted wisdom and virtue to concur in any regular, efficient government. Catch the present moment! Seize it with avidity. It may be lost, never to be regained; and if the union be lost now, I fear it will remain so forever!

THE BIRTHDAY OF WASHINGTON.

RUFUS CHOATE.

The birthday of the "Father of his Country!" May it ever be freshly remembered by American hearts! May it ever re-awaken in them a filial veneration for his memory; ever rekindle the fires of patriotic regard for the country which he loved so well, to which he gave his youthful vigor and his youthful energy, during the perilous period of the early Indian warfare; to which he devoted his life in the maturity of his powers, in the field; to which again he offered the counsels of his wisdom and his experience, as President of the convention that framed our Constitution; which he guided and directed while in the chair of state, and for which the last prayer of his earthly supplication was offered up, when it came the moment for him so well, and so grandly, and so calmly to die. He was the first man of the time in which he grew. His memory is first and most sacred in our love, and ever hereafter, till the last drop of blood shall freeze in the last American heart, his name shall be a spell of power and of might.

Yes, gentlemen, there is one personal, one vast felicity, which no man can share with him. It was the daily beauty, and towering and matchless glory of his life, which enabled him to create his country, and at the same time, secure an undying love and regard from the whole American people. "The first in the hearts of his countrymen!" Yes, first! He has our first and most fervent love. Undoubtedly there were brave and wise and good men, before his day, in every colony. But the American nation, as a nation, I do not reckon to have begun before 1774. And the first love of that Young America was Washington. The first word she lisped was his name. Her earliest breath spoke it. It still is her proud ejaculation; and it will be the last gasp of her expiring life! Yes; others of our great men have been appreciated — many admired by all; — but him we love; him we all love. About and around him we call up no dissentient and discordant and dissatisfied elements — no sectional prejudice nor bias — no party, no creed, no dogma of politics. None of these shall assail him. Yes; when the storm of battle blows darkest and rages highest, the memory of Washington shall nerve every American arm, and cheer every American heart. It shall relume that Promethean fire, that sublime flame of patriotism, that devoted love of country which his words have commended, which his example has consecrated:

"Where may the wearied eye repose,
When gazing on the great;
Where neither guilty glory glows
Nor despicable state? —
Yes — one — the first, the last, the best,
The Cincinnatus of the West,
Whom Envy dared not hate,
Bequeathed the name of Washington,
To make man blush there was but one."

— Lord Byron.

PART IV.

COMIC.

COMIC.

"YOUNG AMERICA" ON PROGRESS.

DOW, JR.

TEXT.—*Drive on your horses.*

MY HEARERS: The spirit of the age is *drive ahead!* If you upset your wagon, and spill your milk, keep up with the popular crowd, and leave the old, slow, careful coaches in the lurch. "Get out of the way, old Dan Tucker!" is all the go nowadays, musically, morally, and mechanically speaking. A flood is upon us that is fast washing all the old works of the old music masters into the dead sea of oblivion. The old heavy drama is too slow a coach altogether for the present day. A lighter and a faster one we must have — a regular trotting concern. Poor Shakspeare! his house is sold, and he has stepped out. His taper shines with a sickly glare in the misty moonlight of the past — a mere glow-worm upon a dark and distant moor. Alas! I am afraid he was not for a time, but for all day; and it 's now about to be all day with him. But good-by, Bill; I must drive on my horses, or take the dust of unpopularity.

My friends, we are a fast people, and live in a fast age. Perhaps you may say we are only riding down hill on a hand-sled: the more we increase in velocity, the sooner we shall reach the bottom; and then have to get back again the best way we can. No; the way is comparatively level, and the road is clear. All we have to do is to keep up steam, and push ahead—*propel.* When I speak of keeping up the steam, I do not mean that you shall fire up with that liquid, the effect of which is to "put a brick in your hat"—in other words, to intoxicate—for thereby you may burst your boilers; but I have reference to maintaining that ambitious spirit of rapid progression, to which neither the everlasting mountains, nor the eternal hills, can set any bounds. Ours is already a great country, but we want to make it a big country. No pent-up Blackwell's Island shall contract our powers; but the whole boundless continent must belong to us. Republicanism, with his new, big boots, is bound to travel—and no power on earth shall say, "Thus far shalt thou come, and no further." Emperors, kings, princes, and potentates! get out of the way, for we are coming with our fast horses! Clear the track for Young America! We intend honestly to vote ourselves farms; but if voting do n't get them, by General Jupiter Jackson, we 'll take them whether or no! Shall we lumber along the road, and allow other nations to pass us with a whiz? No, never!—our horses *are* fast, and we must give the world an awing specimen of their speed. Take care then, by Basil! we are running a race with Britain for Cuba; and if you do n't look out, you may get injured. We must progress—advance—expatiate—till two-thirds of the globe is ours; and then if we are compelled to stop by some unforeseen circumstance, what will be the consequence? Why, we shall fall to fighting among ourselves, and be brought back to the borders of primitive insignificance.

My friends, the world plays us a great game, and every man must look out for his handful. For my part, I take my time, and cheerfully accept of what providence assigns me. But do n't be guided by me—a pauper dependent upon chance.

Drive on your horses; keep ahead if possible, and let the laziest nation be the hindmost. So may it be!

INDEPENDENCE.

DOW, JR.

TEXT. *Independence is the thing,*
And we're the boys to boast on 't.

MY HEARERS: Next Thursday is the birthday of American Liberty — the day upon which our star-spangled banner first waved in the fair breeze of Freedom — the day that the proud eagle of the mountain first looked down from his eyry on a free and independent nation — the day upon which the fat, ragged, and saucy children of Columbia broke loose from the apron-strings of their mother-country, and kicked up their heels for joy, like so many colts released from the bondage of winter confinement. You ought, on this occasion, to be as full of glory as a gin bottle, that this blessed anniversary is about once more to dawn upon your heads, and find you reaping the harvest of those blessings which your fathers sowed in revolutionary soil, watered with their own blood, and manured with their own ashes. Yes, you ought to throw up your caps, and make the halls of Freedom ring with loud huzzas, and then sit down and meditate on the groans, and the pains of travail, which attended this mighty Republic during the delivery of her first-born — LIBERTY.

My friends, next Thursday the celebration will take place. Then the whole nation will be alive like a beggar's shirt; there will be a general stirring up of the genus homo from one end of the nation to another. The fires of enthusiasm will be kindled in every breast; and many of those who look in patriotic glory will, doubtless, supply themselves with the article at the booths round the Park.

But, my dear friends, this sixpenny patriotism is most horrible stuff; it is patriotism of the head, and not of the heart. It makes you feel too independent altogether. It induces you to fight in times of peace, and takes all the starch out of your courage in times of war. While this artificial patriotism is effervescing in your cocoa-nuts, your boasts of independence are loud and clamorous; but when its spirit has evaporated, you are the veriest serviles that ever writhed under the lash of despotism. If you suppose, my friends, that the proper way to observe our national independence is by drinking brandy slings and gin cocktails, you are just as mistaken as the boy was who set a bear-trap to catch bed-bugs.

My dear hearers, I like to hear you boast of your independence, if it be not done in a vain and bragadocial spirit; and my gratuitous prayer is, that you may maintain it as long as you are permitted to squat this side of the deep, still river of death. To preserve your collective strength, your hearts, your feelings, and your pure sympathies must be all joined together, like the links of a log chain. You must all hang together like a string of fish, and stick to one another through thick and thin, like a bunch of burdocks in a bell-wether's fleece. Remember, my friends, that, with all your boasted independence, you are poor, weak, miserable, dependent beings. That same Almighty hand which provides you with soup and shirts, beef and breeches, can take them all from you in a little less than a short space of time, and leave you as naked as an apple-tree in winter. Yes, my friends, you must recollect that you are dependent, as well as independent; and that all the favors you receive are donations from heaven, brought down by angels of mercy, and distributed impartially among the grabbing, snatching, and thieving sons of sin.

EARLY RETIRING AND RISING.

DOW, JR.

TEXT. *Early to bed, and early to rise,*
Makes a man healthy, wealthy, and wise.

MY HEARERS: The text I have chosen for my present discourse is most beautifully homely; but it contains the keen kernels of truth, without husk or chaff. All the brute creation close their peepers at the setting of the sun, save such as see best in the dark; and whose deeds are evil: why should man be an exception, since he is not an owl, nor a bat, that sleeps through the day for the want of properly-adapted optics? I see no reason under the planet of Jupiter, why you should not go to bed as soon as Evening empties her soot-bag upon the earth, and get out of it at the first blush of morn. Even ten hours sleep would do you no harm, after you get used to it; and I know that most of you are able to bear almost twice the quantity without a grunt.

My dear friends, look at that man, the early riser. The rose of health blooms upon his cheek; his eye sparkles with the fire and glow of youth; his step is as elastic as though his legs were set with wire spiral-springs, and his body composed of Indian rubber. He is strong, too; ay, stronger than last winter's butter — stronger than an argument — stronger than a horse, and tougher than bull-beef. He can outjump, outwalk, outrun, and outlive any human being that never leaves his bed-chamber until nine o'clock, I do n't care where you bring him from — whether from the hardy Greenland, or from the soft, sunny clime of the equator. He is infusible. He is not to be fried in his own fat by the melting heat of a midsummer's sun; and he can bare his bosom to the bitter northern blast, with no more sign of a shake or a shiver, than the Bunker Hill Monument in a snow-storm.

Oh, you puny, sickly, saffron-skinned sluggards, that never see the sun rise! You lose a glorious sight — an exhibition that affords more delight to both eye and soul than all the shows ever presented to mortal view, the Northern Lights and Barnum's Museum not excepted. I can't paint the picture. When I think of it, discouraged Fancy drops her pencil at once, and says it's no use. Try and get up and take a peep for yourselves, for once in your lives; then, if you think it a humbug, go to bed again and snooze till the day of judgment, for aught I care. But how do you feel, shaking your feathers, with the sun hard upon the meridian? Rather streaked, I imagine — almost afraid to venture into the streets, for fear your shadows should laugh at you. You muster up courage to sally out. "Shocking steamboat accident that, according to the accounts in the morning papers!" says an acquaintance whom you happen to meet. "What ac— oh — oh, yes, shocking, very shocking, indeed! — good-day," and on you speed, with a most nervous rapidity, for fear of being further interrogated about what you ought to have known hours before. You morning sleepers! know you not that you lose by dribblets the very honey of life, the very quintessence of all that is bright, lovely, and joyful in existence? You do, while others are alive, stirring about, securing health, accumulating wealth, happy and merry as larks; you lie as dead as so many logs, intellectually decaying, morally rotting, and corporeally consuming. Arise ye! Arise ye! Shake off sloth, even as the lion shaketh the dew from his mane; go out and behold the beauties of the morn in all their glory and magnificence, and become healthier, wealthier, wiser, and handsomer human beings than you are.

THE COLD WATER MAN.

JOHN GODFREY SAXE.

It was an honest fisherman,
I knew him passing well,—
And he lived by a little pond,
Within a little dell.

A grave and quiet man was he,
Who loved his hook and rod,—
So even ran his line and life,
His neighbors thought it odd.

For science and for books, he said
He never had a wish,—
No school to him was worth a fig,
Except a school of fish.

He ne'er aspired to rank or wealth,
Nor cared about a name,—
For though much famed for fish was he,
He never fished for fame!

Let others bend their necks at sight
Of fashion's gilded wheels,
He ne'er had learned the art to "bob"
For anything but eels!

A cunning fisherman was he,
His angles all were right;
The smallest nibble at his bait
Was sure to prove "a bite!"

All day this fisherman would sit
Upon an ancient log,
And gaze into the water, like
Some sedentary frog;

With all the seeming innocence,
And that unconscious look,
That other people often wear
When they intend to "hook!"

To charm the fish he never spoke,—
Although his voice was fine,
He found the most convenient way
Was just to drop a line!

And many a gudgeon of the pond,
If they could speak to-day,
Would own, with grief, this angler had
A mighty taking way!

Alas! one day this fisherman
Had taken too much grog,
And being but a landsman, too,
He could n't keep the log!

'T was all in vain with might and main
He strove to reach the shore,—
Down — down he went, to feed the fish
He 'd baited oft before!

The jury gave their verdict that
'T was nothing else but gin
Had caused the fisherman to be
So sadly taken in;

Though one stood out upon a whim,
And said the angler's slaughter,
To be exact about the fact,
Was clearly gin and water!

The moral of this mournful tale,
To all is plain and clear,—
That drinking habits bring a man
Too often to his bier;

And he who scorns to "take the pledge,"
And keep the promise fast,
May be, in spite of fate, a stiff
Cold water man at last!

PART V.

MISCELLANEOUS.

MISCELLANEOUS.

ON THE DEATH OF GENERAL TAYLOR.

RICHARD T. CONRAD.

Weep not for him! The Thracians wisely gave
Tears to the birth-couch, triumph to the grave.
Weep not for him! Go mark his high career;
It knew no shame, no folly, and no fear.
Nurtured to peril, lo! the peril came,
To lead him on, from field to field, to fame.
Weep not for him whose lustrous life has won
No field of fame he has not made his own!
In many a fainting clime, in many a war,
Still bright-browed Victory drew the hero's car,
Whether he met the dusk and prowling foe
By Oceanic's Mississippi's flow;
Or where the Southern Swamps, with steamy breath,
Smite the worn warrior with no warrior's death!
Or where, like surges on the rolling main,
Squadron on squadron sweep the prairie plain,—
Dawn—and the field the haughty foe o'erspread;
Sunset—and Rio Grande's wave runs red!
Or where, from rock-ribbed safety, Monterey
Frowns death, and dares him to the unequal fray;
Till crashing walls, and slippery streets bespeak
How frail the fortress when the heart is weak;
How vainly numbers menace, rocks defy,
Men sternly knit, and firm to do or die;—
Or where on thousands thousands crowding rush
(Rome knew not such a day,) his ranks to crush,

The long day paused on Buena Vista's height,
Above the cloud with flashing volleys bright,
Till angry Freedom, hovering o'er the fray,
Swooped down, and made a new Thermopylæ; —
In every scene of peril and of pain,
His were the toils, his country's was the gain,
From field to field — and all were nobly won —
He bore with eagle flight her standard on;
New stars rose there — but never star grew dim
While in *his* patriot grasp. Weep not for him!
His was a spirit, simple, grand, and pure;
Great to conceive, to do, and to endure;
Yet the rough warrior was in heart a child,
Rich in love's affluence, merciful and mild,
His sterner traits majestic and antique,
Rivaled the stoic Roman or the Greek;
Excelling both, he adds the Christian name,
And Christian virtues make it more than fame.
To country, youth, age, love, life — all were given!
In death he lingered between him and heaven;
Thus spake the patriot in his latest sigh,—
"*My duty done — I do not fear to die!*"

PEACE AND WAR.

SHELLEY.

How beautiful this night! the balmiest sigh
Which vernal zephyrs breathe in evening's ear
Were discord to the speaking quietude
That wraps this moveless scene. Heaven's ebon vault,
Studded with stars unutterably bright,
Through which the moon's unclouded grandeur rolls,

Seems like a canopy which love has spread
Above the sleeping world. Yon gentle hills,
Robed in a garment of untrodden snow;
Yon darksome rocks, whence icicles depend,
So stainless that their white and glittering spires
Tinge not the moon's pure beam; yon castled steep
Whose banner hangeth o'er the time-worn tower
So idly, that rapt fancy deemeth it
A metaphor of peace;—all form a scene
Where musing solitude might love to lift
Her soul above this sphere of earthliness;
Where silence undisturbed might watch alone,
So cold, so bright, so still!

Ah! whence yon glare,
That fires the arch of Heaven?—that dark red smoke
Blotting the silver moon? The stars are quenched
In darkness, and the pure and spangling snow
Gleams faintly through the gloom that gathers round!
Hark to that roar, whose swift and deafening peals
In countless echoes through the mountains ring,
Startling pale midnight on her starry throne!
Now swells the intermingled din; the jar,
Frequent and frightful, of the bursting bomb;
The falling beam, the shriek, the groan, the shout,
The ceaseless clangor, and the rush of men
Inebriate with rage! Loud and more loud
The discord grows; till pale Death shuts the scene,
And o'er the conqueror and the conquered draws
His cold and bloody shroud!

The sulphurous smoke
Before the icy wind, slow rolls away,
And the bright beams of frosty morning dance

Along the spangling snow. These tracks of blood,
Even to the forest depth, and scattered arms,
And lifeless warriors, whose hard lineaments
Death's self could change not, mark the dreadful path
Of the outsallying victors: far behind
Black ashes note where their proud city stood.
Within yon forest is a gloomy glen; —
Each tree which guards its darkness from the day,
Waves o'er a warrior's tomb!

DEGENERACY OF GREECE.

LORD BYRON.

The Isles of Greece, the Isles of Greece!
  Where burning Sappho loved and sung,
Where grew the arts of war and peace,—
  Where Delos rose, and Phœbus sprung!
Eternal summer gilds them yet,
But all, except their sun, is set.

The mountains look on Marathon,
  And Marathon looks on the sea;
And musing there an hour alone,
  I dreamed that Greece might still be free;
For standing on the Persian's grave,
I could not deem myself a slave.

A king sat on the rocky brow,
  Which looks o'er sea-born Salamis;
And ships, by thousands, lay below,
  And men and nations — all were his!

He counted them at break of day,—
And when the sun set, where were they?

And where are they? and where art thou,
  My country? On thy voiceless shore
The heroic lay is tuneless now—
  The heroic bosom beats no more!
And must thy lyre, so long divine,
Degenerate into hands like mine?

You have the Pyrrhic dance as yet;
  Where is the Pyrrhic phalanx gone?
Of two such lessons, why forget
  The nobler and the manlier one?
You have the letters Cadmus gave;
Think ye he meant them for a slave?

'Tis something in the dearth of fame,
  Though linked among a fettered race,
To feel at least a patriot's shame.
  Even as I sing, suffuse my face;
For what is left the poet here?
For Greeks a blush,—for Greece a tear!

Must we but weep o'er days more blessed?
  Must we but blush?—Our fathers bled;
Earth! render back from out thy breast
  A remnant of our Spartan dead!
Of the three hundred grant but three
To make a new Thermopylæ!

What! silent still? and silent all?
  Ah! no; the voices of the dead

Sound like a distant torrent's fall,
  And answer, "Let one living head,
But one arise — we come, we come!"
'T is but the living who are dumb.

NOTE. It has not been thought necessary, by multiplying pieces for recitation or declamation, to make ours a *voluminous* Speaker. There are many others published, containing a great variety of Exercises, *and nothing else;* to which we refer our young friends.

PART VI.

GYMNASTICS AND CALISTHENICS.

GYMNASTICS AND CALISTHENICS.

THE neglect of physical education has been a great practical error in our American system of education.

In the endeavor to secure intellectual culture in the most expeditious manner, due reference has not been had to the health, and physical ability of the young scholar; and, as a consequence of the neglect of proper exercise and physical training, the result has unquestionably been, disease, deformity, and premature death, in no small number of instances.

The body, no less than the mind, demands the enlightened care of all guardians and teachers of youth: both require their appropriate discipline, that health, beauty, and grace, may be found coincident with mental improvement, refinement, and taste.

How seldom is all this realized as the result of our present systematic education of youth? How often is this so called *education* arrested or frustrated by physical infirmities, the legitimate consequences of a violation of the laws of nature, and of neglect of the requisite means for the preservation of the health of the body?

A distinguished English physician affirms that "deficiency of exercise in the open air may be considered as the parent of one-half of female disorders — the pallid complexions, the languid movements, the torpid secretions, flaccid muscles, and disordered functions, and consumption itself," he adds, "attest the truth of this assertion." An American writer, also, speaking of our physical deterioration, says, "We have violated law upon law until we stand amid ruins."

It is certain that women suffer more than men from defective physical training; and inasmuch as the usages of society impose certain restraints upon their free activity in public, it is evident that the evil effects of inactivity will not be obviated, unless *special means* are employed, under the direction of teachers and parents, to improve and perfect the powers and development of the body, as well as of the mind.

In addition, then, to exercise — especially walking — in the open air, together with free expansion of the lungs, and use of the vocal organs, there is nothing that presents so many advantages to the young female as a well devised system of Calisthenics, or exercises having for their end "beauty and strength." By calling into action the various muscles of the body, these exercises are adapted to obviate muscular weakness, and consequent deformity, and to produce an erect and symmetrical figure, as well as ease and grace of manner. Their influence extends also to the nervous system, and to the circulation of the blood, affording a healthful hue to the skin, and a general improvement in all the functions of life.

It may be proper in this connection to allude to the subject of Gymnastics, or exercises for young men, since it is not to be denied that they also suffer too close confinement to study or business, and neglect of free and sufficient activity of body. The great defect of ordinary exercise, undertaken for the promotion of health, is that it lacks an object, and consequently fails of its end; but in gymnastics there is much to excite the mind as well as to employ the bodily powers. These exercises may, with proper care, be resorted to for almost any kind of muscular weakness, while they are also adapted to obviate stiff and awkward habits, contracted by confinement and study.

We conclude these brief and general remarks with another quotation from one of the first English physicians: "Those who can engage in any of the lighter gymnastic exercises should be urged to it by every kind of persuasion, especially in the cool seasons of the year. There are means within the reach of almost all, and the advantages to be derived from such a system are incalculable."— *Dr. Johnson's Economy of Health, p.* 184.

GYMNASTICS AND CALISTHENICS.

A GYMNASTIC GROUND.

GYMNASTICS.

Gymnastics take their origin from the athletic games of ancient Greece. During the best periods of her history, all the youth were regularly trained to these exercises, as a branch of education. In every town, there was a gymnasium or school, supported at the public charge, and furnished with baths, courts, race grounds, and every other convenience. To these seminaries, the youth repaired at a very early period; for we find that even in the great games at which all Greece appeared, boys of twelve years of age obtained prizes. Gymnastics were likewise numbered among the celebrated Olympic games, which sustained and fed the desire of glory that animated all classes of the ancient Greeks.

In modern times, the Germans, Danes, and Swiss, have excelled in gymnastics. Under this general name, indeed, is included every vigorous exertion of the limbs, such as balancing, climbing, leaping, running, vaulting, and walking. The use of gymnastic exercises is to unfold and strengthen the muscular system, by teaching the proper means of employing it to the utmost possible advantage; and the great utility of such recreations will be doubted only by those who are not aware that the health of the body depends upon the full and just exercise of the different members of it. A modern and able writer on this subject, after pointing out the importance of physical exertion, says, that "Exercises, moreover, inspire confidence in difficult situations, and suggest resources in danger. This consequent influence on the moral conduct of a man is such that, by a confidence which is well founded, because it springs from a perfect knowledge of his own powers, he is often enabled to render the most important services to others." When practicing the exercises, it is extremely necessary to guard against performing any one of them in particular, to the exclusion of the others; as, by so doing, the muscles most called into action will become very much developed, while those not exercised will remain weak; and that symmetry and elegance of form which well regulated, active exertion tends so much to improve, must consequently be destroyed. The movements should, therefore, be varied as much as possible; when it will be found that a few hours' practice daily, sometimes at one, sometimes at another kind of exercise, will be sufficient, both for the health of the youthful gymnast and the graceful display of his muscular system.

General Directions.

The best time for practicing gymnastic exercises is either early in the morning or in the cool of the evening; but never immediately after meals.

The pupils should not be permitted to carry knives, peg-tops, or any other toys, in their pockets; neither ought they to be allowed, while warm after practicing, to lie down on the ground, continue without their jackets or coats, sit in a draught, drink cold water, or wash themselves with it; carelessness on these points frequently causing severe illness.

A master or usher should superintend the sports, to keep the pupils from attempting feats beyond such as their strength or practice will enable them to perform with ease and safety. It is a good plan to divide the pupils into classes, according to their size and strength; and they should be made proficient in one exercise before they are allowed to practice another.

The left hand and arm being generally somewhat weaker than the right, the former should be gradually exercised until both become equally strong.

In all gymnastic performances, the pupil should rather endeavor to strengthen the body by exercises taken with moderation, then to exhaust and weaken it by violent and unnecessary displays of force and agility.

The exercises should always be begun and finished gently; abrupt transitions being very dangerous.

Walking.

In walking, the head and body should be carried upright, yet perfectly free and easy, the breast projected, stomach held in, and the shoulders back; and the arms should be allowed to move with freedom by the sides. The knees should be straight, and the toes turned out, but not to an excess; for then they look equally as awkward and ungainly as when they are turned in. In the slow walk or march, the foot should be advanced, keeping the knee and instep straight, and the toe pointing downward; it should then be placed softly on the ground, without jerking the body; and this movement should be repeated with the left foot, and the action continued until it can be performed with ease and elegance. The moderate pace differs from the march in one or two particulars. thus, the ball of the foot, instead of the toe, must first touch the ground, and the toes should not be so much turned out as in the slow walk. In the quick step, the body should be thrown more forward than in the other steps, the toes less pointed out, and the knees allowed to be slightly bent and springy; the head, however, must still be kept erect. All these steps should be practiced until they can be executed with grace and precision.

"In a graceful human step," observes a popular writer, "the heel is always raised before the foot is lifted from the ground, as if the foot were part of a wheel rolling forward; and the weight of the body, supported by the muscles of the calf of the leg, rests for the time on the fore part of the foot and toes. There is then a bending of the foot in a certain degree."

Running.

In running, the body should be inclined forward, the head be thrown somewhat back, and the respiration restrained; the upper part of the arms must be kept close to the sides, with the elbows bent; and they should not be swung about, but moved as rarely as possible, in order that no opposition may be given to the free movement of the body by the fluttering of the clothes. As the pupil advances in proficiency, he may try to run long distances in a given period of time; and he will find running in a circle an exceedingly good practice, if he vary the direction so as to work both sides equally. The pupil should be learned to make his inspirations as long, and his expirations as slow, as possible, long wind being of the utmost consequence to a good runner; but he must invariably cease running the moment his breath becomes short and painful, and perspiration takes place. It is highly injurious to run immediately after meals. A mile in five minutes is reckoned good speed, although it has been achieved in four minutes and a half; and to run four miles in twenty minutes is considered a feat that the best runner would be most happy to accomplish.

The Long Leap

For this exercise, it is usual to have a trench dug in the ground, widening gradually from one end to the other; but it is not essentially necessary to incur such an expense, as two lines marked on the ground, some distance apart from each other, will equally answer the purpose. The gymnasts must try to leap over this trench, following each other in quick succession, taking the wider part as their practice renders them more expert and capable of clearing it. In leaping without a run, the body should be inclined rather forward, the feet close together, and the spring taken from the balls of the toes; the hands and arms should be thrown forward, and as the leaper descends, his body should still be slightly inclined. In performing the long leap with the run, the latter should be from ten to twenty paces, and made in small, quick steps; the spring should be taken from one foot, to be drawn rapidly up to the other, so that the leaper descends upon both feet; the body must be bent, and the arms should be thrown forward toward the spot which the leaper purposes to reach. On level ground, a distance of twenty feet is considered an excellent leap, and twenty-one is very rarely achieved.

Vaulting.

The vaulting horse is a cylinder of wood, rounded off at both ends, and firmly supported on four stout legs. Two ridges of wood are fixed toward the center of the back, leaving sufficient space between them for an ordinary sized person to sit; this space is called the saddle, and the shape of the horse and its saddle will be best understood by referring

Fig. 1. Fig. 2. Fig. 3.

to the above representations; leathern pads, well wadded with wool, should be buckled on the horse at any part on which the exercises are intended to be performed. In Fig. 1, the manner of leaping on the horse is shown to be by placing the hands upon the top, and springing lightly on it. In vaulting into the saddle, the hands must be placed upon one of the ridges, a spring taken at the same instant, and the body turned on one side; so that only one leg passes over the horse, and the performer then descends into the saddle in the proper position: this exercise may be performed either with or without a run. Fig. 2 shows the position in side vaulting; in which the hands are placed on the ridges, and at the moment the spring is made and the feet are thrown over the horse, one hand lets go its hold, as in the illustration, and the gymnast alights upon his toes on the other side of the horse: this should be practiced from both sides. Fig. 3 represents vaulting on or over the saddle, in performing which, the hands are placed on each ridge, and the spring is taken between them; when the body may either rest in the saddle, or go over it.

The High Leap.

The leaping stand is formed of two upright posts, with holes bored through them, about one inch apart, and in which two movable pegs — as shown in the annexed illustration —

may be placed at any height required; weights are placed on the feet of these posts, to keep them from falling, and over the projecting ends of the pegs a line is laid, having a sand-bag attached to its ends, in order to keep it straight; the leap being always taken from the side of the stand toward which the heads of the pegs are turned, if the gymnast's feet should happen to touch the cord, it is, of course, pushed off, and falls immediately. The high leap should be practiced, first standing, and then with a short run; in the standing leap, the feet must be kept close together, and in the leap with a run — which ought not to exceed ten paces — as directed for the long leap. In all these leaps, the performer should alight on the balls of his feet, so as to deaden the shock and descent, which, if not thus broken, might occasion injury.

The Deep Leap.

In practicing the deep leap, the body must be bent, and the hands placed in front of the feet, so that they touch the ground before the latter; or this leap may be made without the hands. This exercise is likely to affect the brain if the descent be made on the heels, instead of the balls of the toes — an effect only to be prevented by constantly practicing progressive exercises, from three or four to twelve feet: for this purpose, a flight of steps is the best adapted; the pupil ascending a certain number, jumping from the side, and increasing the number of steps, or height as he attains proficiency.

Climbing the Upright and Slant Poles.

The upright pole may be two inches and a half in diameter, the slant pole about three inches, and both of them perfectly round and smooth. The climber should take hold of the pole with both hands, as high as he can possibly reach, and raise himself by drawing up his legs; he should then hold very fast on with the latter, and move his hands higher; again draw up his legs, and thus continue ascending, moving his arms and legs alternately. When descending, he should slightly loosen the grasp of his legs, and take his hands from the pole, yet hold them in a guarded manner on each side.

Climbing the Rope.

To climb the rope, cross the feet, and hold the rope firmly between them; move the hands one above the other, alternately, and draw the feet up between each movement of the hands. In the sailor's manner of climbing, the rope from the hands passes between the thighs, and twists round one leg, just below the knee, and over the instep — as shown in the annexed figure; — the other foot then presses upon the rope, and thus an extremely firm support is obtained.

The slant rope is best climbed by placing the sole of one foot flat on the rope, and the other leg across its instep. In descending the rope, the pupil should not slide down, but lower the hands alternately; else they may be injured by the friction.

Climbing the Wooden Ladder.

The learner should seize each side of the ladder, and, by moving his hands alternately, ascend as far as his strength will permit. He should next try to climb the ladder by the

rundles, by bringing the elbow of his lower arm firmly down to the ribs previous to pulling himself up by the other. He may, when perfect in this exercise, try to ascend by seizing one side of the ladder, by its outer and upper part, with both hands, and moving them alternately upward. In these three exercises, the legs must be kept close, and as straight and steady as possible.

Climbing the Rope Ladder.

The rope ladder should have several rundles to keep it spread out, and prevent its getting twisted. The great point to be overcome in climbing this kind of ladder is the method of keeping the body stretched out and perfectly upright; for, from the flexibility of the rope sides of the ladder, its steps, as it hangs, are very easily pushed forward, and the climber is consequently thrown into a slanting position, with his weight upon his hands; the necessary straightening of the body can only be attained by steady and careful practice.

The Inclined Board.

The inclined board should be two feet wide, about two inches thick, and rather rough on the upper surface. The pupil must take hold of both sides of the plank with his hands, and placing his feet flat in the middle, ascend by moving his hands and feet alternately. The board may make an angle of about thirty degrees with the ground, during the first attempts; but when the gymnast has, through practice, acquired power and precision in his movements, the plank may be raised until it is almost perpendicular. When the board is thus slightly, or not at all, inclined, the body should be curved inward, and the legs raised up, so that the highest leg is nearly even with the hand. Ir descending, small and quick movements should be made both with the hands and feet. It is not requisite that the young beginner should climb to the upper part of the board at the first attempt, but stop about half way.

The Parallel Bars.

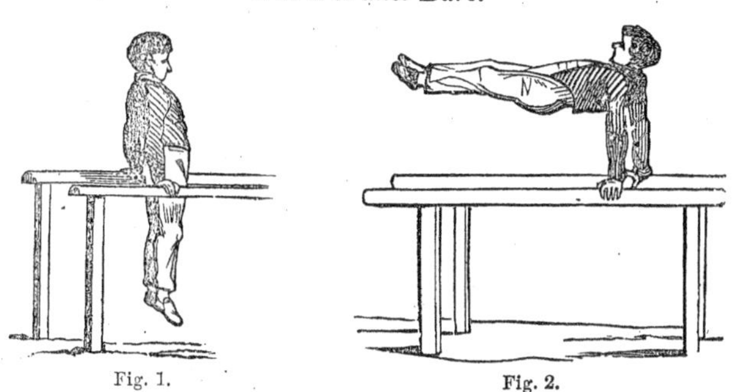

Fig. 1. Fig. 2.

First, raise the body by the hands, as shown in the illustration; then pass from one end of the bars to the other, by alternately moving the hands; and next practice the same motions backward. Afterward, endeavor to pass along, by moving both hands at once, and keeping the legs close and straight. In performing the swing on the bars, support the body on the arms, and swing from the shoulders, allowing the feet to rise equally high before and behind, as in the annexed representation; at the third swing, throw the body over the bar, either to the right or left, loosening hold of the opposite bar at the same instant; and this must also be practiced backward. To lower the body by bending the elbows gradually, let yourself down until the elbows are level with the head; at the same time draw up the feet toward the hams, but without allowing the knees to touch the ground; then straighten the arms, and regain the original upright position on the bars. Another exercise may be performed thus: when the pupil is in the position represented in the first figure, the right elbow should be lowered to the bar, and after that the left; the right arm should then be lifted up, next the left, and the first position resumed.

The Horizontal Bars.

In the exercise on the horizontal bar, the first position is assumed by taking hold, with both hands, of the side of the bar toward you, and raising yourself until you can look over it. When you can perform this easily, place the hands on the further side of the bar, and raise yourself as before. In the next exercise, place your hands on each side of the bar, then raise the body off the ground, and endeavor to pass from one end of the bar to the other, by making a succession of small springs of the hands; and afterward by passing the hands alternately; the legs being, in the mean time, kept close and as straight as possible. Another movement consists in lifting up the legs above the bar, and then allowing them to drop again into the perpendicular position: and when the pupil can swing thus by holding on with his hands and feet, he should try to pass along the bar by moving one hand and one foot alternately; if he can not achieve this, he may slide his feet along the bar, and only move his hands alternately. Next, practice hanging by the right arm and right leg, whilst the left hangs down; and by the right arm and left leg, and left arm and right leg. When perfect in these exercises, take hold of the bar firmly by the right hand, throw the right leg over the bar, hold on steadily by the joint of the knee, and next raise the body and get the left armpit over the bar; then, by a little exertion, you will be enabled to assume a riding position on it. By firmly holding with the hands, while you bring one leg over the bar, you will be in the position shown in the first figure. Swinging round the bar with the head downward, is performed by taking hold of the bar with both hands, swinging the feet backward and forward two or three times, and then throwing them up in front; by which movement the head sinks down backward, as represented in the second figure. Or, take hold of the bar with the hands, swing round, and while doing so, pass the feet between the hands, returning them the same way, or dropping on the toes to the ground.

The Balancing Bar.

Foremost among the preliminary exercises of balancing are the following: standing on one leg, holding one foot high in the hand, kissing the toe, and sitting down. The two first explain themselves sufficiently; to kiss the toe, lift one foot with both hands, and raise it toward the chin, which should be slightly lowered to meet it. In sitting down, both arms and one leg should be thrust forward, and the other leg bent until the pupil can sit down, as shown in the annexed figure; after which he should carefully rise up, keeping his arms and leg outstretched, and steadily preserving his balance all the time. The balancing bar is a long, round pole of wood, about fourteen inches thick at one end, and tapering gradually toward the other, where it is not more than half that diameter. It is supported only at the thickest end and in the middle, from whence to the thinner end it is extremely difficult to perform the

exercises, as the pole yields at each step. In dry weather, the soles of the shoes should be damped, as then the upper surface of the bar is smooth and slippery. Mount the bar either from the ground, or from a riding position on the bar; in the latter case, place the right foot flat on the bar, keeping the heel close to the upper part of the thigh, and allow the left foot and leg to hang perpendicularly down, with the toes pointing to the ground; and then stretch both arms forward, as in the illustration, Fig. 2; next gradually rise on the foot, and keep your balance for a minute or two, before you attempt to walk along the bar. First, try to walk with assistance, then alone, balancing by extending the arms, and afterward with the arms folded behind. When you can walk steadily and easily, endeavor to turn round on the bar, first trying at the broad, and then at the narrow end; and lastly, walk backward. When two persons, in walking on the bar, wish to pass each other, they should join arms, place their right feet forward, and turn quite round, by each stepping with the left foot round the right of the other, as represented in Fig. **1.** All the balancing exercises require great care.

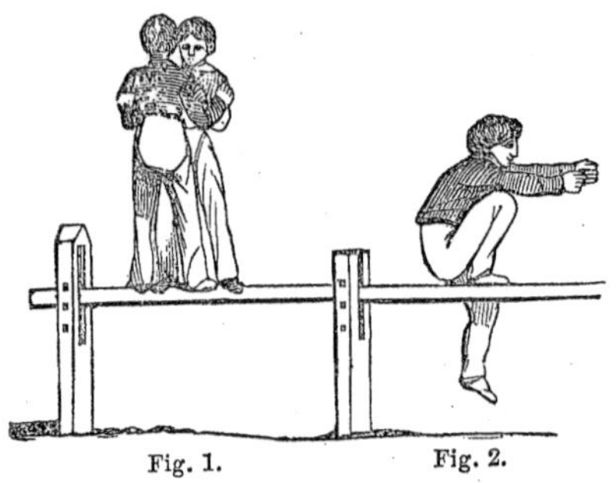

Fig. 1. Fig. 2.

The High Leap with the Pole.

The pole should be from seven to ten feet in length, and made of perfectly sound fir; if it makes the least crackling noise while the leaper is practicing, it is unsound, and should be immediately laid aside. Grasp the pole at about the height of the head with the right hand, and with the left at about the height of the hips; then place the end of the pole to the ground, spring forward at the same instant, and swing round, so that you alight facing the spot you leaped from. When confidence has been attained through practice, the pupil may try to clear over the leaping stand, such as is used in the high leap, already described. In the early exercises over this stand, you may quit the pole, by giving a slight push with one hand, so that it may fall on the inner side of the cord; and try to carry the pole over the cord, which is an exceedingly difficult feat to perform, for you must gradually elevate the pole as you descend, so that when you alight, the end of the pole may be upward. These exercises should be practiced with a short run; and unless you plant the end of the pole on the ground at the very moment that you take the spring, the leap can not be considered perfect.

The Long Leap with the Pole.

This leap requires strength in the hands and arms, and some knowledge of balancing: it is best practiced from a flight of steps. The leaper should take the pole in the usual way, and allow his hands to slide down it until the whole weight of his body rests upon the pole, as shown in the illustration; he should then quit the height with his feet, and swinging round the pole, descend on the balls of his toes, with his face toward the place he sprung from. This leap ought never to be practiced immediately after meals.

The Long Leap with the Pole

Is performed like the preceding, as regards taking the spring and handling the pole. Formerly, in hawking in the woods and coverts, the sportsman carried a stout pole, to assist him in leaping over rivulets. Henry VIII., while one day pursuing his hawk on foot, in Hertfordshire, was plunged into a deep slough by the breaking of his pole.

Walking on Stilts.

Walking on stilts is a very good exercise in balancing, and may be practiced by the pupil when he is expert on the balancing bar. Stilts are easily made: the poles must be about six feet in length; and at or near two feet from the end, pieces of wood, shaped like brackets, should be fastened to them; two or three inches above the brackets, and likewise near the top of the stilts, leather straps with buckles attached must be securely nailed on. To mount these long legs, the balancer must place his feet on the brackets, and buckle the straps closely below his knees, and just above his ankles, so as to confine the upper parts of the stilts to his legs, and keep his feet firm on their resting-places. The long strides which an active youth can take with these additional supports will enable him to keep pace with a four-horsed stage-coach, with comparatively little fatigue.

The Flying Steps, or Giant Strides.

For this exercise, there should be fixed in the ground firmly a stout mast, or upright beam of wood, on the top of which is an iron cap that moves round with facility in a horizontal direction; to this cap are appended four ropes, with short bars of wood fastened to the end. The pupils take hold of these bars, and vault or step out in a circle, increasing their velocity by degrees, and bearing with all their weight upon the ropes. When at their utmost speed, they seldom touch the ground with their toes.

Throwing the Javelin.

The javelin is a tolerably heavy pole, shod at one end with an iron ferrule, or, if you prefer it, with a spike. To throw it, grasp it with the whole hand, so that only the but-end projects from between the fore-finger and thumb, and the other, or shod end, from the little finger; then poise the javelin nicely, elevate it to the height of the ear; draw your arm as far back as you can, and, lastly, hurl the javelin forward with all your strength.

Climbing Trees.

Summer is the proper season for this recreation, as the withered boughs may then be easily detected. Until some experience has been purchased at the expense of a few mishaps, low, stunted trees should be chosen for practice. The kind of wood and strength of branches must always be considered; and as the surface of the branches is either smooth, or moist and slippery, the grasp should never be relaxed for an instant. By practice, the climber becomes so expert that when the branches hang tolerably low, instead of scrambling up the trunk of the tree, by taking a short run and spring, he may seize a branch, swing himself up, and then proceed from bough to bough; or even from tree to tree, should they be planted close enough.

THE EXERCISES FOR THE SCHOOL-ROOM.

These exercises are such as can be performed in the school-room, and in classes. They are to be used in connection with the mechanical gymnastics, or where it is not convenient to arrange the necessary machinery for the latter, and particularly where the more mild and gentle exercises are preferred.

Ling's System of Gymnastics.

For the purpose of showing the practical working of the educational part of Ling's system, which has especially in view the preservation of health, and the prevention of many diseases, we have, with the author's permission, selected from the works of Dr. Roth the following illustrations and descriptions. It is a great feature in Ling's system, that it contains a part, consisting only of such gymnastic exercises as require no technical apparatus or machines. These exercises are called *free*, and are sufficient to produce the harmonious developement of body and mind.

There is a class of *free* exercises in which a support is necessary; but then it is not that of any mechanical contrivance, but a living one, effected by a mutual apposition of the hands, arms, legs, etc., of the individual performing the exercises. The highly celebrated Greek gymnastics consisted, with but few exceptions, of similar free exercises; and the results which were produced by them on the population of Greece are a sufficient proof of their efficiency.

The free exercises are divided into five classes: 1st, movements of the limbs on the spot, and without reciprocal support; 2d, movements from the spot without support; 3d, movements with support; 4th, wrestling exercises; and, 5th æsthetic exercises.

Before we proceed to our practical illustrations of these

various parts, we wish to impress the reader with the idea of a *gymnastic* movement.

Gymnastic movements differ from movements in general in this—that though the latter require space and time, they do not require a determinate space, and determinate period of time, and degree of force. It is this definite amount of space and time in which the movement is to be done, as well as the determinate degree of force with which it is done, that enables us to influence the whole or a single part of the body in the manner necessary for the special purpose.

To raise the arms from a hanging position in a loose, random way, without thinking, and to stretch them in the air, can have little corporeal effect, and certainly no mental one; but to stretch the arms in a manner and direction, and with velocity and force, all previously determined and exactly performed, and then to move the different parts, upper and forearm, hand, and fingers, precisely as determined and commanded—this is a *gymnastic* movement.

To learn to leap very far, or very high, it is not necessary to have special gymnastic instructions; but to leap gymnastically—that is, in a certain way, with the least possible expenditure of power, with great certainty and precision, with nice regard to distance, etc.—this is a matter calling for skillful and systematic instruction; and such a system constitutes rational gymnastics.

Every gymnastic movement has,

1st, *A commencing position*, in which it begins, and from which the preceding movement originates.

2d, *Intermediate positions*, through which the whole or part of the body passes, and which lie in the direction of the movement from its commencement to its end, which forms

3d, *The final position*, in which the moved body, or part of the body, returns to a state of relative rest, and where the movement ceases.

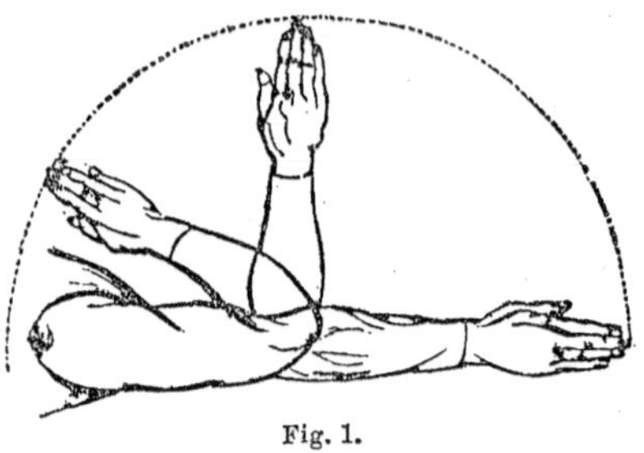
Fig. 1.

The engraving (Fig. 1,) illustrates a movement where the arm is to be bent at the elbow, and which is called *fore-arm flexion*. The stretched arm represents the *commencing position*. The fore-arm bent at a right-angle with the upper, is one of the *intermediate positions;* and the fore-arm forming an acute-angle is the *final position*. When the fore-arm is to be stretched, the previous final position is the commencing position, and the previous commencing position is the final one, the intermediate positions remaining the same in both. The arm is drawn from above, in order to show more distinctly the three positions. We have been obliged to enter into these details, that the reader may the better understand the exercises which follow.

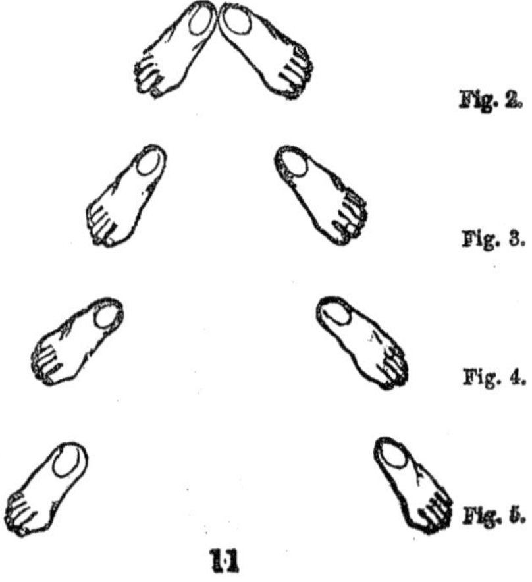

The free exercises are usually done only by healthy persons, and in a standing position. We will suppose that the feet are placed in the *fundamental position* — that is, at a right-angle to each other, (Fig. 2.) From this position originate a great variety of others, in which the feet are always at a right-angle to each other. One foot remains in its original place, while the other is moved either sideways, forward, or backward. The length of the foot of the individual performing the exercise is chosen as a measure of distance at which the foot is to be placed from the other; in this way, we say, *the foot at one, two, three,* (or more,) *distances—place.* The diagram (Fig. 3,) shows the feet placed apart at one *distance,* Fig. 4 at two distances, and Fig. 5 at three distances.

When we place the right foot at one, two, three distances forward, we have the various positions marked, 1, 2, 3, in the sixth diagram. When we choose the close position, in which the feet are placed closely together in their whole length, (Fig. 7,) as our commencing position, then the placing of the feet apart in one, two or three distances, is quite different, as illustrated by Fig's 8, 9, and 10; and the placing of the right foot forward in the various distances is shown by the diagram, (Fig. 11,) where the right foot is placed forward in a straight line with the left, at the distances indicated by 1, 2, 3. By these instances, the reader will understand the importance of the commencing position; because, if this is not taken into consideration, and two persons are to perform, for instance, the movement expressed by the word of command, *feet apart in two distances—place!*

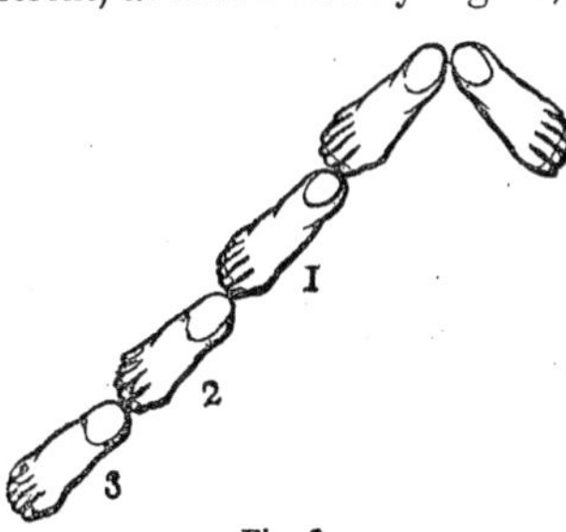

Fig. 6.

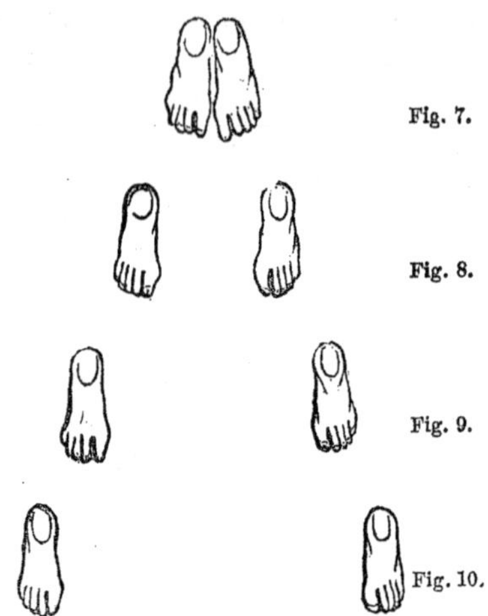

Fig. 7.

Fig. 8.

Fig. 9.

Fig. 10.

the one who chooses Fig. 7 as his commencing position, will place his feet in the position Fig. 9; while the second, having chosen Fig. 2 as his commencing position, will be in the position of Fig. 4.

The Word of Command.

We have mentioned the word of command; this is the order given by the teacher, or person directing the movements, according to which all must move simultaneously. The word of command, or the order, consists of two parts — the first is the announcing, the second the execution order. The *announcing order* describes generally the limb which is to be moved, and the direction of the movement; the *execution order* describes shortly the mode of movement or action. In the command "*feet apart in two distances — place!*" the first five words are the announcing order, at which every individual prepares himself for action, but does not move till the word "*place*," the

Fig. 11.

execution order, is given, when the pupils instantly make the movement. In the order "*right knee upward — bend!*" the first three words are the announcing order, — the word "*bend*," the execution. We advise our readers to place themselves in the various positions described, to keep the head and body upright, the arms either stretched downward, or placed on the hips, when "*hips — hold!*" is the command. By changing the feet at the order "*foot forward — place!*" you have twenty positions, which, if well executed, will increase the strength of the legs, and of some parts of the spine; and this contributes to the better deportment of the body.

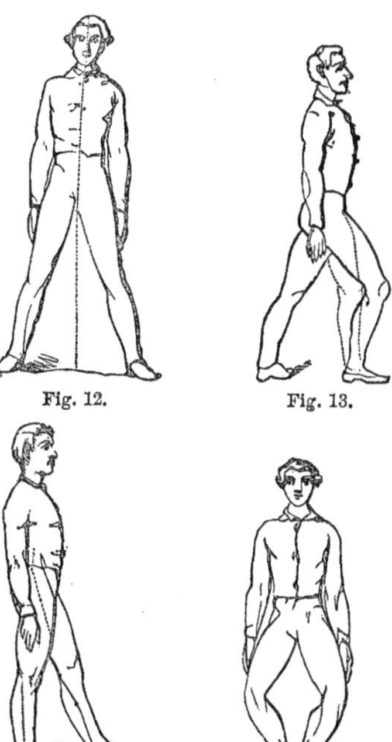
Fig. 12. Fig. 13. Fig. 14. Fig. 15.

Having now a clear idea of the fundamental or rectangular position, (Fig. 2,) and the close position, (Fig. 7,) if you wish to change the rectangular into a close one, the command is "*feet — close!*" and the movement is done at first slowly, and in three motions, thus: The feet being placed heel to heel, with the toes at a right-angle, the toes are a little lifted from the ground, (first motion;) and then brought slowly inward, till the inner edges of the feet touch each other, (second motion;) and finally, the toes again touch the ground, (third motion.) After some practice, these three motions are done so quickly as to form only one. At the order "*feet — open*," the same motions are done in the reverse order—viz., 1st, you raise the toes; 2d, the toes are brought outward to form the right-angle; and 3d, they again touch the ground.

The two movements are practiced as often as the order "*feet — close!*" or "*feet — open!*" is given. The position in which the body is when about to execute a certain movement, is the "*commencing position;*" and there is an infinite variety of such positions. When the feet are placed apart sideways, so that there is at least one distance between the feet, the position is called *strido* position, (Fig. 12.)

The *walk position* (Fig. 13,) is assumed by setting one foot forward, as if going to take a step — the dotted line in the figure shows the position of the leg when stretched.

Half standing position, (Fig. 14.) For this position, one foot is placed with the sole on the ground, while the other leg, perfectly stretched at the knee, is slightly raised, and thrown a little forward, in such a way that it does not touch the floor.

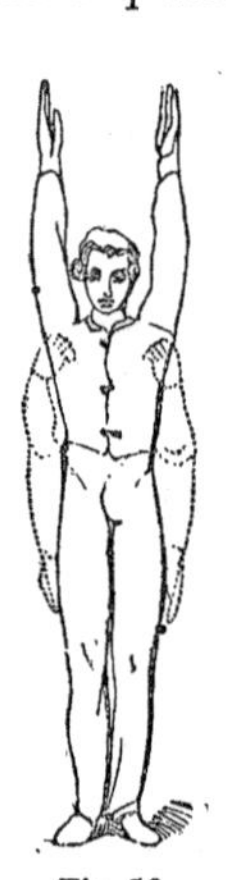

Fig. 16.

Courtesy standing position, (Fig. 15.) The legs are kept together at the heels, the knees a little bent, and directed outward as far as possible, the legs forming, consequently, a regular rhombus.

Stretch standing position (Fig. 16,) has the arms parallel to each other, stretched vertically upward, with the palms directed toward each other. Compound commencing positions are formed of two, or several simple ones; as for instance: *stretch stride position*, in which the arms are in the stretched, (Fig. 16,) and the feet in the stride position, (Fig. 12.)

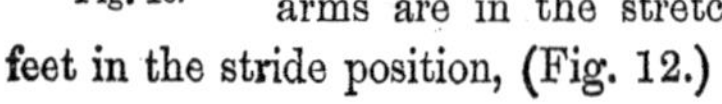

There are hundreds of commencing positions; but those we have quoted are sufficient as instances. Those of our readers who are interested in this matter, we refer to Dr. Roth's works on the subject, where they will find full descriptions and illustrations of a great variety of positions.

The following movements belong to the first class of free exercises — viz., to those done without the assistance of another person, the body remaining on the same spot. We begin with the movements of the head, which it is imperative should always be done in slow time. The following are the words of command applicable to such movements:

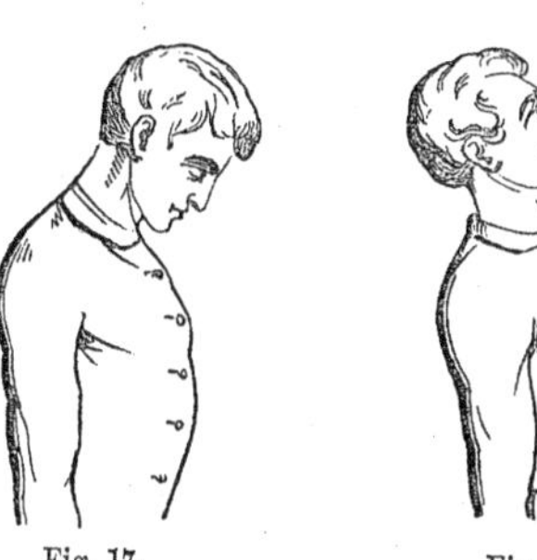

Fig. 17.

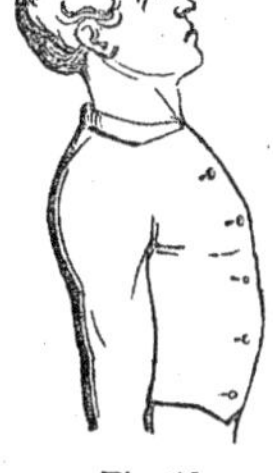

Fig. 18.

Head forward — bend — stretch! (Fig. 17.) The head is held straight, without any twisting of the neck, and must be bent forward until the chin *slightly* touches the chest, (Fig. 17.) The upper part of the body, and especially the shoulders, must be kept firm. At the order "*stretch*," the head is raised into the fundamental position. Both the movements are done steadily, and not by jerks.

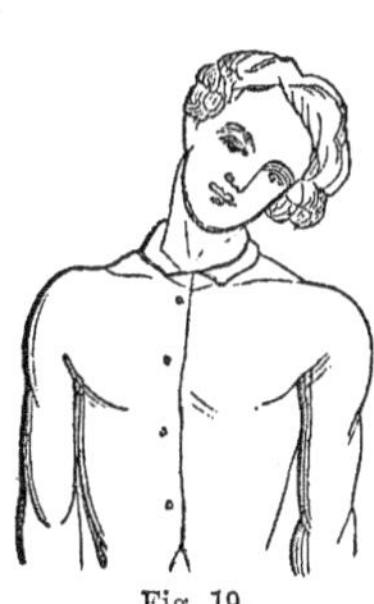

Fig. 19.

Head backward — bend — stretch, (Fig. 18.) The head is slowly bent backward, but without twisting; and at the command "*stretch*," is raised into the previous position. The head must not remain too long in the bent position.

Head right, sideways — bend — stretch!

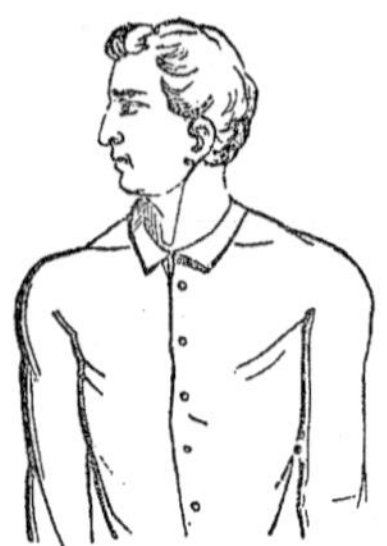

Fig. 20.

Head left, sideways — bend — stretch! (Fig. 19.) The head is exactly bent to the designated side; no twisting of face or shoulders, and no raising of the opposite shoulder, or sinking down of the shoulder on the same side, is permitted.

Head right, turn—forward — turn. (Fig. 20.)

Head left, turn —forward— turn. The head is turned horizontally to the side designated, without the least flexion, if possible, so far that the chin shall be over the shoulder. The shoulders must be kept square in the front line.

CALISTHENICS.

Use of Calisthenics — Cautions —Necessary Apparatus — Dumb-bells — Backboards — Clubs — Wands — The Triangle—The Elastic Cord—Dumb-bell Practice.*

These exercises are carefully accommodated to the delicate organization of the female sex; but in order that our readers may not have any fear with respect to their effect upon the gentler sex, we may remark, that this series of papers have been written under the guidance and supervision of a medical man familiar with such matters, and that the exercises themselves have been conducted by an able and experienced teacher of calisthenics.

It is an admitted physiological fact, that the imperfections in the female form originate, for the most part, in defective

*Calisthenics is derived from two Greek words, signifying beauty and strength.

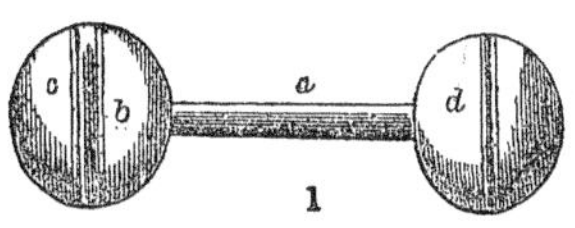

or irregular muscular action. The calisthenic exercises are calculated to cure deformities of the figure, especially of the chest, to invigorate the system, and conduce to elegant deportment and symmetry of form.

All these exercises are based upon physiological and philosophical principles; the former we have already explained, and the latter will be evident as we proceed, for it will be seen that the center of gravity is the ruling principle, as regards many of the postures; in fact, all grace of carriage and attitude depends, in a measure, upon this principle. Dr. Arnold remarks, that "grace of carriage includes not only a perfect freedom of motion, but also a firmness of step, or steady bearing of the center of gravity over the base. It is usually possessed by those who live in the country, and according to nature, as it is called, taking much and varied exercise. What a contrast is there between the gait of the active mountaineer, rejoicing in the consciousness of perfect nature, and that of the mechanic or shop-keeper, whose confinement to the cell of his trade soon produces in his body a shape and air that corresponds to it."

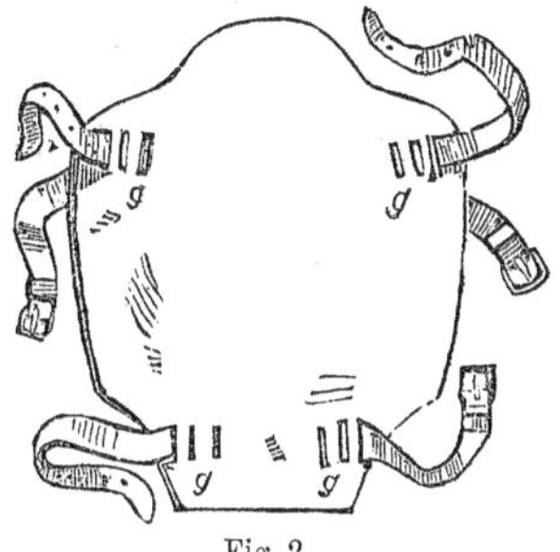

Fig. 2.

These exercises, with great propriety, now form part of the education of the best European seminaries, but unfortunately for the want of a suitable treatise on the subject, have been sadly neglected in our American system of

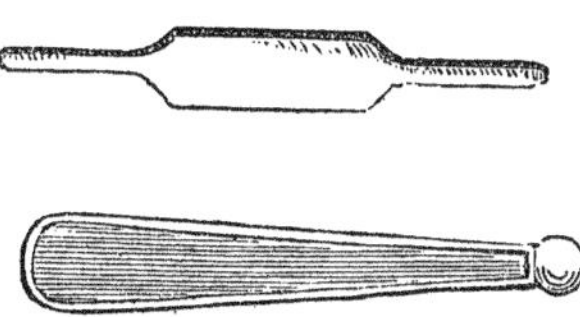
Fig's.3 and 4.

education. Before commencing the series, we must offer some preliminary cautions: 1st, that they should not be performed after a full meal; 2nd, that there should not be any ligatures, or tight strings, straps, etc., on any part of the body, but that the clothes should fit easily and loosely; 3rd, that the body should not be too warmly clothed *during* the exercises, but that an additional wrapper should be provided, to cover the body as soon as they are finished,—by this means, cold will be avoided; 4th, that the exercises should *generally* be performed in a room, in preference to the open air; 5th, that due regard must be paid to the health, age, and strength of the pupils exercised; in fact, to treat them as you would delicate creeping plants—to coax and train, but not to *strain* them.

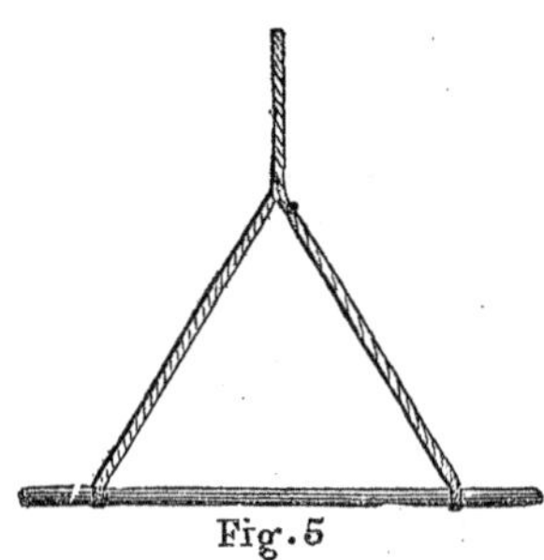
Fig. 5

Our readers and pupils are requested to consider that all the directions furnished with the illustrations, are issued by the calisthenic tutor, and that they are to be minutely performed by the pupil as laid down. It is necessary to explain this now, in order to prevent repetition.

The first things to be attended to are the cautions we have given above; and then the necessary apparatus—consisting of dumb-bells, backboard, clubs, wands, or poles, triangles, and elastic-cord—must be procured.

The *dumb-bells* we advise are constructed as follows: To the staff *a*, (which is made of oak or ash, six inches long, and one and a quarter inches in diameter,) is fixed a hemisphere, *b*, with a male screw, *e*; and to this part is attached at both ends another hemisphere, *c*, fitted with a female screw, so that when these hemispheres are screwed together, they form a complete sphere, as represented by *d*, in Fig. 1. The object of having these hemispheres constructed in the manner we have described, is to admit of their being loaded; and as the total weight of *each* dumb-bell constructed upon this principle is only two pounds,* it is obvious that the most delicate children can use them. In using these dumb-bells, we have usually commenced by loading them with pieces of wood, then with peas, shot, bullets, and sand, according to the age and constitution of the individual; but the heavily weighted ones have never yet been employed for ladies, only for young gentlemen. Of course, after this kind has been used, we recommend, for gentlemen, the ordinary ones, weighted according to age, etc. We mention this, because calisthenic exercises form a very admirable preliminary course to gymnastics.

Fig. 6.

Backboards should be fitted to the person requiring them, unless they are used for the backboard exercise, in which case they will be as represented in Fig. 2. When not used for this exercise, they are fastened to the back and shoulders by means of straps, *a*, *b*, *c*, *d*, which pass round the shoulders, and are made to buckle in front. These straps can be lengthened or shortened, by passing them through holes in the board, *g*, *g*, *g*, *g*, left for that purpose. The lower part of the

Fig. 7.

* They can be constructed as light as three-quarters of a pound each, by having the hemispheres of a less diameter, and made of thin brass.

board is fastened round the waist by a strap, *e*, *f*, which buckles in front.

The dimensions of the short backboard are as follows, for a large size — length, twelve or thirteen inches; breadth, ten inches; lower part, five inches; and upper part, four inches. These measurements can be reduced, according to circumstances, age, etc.

The *long backboard* should be broad in the center, as in Fig. 3, so that the flat part may reach across the back of the shoulders, and the handles, *a*, *b*, be long enough to hold in the hands when the arms are extended. Some of these backboards vary from six feet in length, to only three feet eight inches.

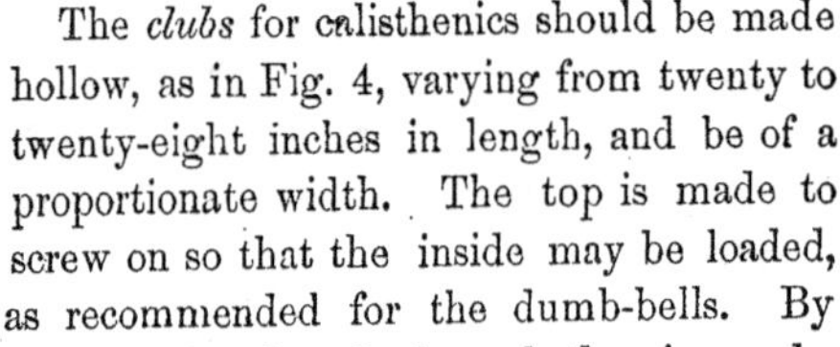

Fig. 8.

The *clubs* for calisthenics should be made hollow, as in Fig. 4, varying from twenty to twenty-eight inches in length, and be of a proportionate width. The top is made to screw on so that the inside may be loaded, as recommended for the dumb-bells. By this means, the weight to be forced through the air can be proportioned to the strength or power of the individual to propel it.

Fig. 9.

The *wands*, or *poles*, should be light, smooth, and sufficiently thick not to bend. They vary in length according to the person's height that is to use them, the rule being, that the poles shall be of the same length as the height of the person requiring them.

The *triangle* is a bar of wood attached to a cord at each end; the two cords meet above, as shown in Fig. 5, so as to form two sides of a triangle, of which the bar forms the third. A cord is attached to the upper part of the triangle, and this passing over a pulley, enables the teacher to lower or raise the bar, so as to suit the height of the pupil.

The *elastic cord* is one of the latest improvements in calisthenic exercises. It consists of two handles, *a b*, of a triangular form, to which is attached an elastic cord, made of vulcanized Indian rubber. They may be obtained at most toy-shops, and vary in price from four to ten shillings, according to the size.

Fig. 10.

Some teachers employ the horizontal bar; but as we disapprove of its use, of course the necessary directions are omitted from our series.

The pupil should commence the exercises with the dumb-bell practice.

The Dumb-bell Practice.

The dumb-bells are not to be used at first; but when the pupil has become proficient in the following exercises, then the dumb-bells are to be held firmly in the hands, which are to perform the same motions directed below.

Fig. 11.

Position of Attention. When the word *attention* is given by the teacher, the pupil is to draw back the shoulders, so as to make them square; the heels are to be placed in a line, and closed; the knees straight, the toes turned out to an angle of sixty degrees, the arms hanging close to the body, the elbows turned in close to the side, the hands open to the front, the little finger lightly touching the dress, and the thumb close to the fore finger. The abdomen is to be slightly drawn in, and the chest advanced, but without constraint; the body upright, inclining a little forward, so that the weight of it may be principally on the fore part of the feet; the head erect, and the eyes looking straight to the front, as in Fig. 7.

First Practice. *One.* At the word *one*, raise the hands, and bring the tips of the fingers in a line with, and pointing toward the shoulders, the body inclining forward, the head erect, and shoulders kept well back, with the elbows close to the side, as in Fig. 8.

Fig. 12.

Fig. 13.

Two. Dart the hands straight to the front, with straight arms, the palms of the hands close together, the thumbs close to the fore finger, nearly in a line with the chin, as in Fig. 9.

These two motions are to be repeated from *two* to *one*, and again from *one* to *two*, several times, before commencing *three*.

Three. The hands are thrown back, with straight arms, in a line with the shoulders, the palms of the hands to the front, the thumbs close to the fore fingers, the head erect, and shoulders kept well back, the body inclining forward, the heels raised off the ground, so that the weight of the body rests on the fore part of the feet, as in Fig. 10. These motions are to be repeated from *three* to *two*, and from *two* to *three*, several times before commencing *four*.

Four. The arms are to be brought gradually by the side to the first position, Fig. 7.

Standing at Ease. When the instructor gives the command to stand at ease, the right foot is to be drawn back about six inches, and the greatest part of the weight of the body brought upon it; the left knee is to be slightly bent; the hands brought together before the body, the palms being struck smartly together, and that of the right hand being then slipped over the back of the left, so as to clasp it; the shoulders are to be kept back and square, and the head to the front; but there is not to be any stiffness or constraint in the position; on the contrary, it is really intended that the pupil should *stand at ease*, the object being to afford a little rest after the performance of any of the exercises.

Fig. 14.

Second Practice. *One.* The hands are to be brought smartly up with the palms of the hands to the front, the tips of the fingers in a line with the shoulder, pointing upward, the elbows to be kept close to the side and well back, so as to square the shoulders; the head is to be held erect, and the body slightly inclined forward, as in Fig. 11.

Two. Raise the elbows a little, so as to draw them upward and backward, then bring the hands smartly down to the side, as in Fig. 12, and assume the position of attention, Fig. 7.

Long Backboard Exercises.

The pupils are to stand at ease, as directed before, and then the instructor will give them the long backboards, Fig. 3, which are to be held by the handle with the left hand, and the right hand is to be placed on the top of the backboard, while the other end rests upon the ground between the feet, as in Fig. 13.

Attention. When this word is given, the heels are to be brought in a line, and the backboard brought across in front of the thighs at the full extent of the arms, holding it by the handles with both hands; the back of the hands to be front, as in Fig. 14.

One. The backboard is to be gradually raised from the position of attention, with the arms straight, until the flat part of it is horizontal and over the head, the tips of the fingers in front, and the knuckles behind; the body is to be kept well forward on the fore part of the feet, and the head erect, as will be seen in Fig. 15.

Fig. 15.

Two. At this word the backboard is to be lowered from position *one*, the arms being contracted, and it is to be brought across the back part of the shoulders, as in Fig. 16, still keeping the body well forward, and the head erect. In the last position, the pupil will be required to walk slowly round the room, then quickly, and to practice the balance step without gaining ground.

Fig. 16.

When the various exercises have been frequently repeated, the word "steady" will be given, when the position of attention, Fig. 14, is to be resumed, and at the command "stand at ease," that position, Fig. 13, with the backboard, is at once to be taken.

Short Backboard Exercises.

The short backboard, Fig. 2, being strapped on as before directed, the pupil is to hold the head erect, and to be practiced in the balance step, with and without gaining ground, for half an hour at least; after which the muscles of the arms and shoulders should be exercised by the club practice.

The Club Practice.

The clubs, Fig. 4, are to be placed in the pupil's hands, with their wrists turned out, and having a firm hold of the handles; the heels are to be kept close, the knees well pressed back, the weight of the body resting on the fore part of the feet, the head erect, and the body perfectly steady.

Fig. 17.

First Practice. *One.* Turn the back of the right hand to the front, raise it gradually with a straight arm in a line with the shoulder, carrying the club in a circular direction round the head, the arm extended to the front, the club resting on the right shoulder, as in Fig. 17.

Two. Turn the back of the left hand to the front, raise it gradually with a straight arm in a line with the shoulder, and carry the club in a circular direction round the head, the arm extending to the front, the club resting on the left shoulder. In this position, both hands must be kept close together, the arms straight, the body inclined forward, and the head erect.

Three. Separate the hands, and carry them backward, with the arms straight, and in a line with the shoulders, as in Fig. 20, the clubs hanging perpendicular, being held between the fore fingers and thumb; the palms of the hands upward, and the fingers straight, body well forward on the fore part of the feet, the head erect, and shoulders well pressed back.

Four. Let the arms fall gradually to the side, with the

Fig. 18.

wrists turned out, and the clubs beir.g held with a firm grasp, as in Fig. 18.

SECOND PRACTICE. *One.* Bring the hands close together in front of the body, the arms straight, the thumbs in a line with the chin, and the clubs held perpendicular, as in Fig. 21; the body being well forward, and the head erect.

Two. Separate the hands, carrying them off with straight arms in a line with the shoulders, as in Fig. 20.

The same motions are to be repeated as directed for *three* in the first club practice.

Three. Let the ends of the clubs fall to the back of the hips, as in Fig. 22, keeping a firm grasp of the clubs, with the arms straight, the body kept forward, the head erect, and shoulders pressed well back.

Four. Let the arms fall gradually to the side, with the wrist turned out, the clubs being held firmly, as in Fig. 18.

THIRD PRACTICE. *One.* Carry the right hand, with the wrist well turned out, straight to the front, and circle the club round the right shoulder; then let the arms fall gradually to the side, at the word "steady."

Fig. 19.

Two. Carry the left hand, with the wrist well turned out, straight to the front, and circle the club round the left shoulder; then let the arms fall gradually to the side, at the word "steady."

Three. Carry both hands, with the wrists well turned out, straight to the front, and circle both clubs round the shoulders, swinging them independently; then, at the word "steady," let the arms fall gradually to the side.

Wand or Pole Exercises.

Fig. 20.

The pupils are to stand at ease, as we have before directed, and when the poles are delivered to them, they are to remain in the same position, with the poles between their hands and the body. When the word "steady" is given, the poles are to be held in the center, with the thumbs turned inward, and close together.

FIRST PRACTICE. *One.* Slide the hands smartly up the pole to the top, which is to be grasped firmly; then dart the hands straight to the front, with straight arms, the thumbs close together and uppermost; the knuckles to the front, as in Fig. 23.

Fig. 21.

Two. Throw the hands well back, the same as directed for dumb-bell practice, (First Practice, "*Three*,") keeping the knuckles to the front.

Repeat these motions from *two* to *one*, and from *one* to *two*.

Three. Slide the hands down the pole to its center, and resume the position you had before the word "*one*" was given.

SECOND PRACTICE. *Attention.* When this word is given, the heels are to be brought in a line, and the pole brought across the front of the thighs, at the full extent of the arms, the same as in the backboard exercise, Fig. 15.

One. Raise the right hand until it is above the center of the head, and move the left hand from left toward the right, until it is under the other hand, and the pole held quite perpendicular, as in Fig. 25; the back of the left hand being toward the teacher, and the back of the right hand toward the body.

Two. Reverse the last exercise, by raising the left hand first.

These motions are to be repeated from *two* to *one*, and from *one* to *two*.

THIRD PRACTICE. *One.* Raise the pole gradually from the position of *attention*, to above the head, as in the long backboard exercise, Fig. 15.

Two. Lower the pole from the position "*one*," the arms being contracted, until it is brought across the back part of the thighs at the full extent of the arms, as in Fig. 26; the thumbs being at the back, the little finger in front, and the palms of the hands upward. Repeat the exercise from *two* to *one*, and from *one* to *two*.

FOURTH PRACTICE. The first word given is *attention*, when the pupil is to come smartly into this position, as in the back-board exercise, Fig. 16.

One. Reverse the hands one at a time, beginning with the right hand, so as to bring the tops of the fingers in front, and looking upward, the knuckles to the rear, and the thumbs crossing the fore and middle fingers; the body well forward on the fore part of the feet, the head erect, and shoulders well pressed back.

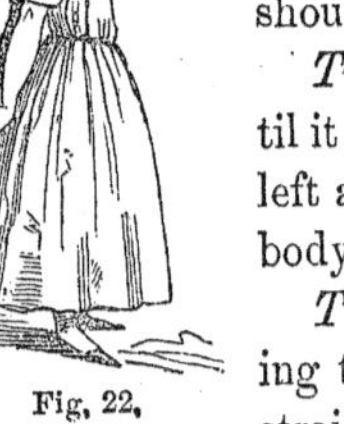

Fig. 22.

Two. Raise the right hand smartly, until it comes in a line with the chin; keep the left arm straight, and hand steady, and the body in the same position as the last.

Three. Reverse the last exercise, by raising the left hand, and keeping the right arm straight, and hand steady.

Repeat the exercise from *three* to *two*, from *two* to *one*, and from *one* to *two*, and from *two* to *three*, first slowly, and then rapidly.

Walking.

Position. In walking, the arms should hang close to the body, the elbows turned in and close to the side; the hands rather open to the front, and the little finger lightly touching the dress; the chest advanced, but without constraint; the body upright but inclined a little forward, so that the weight of it may principally bear on the fore part of the feet; the head to be erect, and the eyes straight to the front.

The arms should not be allowed to swing about like a pendulum; the movement of the leg and thigh must spring from the hip, and be free and natural. The foot should be raised high enough to clear the ground without grazing it, carried straight to the front, and without being drawn back, placed softly on the ground on the fore part or ball of the great toe, and the heel allowed to come gradually to the ground, so as not to jerk or shake the body in the slightest degree.

The Elastic Cord Exercises.

These exercises are performed nearly the same as part of the club and backboard exercises, but are arranged as follows:

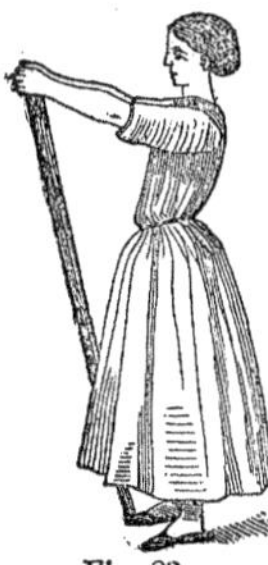
Fig. 23.

Attention. The heels will be brought in a line, the handles of the elastic cord are to be firmly grasped with the hands, and the cord brought across in front of the thighs, to the full extent of the arms, the back of the hand being outward, the thumb and fore finger to the front, and the little finger to the rear.

One. Dart the hands straight to the front, with straight arms, the thumbs touching each other, and the cord hanging perpendicular. See "*one*," second practice of the club exercise, Fig. 2.

Two. Raise the hands gradually from the former position, together with a straight arm over the head. See "*one*," fourth dumb-bell practice, Fig. 7.

Three. Lower the hands, until both little fingers are behind the back of the head, then separate the hands gradually, and bring the elbows close to the side, the knuckles to the rear, the shoulders and head well back, the body inclining forward, and the elastic cord across the back, the same as in the backboard exercise. See "*two*," long backboard exercise, Fig. 16.

Four. Bring the knuckles together in front of the body in a line with the chin, the elbows close together in front of the chest.

Repeat the exercise from *four* to *three*, several times, so as to bring the shoulders well back, the head being kept erect.

Repeat the exercises slowly at first, and then quickly, from *four* to *three*, from *three* to *two*, and from *two* to *one*, and afterward back again to *four*, commencing with *one*.

The Balance Step.

First Practice.—The pupil being placed in the first position, (attention, Fig. 7,) the instructor should explain and instruct her in the balance step, the object of which is to give a steadiness to the body, and remove that rolling motion so frequently observed in those who have not learned Calisthenics, and impart a free and graceful motion to the limbs. Care should be taken to prevent the pupil throwing back the one or

Fig. 24.

both shoulders during this exercise, or of acquiring inelegant postures.

1. *Without gaining ground.* The pupil commences by balancing the body upon the right foot. At the word

"*Front*," the left foot is brought gently forward, the heel in a line with the right toe, and about three inches above the ground; the toe turned out, and pointing to the ground;

"*Rear*," the left foot is brought slowly to the rear, the toe in a line with the heel of the right foot, and the knee a little bent.

When these two motions have been practiced for several times, the pupil should balance upon the other foot.

Fig. 25.

"*Halt.*" When this word is given, the foot, whether advanced or to the rear, is to be brought to the ground, and the heels kept square.

2. *Balance step, gaining ground by the word "Forward," "Front."* When this word is given, the left foot is to be carried gently to the front, as before, the knee is to be gradually straightened as the foot is brought forward, the toe turned out a little to the left, and remaining about three inches from the ground. This position is to be maintained for about three or four seconds; then, at the word

Fig. 26.

"*Forward*," the left foot is to be brought to the ground (eighteen inches from heel to heel,) softly, resting the first on the ball of the great toe, and then lowering the heel gradually. This must be done so as not to shake the body; and at the same time, the right foot is to be raised, and kept extended to the rear.

"*Front.*" At this word, the right foot is brought to the front, and at the word

"*Forward,*" the right foot is brought to the ground, and so on, remaining about three seconds between the words, until the length of the room has been passed through; then the pupil should be requested to turn round, and retrace her steps, the words being given, "*front*" and "*forward,*" alternately.

Fig. 27.

The number of paces taken in a minute should be seventy-five, and the distance between each, eighteen inches.

SECOND PRACTICE. When the pupil has performed the balance step well, she should be made to walk quicker, so as to take one hundred and eight steps in a minute, and during her progress the word should be given,

"*Change Feet.*" The object of this is to exercise a person in keeping step in walking, for example, when she is stepping with a different foot from her companion.

At this word, the ball of the rear foot is brought up to the advanced heel; then a step is made forward again with the advanced foot, so that two successive steps are made with the same foot.

Fig. 28.

THIRD PRACTICE. The pupil should be made to place the hand upon the hips, with the thumbs turned back, and the tips of the fingers to the front, as in Fig. 27; the heels are then to be raised gradually from the ground, and the pupil must move forward by successive short jumps, of two inches at a time, performed on the toes.

This exercise must not be performed until after the others have been executed, and only for five or ten minutes at a time, the object being to strengthen the knees, ankles, and muscles of the legs, but not to tire them.

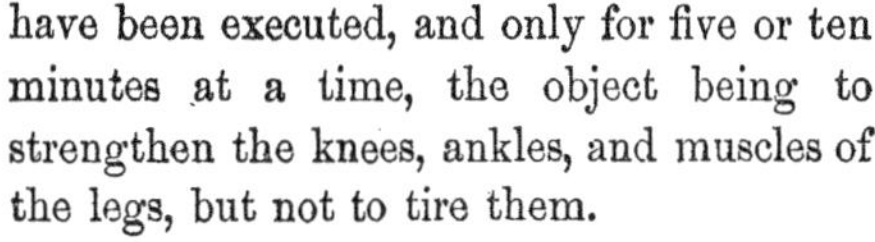

Fig. 29.

FOURTH PRACTICE. The pupil should be made to walk up and down the room with a heavy book balanced on the head, for about ten minutes every day, the hands being rather open to the front, and the little finger touching the dress, as in the proper position for walking.

This gives a graceful carriage to pupils, and prevents their becoming round-shouldered; in fact, counteracting the ill effects likely to arise from their ordinary school exercises.

Exercises with the Triangle.

FIRST PRACTICE. *One.* The bar being lowered to a little above the knees, the pupil should be requested to grasp the bar firmly with both hands, the backs of the hands being uppermost, the arms straight, and the body erect.

Two. The arms are to be gradually bent, and the bar raised until it is about breast high; then the pupil should incline the body forward, and step round upon the toes, gradually increasing her speed until she has acquired a tolerable velocity, when she must stop herself, by throwing the body backward, as in Fig. 28, and stepping shorter.

Three. Repeat the last exercise, but incline the body backward instead of forward at starting.

SECOND PRACTICE. The triangle being raised to the same height as the pupil's head, the bar is to be grasped firmly with both hands, near to the cord, the back of the hands being to the rear, and the thumbs inside. The heels are to be brought in a line and closed, the knees straight, the toes turned out at an angle of sixty degrees, and the head erect.

One. Raise the left heel until the leg is parallel to the floor, both knees in a line, and the sole of the left foot perpendicular, and looking backward.

Fig. 30.

Two. Reverse the last exercise, by raising the right foot instead of the left.

Repeat the exercise from *two* to *one*, and from *one* to *two*, several times before commencing three, and each time remain in either position for a minute or more.

Three. Raise both heels off the ground, and remain on the toes, while the instructor counts ten slowly; then bring the heels *gradually down.* Repeat this exercise several times for ten minutes.

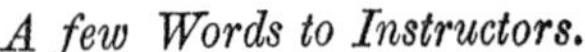

A few Words to Instructors.

Fig. 31.

In conclusion, we would remark that the instructor should give the orders clearly, firmly, and concisely, avoiding all unnecessary words, and always performing the exercise *before* the pupils, while another person, generally a proficient pupil, imitates the motions *at the side* of the pupils.

Hastiness of temper can not be too strongly censured, for it is possible that many of the pupils will catch the ideas of the instructor quicker than others; while blustering and severity of manner is apt to confuse rather than instruct some pupils. Remember that practice makes us all perfect, and in time, no doubt, many of your apparently dull pupils will be better versed in the exercises than the others, who, relying upon their facility in learning, soon forget them, because they cease to think.

Always explain everything as you proceed. Do not hurry the pupils through the exercise — they should understand one practice well before commencing another — but do not run into the opposite extreme of keeping them too long at one exercise, and thus give them a disgust for calisthenics. Long lessons are injurious to health, and tend to distract the attention rather than fix it. We consider an hour's exercise quite long enough for any one.

Fig. 32.

THIRD DUMB-BELL PRACTICE. *One.* Bring the hands up, with the fingers clenched, the knuckles being in front and in a line with the chin, the elbows close together in front of the chest, and the head kept well back, as in Fig. 29.

Two. Separate the arms, carry them back with the fingers clenched in a line with the shoulders, the knuckles behind, the shoulders and head well back, the body inclining forward, with the elbows close to the side, as in Fig. 30.

Fig. 33.

These two motions are to be repeated from *two* to *one*, and from *one* to *two*, before commencing *three.*

Three. Dart the hands up in the air with a straight arm, the palms of the hands being in front, and the fingers pointing upward, as in Fig. 31.

These motions are to be repeated from *three* to *two*, and from *two* to *three*, before proceeding to four.

Four. Bring the arms gradually down to the side, so as to come to the first position, (Fig. 7.)

All the motions of the first three practices are to be performed slowly, and with precision.

Fig. 34

FOURTH DUMB-BELL PRACTICE. The following exercises are to be performed quicker than the preceding ones — generally about three times as quick — great care being taken to make each pupil perform them separately at first.

One. Bring the palms of the hands smartly together, with the arms as straight as possible over the head, as in Fig. 32; the body is to incline forward, and the head to be kept well back.

Fig. 35.

Two. Separate the hands from above the head, and let them fall quickly to behind the hips, with a straight arm; the back of the hands being behind, and meeting each other; the heels are to be raised off the ground, so that the weight of the body rests upon the fore part of the feet; the head must be kept erect, and the shoulders well back, as in Fig. 33.

These motions must be repeated, from *two* to *one*, and from *one* to *two*.

When the pupil is in the second position, Fig. 33, the teacher gives the word — "*steady!*" when the arms are to be gradually brought down by the side, and the "attention position" resumed. See Fig. 7.

Fig. 36.

FIFTH DUMB-BELL PRACTICE. *One.* Close the fingers of both hands; then bring them to the front, so that the two thumbs may touch, and the knuckles be to the front; raise the right arm slowly, until it is perpendicular, as in Fig. 34, and then bring it down backward, as in Fig. 33, and finally let it hang by the side; repeat this exercise with the left arm, then with both together, Fig. 35, taking care to do so slowly and steadily at first, and afterward in quicker time.

Two. Raise the hands slowly over the head, Fig. 35, and when they are perpendicular, bend the body over, until the hands nearly touch the feet, keeping the arms and knees straight; then raise yourself until you resume the position, Fig. 35, of the first motion, and bring the hands down to the side, Fig. 7, with the palms to the front.

The attention of School Committees, Superintendents, principals of Academies, High Schools, and Teachers, is invited to the following valuable *School Books*, embracing some of the best and most reliable in the United States.

NORMAL SERIES OF SCHOOL BOOKS

PUBLISHED BY

SHELDON, LAMPORT & BLAKEMAN,

115 NASSAU STREET, NEW YORK.

STODDARD'S ARITHMETICAL SERIES,

By John F. Stoddard, A. M., President of the University of Northern Pennsylvania

COMPRISING

THE JUVENILE MENTAL ARITHMETIC, 12½ cents, 72 pp., for Primary Schools, to precede

THE AMERICAN INTELLECTUAL ARITHMETIC, 164 pp., an extended work, designed for Common Schools, Seminaries, and Academies, 20 cents.

STODDARD'S PRACTICAL ARITHMETIC, half-bound, which embraces every variety of exercises appropriate to written Arithmetic, 40 cents.

STODDARD'S PHILOSOPHICAL ARITHMETIC, a higher work for Colleges and advanced Classes in Union Schools, Seminaries and Academies, 60 cents.

☞ This Arithmetic has neither Rules, Answers, nor Key.

The first two numbers of the series constitute a complete treatise on the subject of Mental or Analytic Arithmetic.

The last two are no less thorough in their treatment of Practical or Written Arithmetic.

The series, as a whole, by a truly progeessive arrangement and classification of examples, including the various kinds and combinations in compound and complex ratios, or "Double Position," original methods of computing interest discount and percentage in all their variations, together with a variety of Algebraic exercises, is carefully designed to conduct the learner from initiatory steps, by an easy and gradually progressive system, to the more advanced attainments in Mathematical Science.

The arrangement of "The Philosophical Arithmetic," without "Rules, Answers or Key," in which the examples are met with in the same manner as in practical business life, is adapted to the use of advanced classes in all Schools where there is a desire to take an independent course, and prove the scholars master of the subject.

☞ Such a work has long been solicited by the most able and prominent Teachers throughout the country.

A whole volume of the most exalted recommendations of this series of Arithmetics, from the best Educators in all sections of the country, who have used them, can be shown. The following will be sufficient for the present purpose.

TESTIMONIALS FROM THE STATE OF NEW YORK.

NEW YORK CITY SCHOOLS.

I have examined with much pleasure a work entitled "Stoddard's American Intellectual Arithmetic." It closely resembles in the nature of the exercises Colburn's Mental Arithmetic, a work that has met with the unbounded approbation of the ablest teachers in the country. I observe that Stoddard's contains many decided improvements on Colburn's ; it is more systematic in its arrangement, passing from what is easy, more gradually to what is difficult ; some very important omissions are supplied, and very considerable additions in Interest, Discount, Percentage, etc. I see that it is also adapted to Federal Money.

It seems to me to be the best book on Intellectual Arithmetic now in use, and I hope for the good of education it will be used in every school where Arithmetic is taught.

DAVID PATTERSON, M. D.,
Principal of Public School No. 3, and one of the Teachers of the Male Normal School
NEW YORK, July 26, 1853

Concurred in by

HENRY KIDDLE,	Principal P. S.	No. 2.	P. D. DEMILT,	Principal W. S.	No. 34.
H. FANNING,	"	No. 13.	N. P. BEERS,	"	No. 15.
C. W. FEEKS,	"	No. 4.	E. McELROY,	"	No. 32.
A. MURPHY,	"	No. 17.	SAML. ST. JOHN,	"	No. 26.

NEW YORK, July 13, 1853.

After a careful examination of "Stoddard's Practical Arithmetic," I have no hesitation in pronouncing it a work of very superior merit. The brevity and clearness of its definitions and rules, its lucid analysis of every operation, and the great variety of its examples comprising almost every possible combination of arithmetical principles, render it one of the best books to discipline the mind of the scholar, in mathematical reasoning, I have ever seen.

HENRY KIDDLE, Prin. P. S. No. 2.

I entirely concur with Mr. Kiddle in his opinion of "Stoddard's Practical Arithmetic."

H. FANNING,
Principal P. S. 13.
July 15, 1853.

I also concur with Mr. Kiddle in his opinion of "Stoddard's Arithmetic."

DAVID PATTERSON, Prin. P. S. 3.

I concur in the above. GEO. MOORE, W. S. 10.

BROOKLYN SCHOOLS.

Having submitted "Stoddard's Intellectual Arithmetic" to the practical test of the school room, we have no hesitation in expressing a strong preference for it over all Text-books on the subject. The author has taken a decided step in advance of those who have preceded him ; and his labors are likely to do much towards popularizing a study, the importance of which as a mental discipline can hardly be over-estimated. The works formerly in use were deficient of systematic arrangement, were neither gradual enough in their transitions, nor sufficiently comprehensive and varied as regards their examples. Stoddard's on the other hand, is an eminently practical book ; philosophical in its arrangement, natural and lucid in its analysis, original in its design, adapted at the commencement to the comprehension of beginners and carrying the pupil by easy inductive steps through the most complicated operations : it seems invulnerable to criticism, and leaves little or nothing to b accomplished by future authors on this subject. The examples are numerous and varied, embracing all cases likely to arise in business ; and there are not less than fifty pages of questions capable of Algebraic solution. The Chapters on Percentage, Interest and Discount, are worthy of special commendation. In these the author has an entirely original plan, which enables the pupil to solve mentally, with perfect ease, questions which, without this drilling, few are able to manage even on the slate.

In view of these striking and excellent features, we warmly commend Prof. Stoddard's work to all who are interested in the education of youth.

S. C. BARNES,	Principal P. S.	No. 4.	GEO. H. STEBBINS,	Principal P. S.	No. 12.
JOSIAH REEVE,	"	No. 8.	F. D. CLARKE,	"	No. 3.
J. T. CONKLING,	"	No. 5.	CHAS. H. OLIVER,	"	No. 11
DAVID SYME,	"	No. 6.	PETER ROUGET,	"	No. 10.
A. B. CLARKE,		No, 13.	E. C. SEYMOUR,	"	No. 7.

WEBB'S SERIES OF NORMAL READERS.

NORMAL PRIMER, Beautifully Illustrated, 12mo. 24 pp. Paper covers 5 cents, stiff covers 6 cents.

PRIMARY LESSONS, a Series of Cards to be used in connection with No. 1. Price one dollar per set.

NORMAL READER, No. 1. 12mo. 90 pp. 12½ cents.

NORMAL READER, No. 2. 12mo. 168 pp. 25 cents.

NORMAL READER, No. 3. 12mo. 216 pp. 37½ cents.

NORMAL READER, No. 4. 12mo. 312 pp. 50 cents.

NORMAL READER, No. 5. 12mo. 490 pp. 75 cents.

These Readers are used in the principal cities and villages throughout the United States, and are rapidly coming into use in the smaller towns of the country. Their merits have been fairly tested, and they have universally been pronounced superior to any series of Readers extant, not only for the improvement in the system of teaching, which is the WORD METHOD; but also in the high moral tone and inspiriting character of the pieces selected. The author, Mr. WEBB, was recently from the State Normal School, at Albany.

They are THE BEST Practical Readers that have come under my notice; they are ALL and EVERY THING they should be. HON. S. S. RANDALL, *Deputy State Supt. Com. Schools.*

Webb's Readers are the best books of their kind for our schools.
D. M. CAMP, *Ex-Governor of Vermont.*

I am happy to command Webb's Readers to the favorable regard of all Educators.
J. R. BOYD, *Author of Rhetoric, Moral Philosophy, &c.*

We have used "Webb's Normal Readers," and believe them superior to any with which we are acquainted, and would cheerfully recommend their general adoption to all of our schools. ROSMAN INGALLS and E. S. INGALLS. *Teachers of Select School.*

Having examined "Webb's Normal Readers," we believe them to possess many advantages over any other series of Readers which has come under our notice, and would therefore recommend their introduction into the schools of Binghampton.
A. D. STOCKWELL, A. W. JACKSON. *Trustees of District No.* 2.
GEORGE PARK, R. S. BARTLETT, *Trustees of District No.* 1.
T. R. MORGAN, WM. E. ABBOTT, *Trustees of District No.* 4.

Dear Sir—I have examined "Webb's Normal Readers," and consider the system superior to any now in use. Respectfully yours, H: G. PRINDLE,
Town Supt. Common Schools, Norwich.

Sir—I have examined, with considerable care "Webb's Series of Readers," and can cheerfully recommend them, as in my opinion, superior to any others with which I am acquainted.
Yours, &c., MARSENA STONE, *Pastor Baptist Church, Norwich.*

At a meeting of the Town Superintendents of the County of Chenango, held in the village of Norwich, on the 16th of August, the following Resolution was adopted:—
Resolved, That we consider the uniformity of text books a matter of infinite importance to our common schools; and believing "Webb's Normal Readers," to be superior in many respects to any extant, for teaching the principles of reading and instilling sound moral principles in the mind of the scholars, we therefore recommend their general adoption in the schools of the county.

FROM THE CITY SUPERINTENDENT OF SCHOOLS, UTICA, N. Y.

Dear Sir—Having somewhat carefully examined "Webb's Normal Readers," I have no hesitation in saying I consider them to rank high among the best Practical Readers that have come under my notice. We have lately introduced two numbers into some of our public schools of this city, which have thus far given good satisfaction. D. S. HEFFRON.

GOODRICH'S GEOGRAPHIES.

THE NEW NATIONAL GEOGRAPHY, with a Catechetical Introduction and Colored Maps. In the elegance of its numerous illustrations, and the clearness and beauty of the Maps, it is not excelled, if equaled, by any similar work. New Edition, with the late Census. Price 50 cents.

A COMPREHENSIVE GEOGRAPHY AND HISTORY, ANCIENT AND MODERN. This work contains 272 quarto pages, equal to 1000 common 12mo. pages, and is Illuminated with Seventy-nine beautiful Maps, and numerous Engravings. It is the most complete and comprehensive work for High Schools, Families, Merchants, Travelers, and Emigrants, that has ever appeared. It contains the Geography and History of every Country. The work has received the highest commendations at the hands of scientific men, in America and Europe, and is regarded as one of the most useful, convenient and valuable which the author has given to the public. Price $2 50 half-bound.

PRIMER OF GEOGRAPHY. A new and elegant ILLUSTRATED "FIRST BOOK" in Geography. Price 20 cents.

PARLEY'S GEOGRAPHY FOR BEGINNERS. New Edition, with Catechetical Introduction and Colored Maps. Price 30 cents.

⁂ Any number of testimonials, from the highest sources, could be added, if thought necessary.

☞ This complete Series of Geographies, by S. G. GOODRICH, ESQ., is not surpassed, if equaled, in beauty, interest, and cheapness, by any now published.

FIRST LESSONS IN GEOGRAPHY. By GEORGE W. FITCH. Colored Maps. 40 pp. quarto, price 45 cents.

In this book the learner's attention is mainly directed to one thing—the study of maps. It embraces very little descriptive information. It is believed the definitions are sufficiently extensive for all useful purposes, and as exact as is consistent with simplicity. The author has endeavored to embrace nothing which should not be studied and retained, and nothing which may not with reasonable effort be remembered. With the hope that it will prove itself a useful manual in the school-room and at the fireside,the author respectfully submits it to the examination of teachers and parents.

FITCH'S MAPPING PLATES: Designed for Learners in GEOGRAPHY, being a collection of Plates prepared for Delineating Maps of the World, and Countries forming its principal subdivisions, viz :—1. The World. 2. United States. 3. North America. 4. South America. 5. A State. 6. Mexico and Guatimala. 7. Great Britain and Ireland. 8. Europe. 9. Southern Europe. 10. Germany. 11. Africa. 12. Asia. 13. Atlantic Ocean. 14. Pacific Ocean. By GEORGE W. FITCH. Price 30 cents.

The attention of the public are respectfully called to the above Plates, and to the advantages they are calculated to afford in the study of Geography. They are prepared with the suitable and requisite lines of latitude and longitude, for maps of the world, and the countries forming its principal subdivisions, and are designed to be used in connection with the school atlases in common use, as well as with outline maps. With these Plates, the pupil is able to commence, at once, the delineation of maps, without the difficult and perplexing labor of drawing the meridians and parallels—a labor which generally consumes the time of both teacher and scholar, to an extent entirely disproportionate to any good which may be derived thereby.

SPELLERS.

THE SPELLER AND DEFINER. By E. Hazen, A. M. Price 20 cents.

SYMBOLICAL SPELLING BOOK. With 553 Cuts. Price 20 cents.

" " " Part 1st, 288 Cuts. Price 10 cents

" " " Part 2d, 265 Cuts. Price 12½ cents

MILES' UNITED STATES SPELLER, a new work, containing upwards of fifteen thousand of the most common English Words. Price 13 cents.

The author of this work is an old PRACTICAL TEACHER; the arrangement and classification are original and strictly progressive; and in Orthography and Pronunciation, the best Standard Authors, Writers and Speakers have been consulted.

These Spelling Books are designed to accompany Webb's Series of Normal Readers.

LOOMIS' ELEMENTS OF ANATOMY, PHYSIOLOGY AND HYGIENE. By Prof. J. R. Loomis, of Waterville College, Maine. Price 75 cents.

This is a new work, beautifully Illustrated with Colored Plates, and many Original Drawings.

The author has been a practical instructor of this science for many years; but having met with no Text Book of the kind which, in his judgment, was completely adapted to the *use of classes*, he has prepared a small volume of about 200 pages, that can be gone thoroughly through in one term of three months, a *desideratum*, in which he has presented in a most lucid, concise and comprehensible manner, the entire subject, as far as it is practicable to be taught in Common Schools, Seminaries or Colleges.

This treatise is already introduced in some of the best schools and academies, in New York and Ohio, and is rapidly gaining popularity.

PHELPS'S LECTURES ON PHILOSOPHY AND CHEMISTRY, Each 300 pp. 12mo. Are highly esteemed, and used extensively. Price 75 cents

CHEMISTRY AND PHILOSOPHY FOR BEGINNERS. By Mrs. A. Lincoln Phelps. Each 218 pp. 18mo. Price 50 cents.

These admirable books, by the distinguished authoress of "Lincoln's Botany," are unquestionably among the very best works of their kind. The great elementary truths which are the basis of these most interesting departments of study, are presented with such directness, clearness, and force, that the learner is compelled to perceive and apprehend them; at the same time he is attracted, charmed, and indelibly impressed with that indescribable felicity of language, which none but an accomplished lady or mother can ever address to delighted and instructed youth. To be approved and adopted, these books need only to be universally known. Though but recently published, their circulation, already extensive, is rapidly increasing.

GRAMMAR MADE EASY FOR BEGINNERS. By Mrs. Sarah L. Guernsey. 108 pp. Price 25 cents.

This is the title of an attractive little book, in which the author has fairly sustained her right to the title she has selected. The too commonly dry subject of grammar has been rendered agreeable, instructive, and entertaining by the manner in which Mrs. Guernsey has presented its primary truths. This book therefore will be found a very useful and appropriate introduction to the study of language, the most useful and important of all departments of knowledge, for unless the laws of language are clearly understood and observed, no person can either acquire or impart knowledge to others. The mechanical execution of this little book is unusually neat and attractive. It has met with great favor.

NELSON'S INTRODUCTION TO PENMANSHIP Designed for the Use of Schools. In Five Books, consisting of an *elementary*, and No. 1, for Beginners; No. 2, for Boys; No. 3, for Girls; and No. 4, Course Hand, each 12½ cents.

These Copies are all Lithographed, and not Stereotyped like most other Copy-books in use, and thus like the Daguerreotype of the face, an exact copy of the original is taken. But in Stereotyping the hair stroke cannot be copied.

COLT'S SCIENCE OF DOUBLE-ENTRY BOOK-KEEPING, Simplified, Arranged, and Methodised after the forms of Grammar and Arithmetic; explained by different rules, and illustrated by entries classed, in a manner materially different from any work ever before offered to the public. Containing also a KEY, explaining the manner of Journalizing, and the nature of the business transactions of each of the Day-Book entries, together with practical forms for keeping books, as circumstances may require in different commercial houses. By John C. Colt. School Edition, price $1 00. Teachers' and Clerks' Edition, $1 50.

J. C. Colt, Esq., *Albany.*

Sir—Having been presented with a copy of your Treatise on Book-Keeping,—with a request that I would examine it, and give an expression as to its merits,—I have examined the work, and every page has afforded new evidence that it is the work which is to fill a void in the public schools of our country, hitherto left blank, more for the want of a *proper text-book*, than any other cause. With your book the study may be prosecuted in all our schools, with as much confidence and success, as the study of arithmetic, grammar, or any ordinary study,—and with little additional labor to the teacher. I shall use the work in my school.

Respectfully yours, J. W. BULKLEY.

Equally flattering and complimentary recommendations as the preceding, have been received from the following gentlemen:—

Gazzam & Butler, Merchants, Cincinnati, Ohio.
Delafield & Burnet, Bankers, " "
Hartwell, Lawrence & Co., Merchants, "
A. H. Wheeler, Teacher of Book-Keeping, 251 Broadway, New York.
Wm. Hiller, Teacher, 126 Allen Street, N. Y.
James Lawson, Teacher, New York.
E. B. Tanner, " "
Henry Swords, " "
J. Taft, Principal of Halcyon Seminary, N. Y.
B. Fowler, Teacher, New York.
N. Mowry, " "
John Oakley, " "
E. F. Mitchell, " "
J. Healy, " "
W. Marsh, " "
Robert Smitharst, Accountant, Philadelphia.
John G. Pearson, " "
J. L. Orcutt, Teacher of Book-Keeping, "
Edward Knowlton, " " Southwork, "
Wm. B. Wedgwood, A. M. Teacher of Poughkeepsie Classical School, New York.
Wm. Jenney, Principal Dutchess Co. Academy, Poughkeepsie, New Youk.
J. Grant, Esq., Cashier Farmers' and Manufacturers' Bank. Poughkeepsie, New York.
E. B. Brigamin, Esq., Cashier Bank of Poughkeepsie, New York.
F. S. Pease, Esq., Book-Keeper Commercial Bank, Albany, New York.
Carlo Green, Principal of a Select School, Hudson, New York.
A. B. McDonal, Teacher of Book-Keeping, Albany Academy, Albany, New York.
Joel Marble, Teacher State St. Public, Albany New York.
Wm. H. Hughes, Teacher of Book-Keeping, Albany, New York.
George W. Francis, Teacher of a Select School, Troy, New York.
James Park, Teacher, and Secretary of the Troy Teachers' Society, Troy New York.
Joseph Childs, Jr., Teacher, Fifth Street, Troy, New York

MUSIC BOOKS.

THE LADIES' GLEE BOOK; A Collection of choice and beautiful GLEES, for Three Female Voices, in *English*, *French* and *Italian*. Designed for the use of Classes, School Exhibitions, and to add to the pleasures of the Home Circle. An extra part is added, which may be sung by a baritone or tenor voice, when the third female voice cannot be procured. Translated, adapted, arranged and composed, with an accompaniment on the Piano Forte, by HENRY C. WATSON. Quarto, 112 pp. Price half-bound $1 00, cloth $1 50.

I cordially recommend the work to my friends and the public. W. V. WALLACE.

I wish the "Ladies' Glee Book" every success, feeling assured that its merits, its beauty, and its usefulness, will cause it to be generally used and extensively circulated. MAURICE STRAKOSCH.

As soon as the "Ladies' Glee Book" is known, it will, in my opinion, find its way into every drawing-room. MRS. EDWARD LODER.

I recommend the work to my friends with great pleasure. MAX MARETZEK.

I believe the "Ladies' Glee Book" will be generally adopted in the Ladies' Schools and Institutes, and also in private circles. E. WALLACE BOUCHELLE.

THE MILLIONS' GLEE BOOK, OR NEW YORK MELODEON; Consisting of a choice selection of Glees, Quartettes, Duets, Songs and Ballads, many of which have never before been published in this country. By I. B. WOODBURY, author of the "Dulcimer" and other Musical Works. Price 50 cents.

THE NEW YORK NORMAL SCHOOL SONG BOOK, containing a New Oratorio, founded on incidents of the American Revolution, with original words; also, a great variety of Miscellaneous Music, both Secular and Sacred, with new instructions, adapted to the use of *Public Schools*, *Singing Schools*, and *the Social Circle*. By L. A. BENJAMIN and I. B. WOODBURY. Price 38 cents.

THE CRYSTAL PALACE AND FLORAL QUEEN: Containing a New Oratorio of the Crystal Palace, or the Spirit of the World's Fair; also, a Grand Coronation Festival, The Village Queen, and a variety of Miscellaneous Music, Sacred and Secular, adapted to Public Schools, the Concert-room, and the Social Circle. By L. A. BENJAMIN. Price 38 cents.

THE INSTRUMENTAL PRECEPTOR; Designed for the Violin, Bass-viol, Flute, Clarionette, Bugle and Trombone, together with the greatest collection of Martial Music now in modern practice, consisting of a great variety of *Band Music*, Duets and Waltzes, carefully selected and prepared, by WILLIAM L. BALES. Price 75 cents.

THE SABBATH SCHOOL MINSTREL; A Choice Collection of MUSIC and HYMNS, by a Sabbath School Teacher. Price 75 cents per dozen.

This book has been exceedingly popular, over 100,000 copies having been sold. The ollection of Music and Hymns embraced in the following pages has been made with especial reference to the wants of the Sabbath School. The style of the music is simple and devotional; and while it will gratify those somewhat advanced in the science, it may be learned with facility by even the youngest scholar. The object has been to introduce as large a number of appropriate Hymns as possible, varying in length and in measure, and all adapted to the exercises of the Sabbath School, its anniversaries, celebrations, &c.

PRESTON'S INTEREST TABLES.

PRESTON'S SEVEN PER CENT. New Edition, Enlarged. 256 pp. Price $1 75.

PRESTON'S SEVEN PER CENT. Abridged. 76 pp. 8vo. Price $1 25

PRESTON'S SIX PER CENT. Large. 250 pp. $2 50.

PRESTON'S SIX PER CENT. Abridged. 132 pp. $1 50.

During twenty-five years "Preston's Tables of Interest" have been regarded by the public with much favor. The first editions of this now standard work appeared in the year 1828, and such was the rapidity of its sale, that a second edition was called for soon after the publication of the first issue, and that, too, soon found its way into the hands of those who learned to appreciate its value. It was then thought best to enlarge the work, and to stereotype it. Accordingly it was enlarged and then stereotyped in 1836. The improvements of the work at that time consisted in part of an extension which comprehended facilities for obtaining about 71,000 calculations of interest, and in part of 133,225 calculations of time. The work had now been in use eight years, nor had the prophetic assurance of the unbelievers in its merits, that it would soon be "pushed off in the auction rooms at one shilling a copy," been realized in the results; on the contrary, though the price had been *increased*, the demand continued to be encouraging. Thus it continued to prosper eight years more, when, in 1844, another improvement was made in the work, which comprehended facilities for obtaining 143,000 additional calculations of interest; and what we wish to have particularly borne in is, that we have again increased the capacity of the work by adding 143,000 more calculations to its former contents. So that now including the twelve pages of time, we exhibit facilities for obtaining 1,133,225 calculations. If we add to this results obtained by doubling, to the full capacity of the book, confining its application to within practical limits, we shall find that PRESTON'S TABLES OF INTEREST, at 7 per cent. accommodates us with upwards of *four hundred millions* of calculations ready made.

We deem it in place to inform the public that the plates of this work have recently been reviewed, for the purpose of correcting any imperfections which might be found in them, as the result of long use, and that the few blemishes which was found have been restored to a sound condition.

"Preston's Six per cent Interest Tables" are distinguished by the same characteristic features that have secured to his Seven per cent. Tables such an extensive and increasing demand.

DIARY FOR 1856	18mo.	Tuck, gilt edge.	Price 37½ cents.
" "	12mo.	" "	50 "
" "	8vo.	" "	75 "
" "	Large 4to.	"	75 "

These Diaries are made in a superior style, and beside the usual matter, are furnished with a Cash Account for each month, Annual Summary of Cash Account, and Bills Payable and Receivable, rendering them more complete than others, and invaluable to every business man

www.ingramcontent.com/pod-product-compliance
Lightning Source LLC
LaVergne TN
LVHW010232110826
845151LV00004B/1271

* 9 7 8 1 4 2 5 5 2 5 6 2 0 *